MW00980418

Prince George:

A Social Geography of B.C.'s Northern Capital

Prince George:

A Social Geography of B.C.'s Northern Capital

edited by Greg and Regine Halseth

UNBC Press

1998

Copyright © Greg and Regine Halseth for selection and editorial matter;
Copyright © contributors for their individual chapters

All rights reserved. No part of this book may be reprinted or reproduced or utilized in any form or by any electronic, mechanical, or other means, now known or hereafter invented, including photocopying and recording, or in any information storage or retrieval system, without written permission from the authors or publishers.

The editors would like to recognize the University of Northern British Columbia and the UNBC Northern Land Use Institute for their support.

Cover Design and layout by Carol Fairhurst, Meridian Visual Communications
Printed by UNBC Copy Services

UNBC Press
3333 University Way
Prince George, B.C.
CANADA V2N 4Z9

Canadian Cataloguing in Publication Data

Main entry under title:

Prince George:
a social geography of B.C.'s northern capital

Includes bibliographical references
Paperback ISBN 1-896315-06-2

1. Prince George (B.C.)-- Social conditions. 2. Human geography--British Columbia--Prince George. I. Halseth, Greg, 1960- . II. Halseth, Regine, 1961-

GF512.B7P75 1998 971.1'82 C98-900849-5

This book is dedicated to
the People of Northern British Columbia
whose spirit and foresight
helped found a new university.

ACKNOWLEDGEMENTS

In any large project such as this, a successful product rests on the contributions and input from a great number of people. We gratefully acknowledge the kind and generous assistance offered to us and the chapter authors by so many people and organizations in Prince George. Collectively, we offer this book as our thank you.

Many individuals such as Armenio Sardinha, Leo Hubert, Baljit Sethi, Bill Kennedy, Iona Campagnolo, Murray Krause, and others freely offered time, information, or assistance. As well, many of the local organizations active in Prince George such as the Prince George Native Friendship Centre, the Immigrant and Multicultural Society, and others also provided information and assistance when asked.

One of the special strengths of this book is its maps. These maps, showing the spatial distribution of Prince George's people and services, are the most fundamental tool available to geographers. Nothing in a community happens in isolation, and it is through maps that we can often identify the linkages and relationships between locations and activities that together function to make our community a diverse and vibrant place to live. To assist readers, two base maps have been included on the front and back inside covers of the book for reference and referral while reading the text.

The maps in this book truly are portraits which "can say a thousand words". Two individuals deserve special thanks in this regard. Brian Stauffer produced most of the graphics figures, designed and developed the base maps used in the book, and undertook some special mapping assignments such as the expansion of City jurisdictional boundaries and the police statistical area maps. Kevin Driscoll completed this work and produced most of the final maps which are reproduced on the pages which follow. Both Brian and Kevin were able to make this contribution because of the fine training and facilities available at UNBC. Roger Wheate, the geographic information systems (GIS) faculty member at UNBC manages a state-of-the-art GIS Laboratory. This is a tremendous resource to have available for research on northern landscapes and communities.

The editors would like to acknowledge the financial support of the Northern Land Use Institute (NLUI) at the University of Northern British Columbia. Without the assistance of Max Blouw (Associate Vice President of Research and Dean of Graduate Studies) and NLUI Director Bob Pfister, publication of this book would not have been possible. We would also like to acknowledge the support given by the UNBC Geography Program. This book is part of a continuing commitment to community outreach on the part of our geography faculty. As well, Fred Gilbert, former Dean of the Faculty of Natural Resources and Environmental Studies, gave this project enthusiastic support from its earliest stages and this support was continued by Lee Keener, Acting-Dean of the College of Science and Management and by Deborah Poff, UNBC Vice President Academic.

Production of this book was assisted by Clive Keen, Rob van Adrichem, and Jennifer Hammond of the Office of Communications at UNBC. We felt from the start that it was important for this book to be published by the University of Northern British Columbia Press. Somehow, a book about one of B.C.'s northern communities, written for the people of northern B.C., just wouldn't feel right if published in Vancouver or Toronto.

It is our sincere hope that this book will be the first in a series detailing the lives and landscapes of B.C.'s northern communities. In this respect, the book is dedicated to the people of northern British Columbia who petitioned the provincial government to establish UNBC and who have since supported *their* university in so many ways.

TABLE OF CONTENTS

LIST OF MAPS

continued next page

LIST OF MAPS

continued

LIST OF TABLES

continued next page

LIST OF TABLES

continued

LIST OF FIGURES

Contributors

CHERIE ALLEN graduated from UNBC with a Bachelors of Arts General degree. She has since gone on to complete her teacher training certificate through Simon Fraser University's Professional Development Program as offered in Prince George. Presently, Cherie is teaching at the secondary school level in Prince George.

LEON GEISLER graduated from UNBC with a Bachelors of Arts General degree and a Minor in human geography. He has since completed teacher training through Simon Fraser University's Professional Development Program and is teaching elementary school in Prince George. Presently, Leon is also working towards his Bachelors of Education degree through Simon Fraser University.

GREG HALSETH teaches human, social, political, and small town geography at the University of Northern British Columbia. His most recent book is *Cottage Country in Transition,* published by McGill-Queen's University Press. His research work looks at the ways rural and small town communities in northern BC are reacting to the challenges and opportunities arising from the restructuring of resource based industries.

KERRY KILDEN graduated from UNBC with a bachelors degree in English. She has completed teacher training through Simon Fraser University's Professional Development Program and is teaching elementary school in Prince George. Kerry is also presently working on her Bachelors of Education degree through Simon Fraser University.

KATHY MARCHUK graduated from UNBC with a bachelors degree in Geography. She has recently completed teacher training through Simon Fraser University's Professional Development Program and is teaching at both the elementary and secondary school levels in the Prince George region.

J. ALISTAIR MCVEY is currently Dean of Science and Technology at the College of New Caledonia in Prince George. He has been teaching and studying the geography of the central interior of British Columbia for the past 25 years. He served as a

Commissioner on the BC Utilities Commission's review of the Kemano Completion Project, and has most recently chaired a committee studying the revitalization of Prince George's downtown core. He has a special research interest in new town planning models in resource community settings.

BRANNON RENNIE graduated from Simon Fraser University with a Bachelors of General Studies degree. While doing her studies at SFU Brannon also completed a Minor in Early Childhood Education and a Minor in Learning Disabilities.

LAURA RYSER graduated from UNBC with a bachelors degree in Geography. While at UNBC she participated in the Model United Nations program and has since gone on to spend time on a United Nations Internship to Mongolia as a liaison worker with their Agenda 21 environmental initiative. Laura has recently enrolled in graduate studies at UNBC with an interest in Winter Cities planning.

JOHN SARDINHA graduated from UNBC with a bachelors degree in Geography and a Minor in Environmental Planning. After completing a year of background studies, John has recently entered a Masters Degree program in City Planning at the University of Portugal in Lisbon.

BRIAN STAUFFER graduated from UNBC with a bachelors degree in Geography. His interest in Geographic Information Systems (GIS) technology was translated into a job with CANFOR at their Fort St. James offices doing computer based mapping for their forest operations planning. Brian has recently enrolled in graduate studies at UNBC as a way to develop and extend his GIS skills.

PREFACE TO A SOCIAL GEOGRAPHY OF B.C.'S NORTHERN CAPITAL

J. Alistair McVey

In many ways, this book may be said to have its roots in a geographical tradition that was first introduced to the Central Interior in the 1960s. When I was appointed as the first Geography Instructor at the College of New Caledonia in 1969 (the first year of its operation), I immediately became aware of a small, but dedicated and highly-motivated, group of Geography teachers who taught Social Studies and Geography in several secondary schools within the large region served by the College. In particular, Keith Gordon, Peter Thrift, Roy Hooker in Prince George and George Worobey in Quesnel generated an enthusiasm for the discipline that resulted in a steady stream of students coming to the College to continue their studies. Many of these have gone on to complete their degree (or, in several instances, degrees) in Geography at various universities in the Province and, indeed, elsewhere. As a result of the enthusiasm of such students and the dedication of a small number of instructors during the past 28 years, Geography has developed a significant presence within the College, with nearly 400 students and 3 full-time instructors in the Department.

For me, teaching Human Geography in Prince George through that time has been a most fascinating and rewarding enterprise, primarily because of the many changes that have taken place in the city's urban landscape since the heady expansion of the 1960s. Of particular interest to the urban geographer is the fact that, almost alone among cities in British Columbia, much of post-1960 Prince George has developed according to many of the principles of "new town" planning that have diffused from Europe - land-banking, green belts, neighbourhood planning, and so on. More recently, this medium-sized community has experienced inner city decay in the face of suburban mall and "box" store development, the loss of many heritage buildings despite gentrification around the core, the development of an urban-rural fringe, and other processes and manifestations of urban change that can be discerned in cities of much larger size within the Canadian urban system.

To have a deeper understanding of how our communities are developing, a geographic perspective is, in my view, of immense value. Cities are obviously "people places" and the imagination of the human geographer can be most useful in mapping the fascinating patterns that people create in an urban setting. In addition, he or she can discover that special sense of place that individuals and groups may possess as they occupy and change their urban landscape. As the City continues to grow, it is vital that municipal authorities and elected officials be in possession of as much valid and reliable information as possible. Yet, until recently, very little research by geographers has been conducted in the Central Interior, with the Lower Mainland, Vancouver Island and the Okanagan Valley receiving most of the attention from the province's metropolitan-based geography departments. Furthermore, government agencies have not had the resources to undertake the kind of research that has been needed. As a result, residential segregation, demographic change and other indices of the social geography of Prince George have received little or no attention.

The establishment of the University of Northern British Columbia in 1990 created a wonderful opportunity for the nature of the Central Interior to be more completely understood through research activities. The inclusion of the Geography Program at the University has added a new dimension to a discipline that, as we have seen, has become a vital part of the academic life of the region. This book is the first of what will be a short series of social geography studies on Northern British Columbia and its roots lie in the geographical tradition mentioned above. Of particular significance is the fact that the contributing authors are graduates of UNBC, many of whom have strong links with the College of New Caledonia in that they were university transfer students in the College's Geography Department prior to completing their degrees at UNBC.

This book is a most welcome contribution to our understanding of the social geography of Prince George. I am confident that it, and others like it, will contribute a great deal to an already vigorous and solid geographical tradition in the Central Interior of British Columbia.

J. Alistair McVey
College of New Caledonia
February 1998

INTRODUCTION

Greg Halseth

INTRODUCTION

The study of human geography is the study of people and the places in which they live. It represents an attempt to understand something of the character and sense of place which defines individual communities. This specific volume represents a "social geography" inquiry, that is, it explores some of the central social processes and outcomes responsible for creating and maintaining the local communities within which we live. The City of Prince George is an especially suitable community for a social geography inquiry. In recent years, Prince George has experienced considerable growth, and there is a strong sense in the media, among decision-makers and in the community, that the City is undergoing fundamental changes as it grows and develops into "B.C.'s Northern Capital". This study of Prince George is, therefore, timely as it provides not only some information and a context for interpreting changes the City has experienced in its recent past, but it also provides a foundation from which to view and assess the kinds of changes that may occur in the future. Certainly, the issues of growth and change are not new ones for Prince George and it is hoped that this book will make a contribution to understanding the City and the communities which comprise it.

SOCIAL GEOGRAPHY

Social geography is a comparatively young field of inquiry. As it has evolved, social geography is interested in the way social processes create a physical or "spatial" community and the way in which social resources and phenomena are distributed within that community. Among the topics often considered are: work, housing, and social services, as well as concerns for the role of gender and ethnicity in shaping our communities. In setting the foundation for any social geography study we need to be aware of the general perspectives being employed and the range of possible topics to be included.

Social geography inquiry is grounded in two intersecting perspectives. The first, quite naturally, is the spatial perspective. Geographers have long been interested in how resources, settlements, goods and services are distributed across the land. By extension, social geographers are interested in how social phenomena are distributed across our community landscape. Social geographers also recognize that such patterns and distributions come into place slowly, and that once in place, they have a certain momentum that resists change. Therefore, social geography also adopts something of a historical perspective. Community change, after all, happens *in* places *over* time. It is important to bear both perspectives in mind when interpreting any community's social geography.

Studies of social geography generally focus upon a limited number of topics or social attributes. Most often these include patterns of population distribution, housing type and affordability, employment and poverty, social services availability, gender, ethnicity and racism, and crime. These are, of course, not the only topics social geographers study but they are most often selected because they are highly influenced by, and have a strong reciprocal influence upon, the social processes shaping our communities. Take for example a high status housing neighbourhood. In this neighbourhood there is likely to be a strong similarity, or homogeneity, both in terms of house types and the households living there. Occupied by relatively affluent residents, such neighbourhoods are often able to block plans to locate alternative (or social) housing or social services nearby. In turn, this creates pressures to further segregate such services in particular parts of the community. When a large number of such interacting issues and pressures are considered, we can start to see patterns which help us to interpret why the spatial organization of our community has evolved as it has. In this sense, the outcomes studied in social geography are said to be "socially produced". They are the result of local social and political interaction and debate. The chapters in this volume very clearly focus upon some of these socially produced spatial outcomes within the City of Prince George.

PRINCE GEORGE

The City of Prince George is located at the heart of British Columbia's Central Interior (Map I.1). Over the past 30 years, the City has experienced tremendous growth and an increasing diversity of economic activity; so much so that it has recently adopted the civic motto: "B.C.'s Northern Capital". It is against this backdrop of recent and rapid growth that this study of Prince George's social geography is set. New economic opportunities, and the in-migration by many individuals, families, and groups seeking to participate in these new opportunities, have created a complex, fascinating, and multi-faceted community.

Prince George's physical setting and location have been, and continue to be, critical to its development. The City is surrounded by tremendous natural resource wealth and is located at a provincially important natural transportation crossroads. The forests, rivers and lakes surrounding Prince George have long been the foundation for an economy based on the land. From the early Carrier-Sekani inhabitants, to the coming of the fur-trade, to the large scale development of the lumber and pulp and paper industries, the rich natural resource base has been at the heart of the local economy. In terms of recent growth, the construction of the three pulp mill operations and their associated support industries in the early and middle 1960s have been of key importance. Prince George's location at a natural hub in British Columbia's

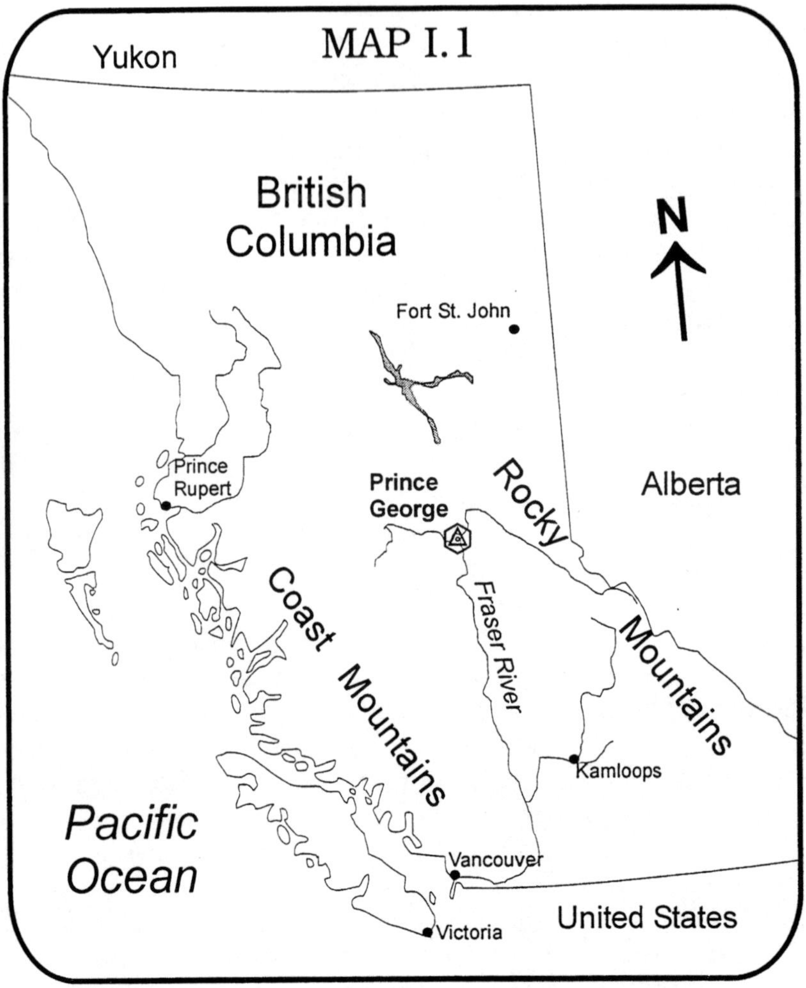

transportation and communications system has also been of tremendous benefit. In its early days, when water transportation played a significant role in the development of trading routes and communities, Prince George's location at the confluence of the Fraser and Nechako River systems afforded considerable advantage. It is also only a short distance from an easy crossing of the continental divide into the arctic watershed of the Peace River system at Giscome Portage.

Canoe and paddlewheeler routes have now been supplanted by rail and highway systems. The City now acts as a central supply, distribution, and service centre for much of the Central and Northern Interior of the Province. Taken together, a strong resource economy base with a burgeoning service centre function give credibility to Prince George's boast of being "B.C.'s Northern Capital".

OUTLINE OF CHAPTERS

The eight chapters in this book cover those topic areas most commonly discussed in social geography. Most of the eight chapter contributors grew up in Prince George and all are University of Northern British Columbia graduates. The book has grown out of a class project in Greg Halseth's "Social Geography of Northern Communities" course. The organization of each chapter is relatively similar in that a brief review of general concepts is followed by specific information on Prince George. Readers should notice a good deal of interlinkage between individual chapters. While the topics described in each chapter are of necessity all dealt with individually, it is important for us to keep in mind that they are all indivisible components of that larger whole which is our community. Something else the readers should notice is that numbers of changes have occurred in the community since the time the research for the individual chapters was undertaken. Most research was completed in 1996, with some items updated in 1997 and 1998. Change is of course a normal and usual part of community life and, therefore, our collective goal is provide a "snapshot" of Prince George at one point in its development and to link this snapshot to some general ideas about how communities grow and how their social geography evolves.

The first chapter, by Stauffer and Halseth, introduces some of the basics of population change in the city. Tracing population growth over time, links are made to important local historical events such as the arrival of the Grand Trunk Pacific railroad and the construction of the pulp mills. The chapter also discusses basic population data collection processes and describes the changing structure of the City's population. As such, this chapter sets the foundation for much of the detail and data used in the rest of the book.

Chapters 2 and 3 outline two of the more basic components of a community's social geography. In Chapter 2, Rennie and Halseth cover the topic of work and employment. This includes an introduction to the major employers in the community and a review of the occupational structure of the Prince George labour force. In Chapter 3, Marchuk describes the social geography of housing in Prince George. It is through housing that many of the socio-economic differences between neighbourhoods are physically imprinted onto the city landscape. Marchuk's chapter describes patterns of housing construction, costs, and tenure across Prince George's neighbourhoods.

Chapters 4 and 5 begin to introduce some of the social issues often discussed and debated within both small towns and large cities. Chapter 4 develops directly out of the topics raised by the chapters on work and housing, with Geisler and Kilden examining the issues of poverty and homelessness in Prince George. Besides highlighting the complexity of these concepts, they also describe a range of services and support structures which are in place and working to alleviate the very real needs of some members of our community. Readers will note that the tenuous aspects of being homeless are reinforced by the rapidity with which some local service providers have come and gone within Prince George. In Chapter 5, Kilden examines a series of issues connected with the study of gender. Drawing specifically upon the needs and experiences of women, the chapter examines such issues as lone-parent families, as well as the support networks and services which are available to women in Prince George.

In Chapter 6, Sardinha looks at the importance of ethnicity to communities of people within Prince George. Ethnicity and ethnic identity have been the foundation for development of many groups, clubs, and facilities, yet it is a complex concept and one which needs to be better understood.

In Chapter 7, Allen bring together a number of themes raised in earlier chapters in her study of Prince George's social services. One of the important findings in her chapter is the reciprocal relationships which together underscore why the City's social services are clustered in the downtown core. The complex interrelationships between social services, transportation, housing, retail activity, public facilities, and dependent populations must be clearly recognized if debates over downtown redevelopment or the siting of social services are to move forward.

In the final chapter, Ryser tackles the difficult issue of crime. As the study of crime is complex and fraught with concerns over how statistics are collected or how explanations are linked to individual behaviours, much of this chapter is spent on the topic of crime prevention through environmental design.

It is hoped that readers will find this volume a timely and interesting contribution to understanding Prince George as a community. In the following eight chapters a tremendous amount of information is communicated through text, tables, charts and maps. In reading through the volume it is very much hoped that readers will not only learn about the community, but also will find themselves asking questions like 'why did it happen like this?', and 'why is this pattern seen?' Above all, it is hoped that this volume will stimulate thinking, questions, and perhaps even further research and study into understanding the Prince George community. After all, one of the best purposes of social science inquiry is less to provide answers and more to provide a foundation for asking new and better questions.

Chapter 1

POPULATION CHANGE IN PRINCE GEORGE

Brian Stauffer and Greg Halseth

INTRODUCTION

Population growth in Prince George is an important part of the social geography of the City. Changes in population levels can show significant events in a city's development, and from before the Fur Trade to the opening of the University of Northern British Columbia, the various reasons for people coming to Prince George provide an interesting "time map" of the history and culture of the City. The purpose of this chapter is to try and develop some insight into the social geography of Prince George by analysing some of the changes in its demographic characteristics. An attempt will also be made to see if some of these changes correspond to significant events in the City's history. For example, how did the construction of one, and then two more, pulp mills relate to local population increases. In this respect, population information provides a foundation for understanding a range of issues important to the overall social geography of Prince George. The numbers and distribution of people in the City underlie relationships between ethnicity, housing and labour. As the population increases through time, the boundaries of the City move outwards and services are developed and extended. Also, the problems of the City may increase along with the size of the population. For example, the type, location, distribution and frequency of crime may change as a city grows.

BACKGROUND

Much of the data presented in this chapter comes from Statistics Canada census data for the years between 1921 and 1991. The older information is less complete and some comparisons over time are difficult. From 1961 to 1991 more detailed information is available and is compiled at 5 year census intervals. The use of census data over such a long period of time is important if we are to gain an understanding of changes and trends within Prince George. The value in using a standard data source like the census is seen throughout this book as similar census boundaries and time frames allow comparisons between issues. Also, the census data is broken down into detailed categories and also into smaller geographic areas which allows for study of variations across the City's neighbourhoods.

A number of data issues and problems were encountered when doing the research for this chapter. These included the fact that census data is only collected every five years, and therefore, developing a relationship between population increases and significant historical events was difficult. For example, if an event occurred in 1972, the population effect would not be measured until 1976 when the next census was taken. Further, certain sectors of the local population may not be well accounted for in census statistics. Homeless people, and in the past a significant portion of indigenous peoples, have not been well represented in the census data. Rather than a continuous record of population change, it would be better to think of census data as a window, opened every five years, through which we can glimpse a snapshot of Prince George.

Throughout this chapter, and many of those which follow, maps have been produced using the Statistics Canada census map as a base. Map 1.1 identifies the boundaries and locations of the 23 "Census Tracts" which make up the City of Prince George. The boundaries on the census map tend to follow natural breaks in the community such as major roads and

Map 1.1
Census Tract Boundaries, 1991

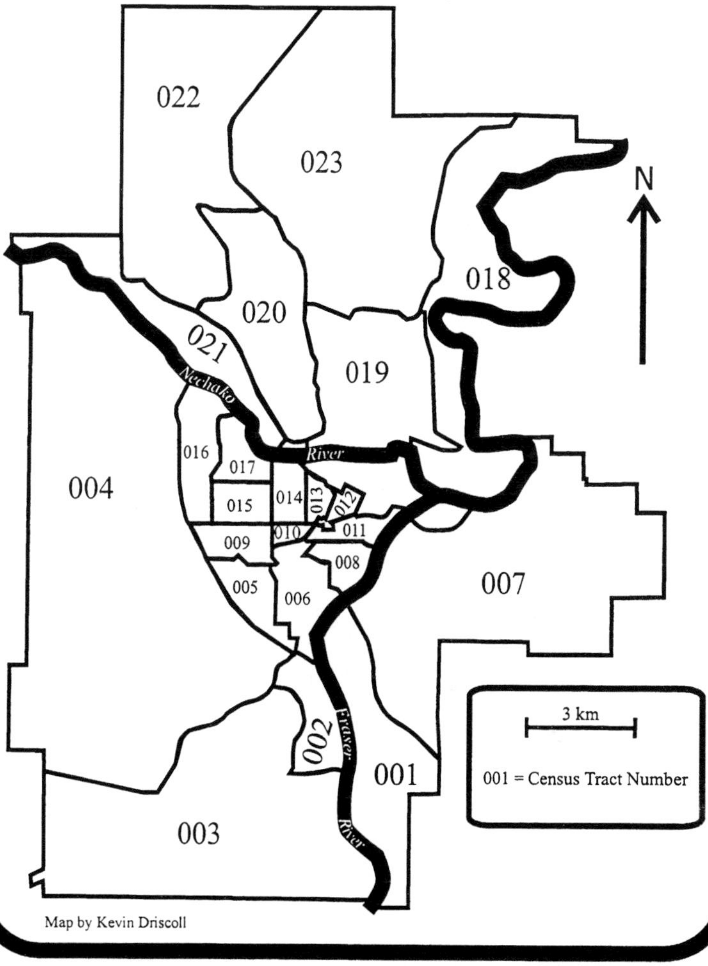

natural features like rivers and escarpments. The outside boundary conforms with the City boundary. By dividing Prince George into 23 smaller segments, this map is a useful tool for looking at neighbourhood level population issues and the differences between such neighbourhoods. These census tract boundaries are accurate for the 1981, 1986, and 1991 census dates. Previous census information is only available City wide.

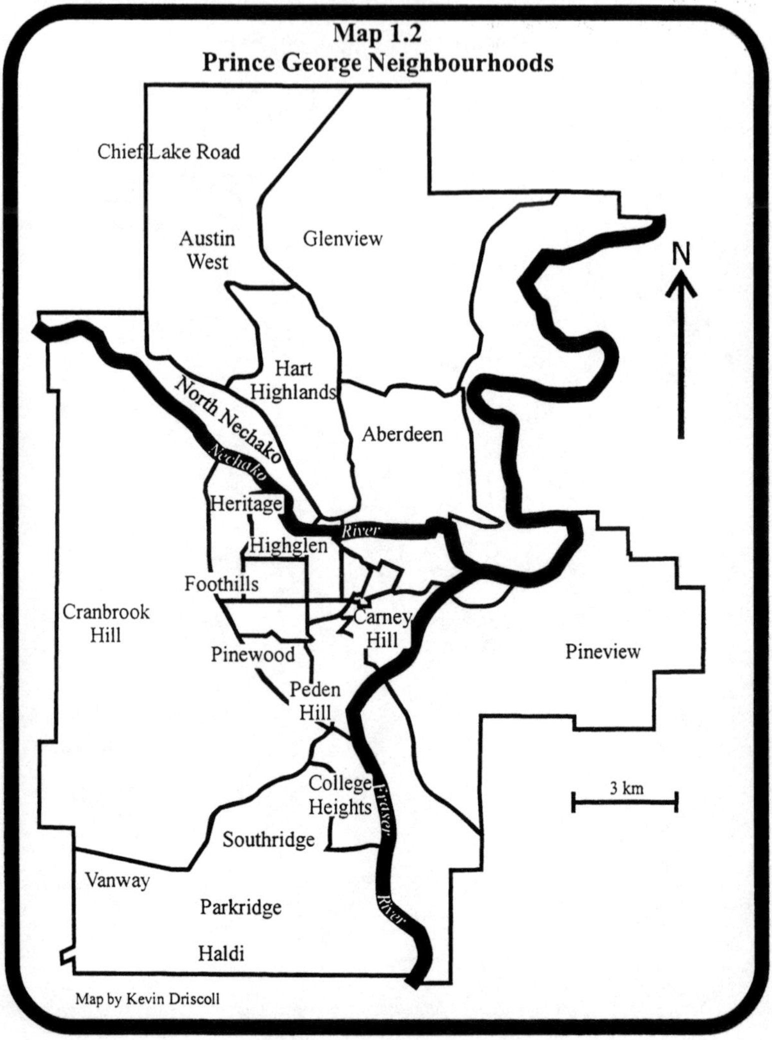

Map 1.2
Prince George Neighbourhoods

Some historical maps are also included to give perspective on the physical development of the City. Map 1.2 shows how these census tract boundaries relate to neighbourhood areas within Prince George.

Other constraints on understanding local population growth include physiographic barriers to growth. The Cutbanks, Cranbrook Hill, the Nechako and Fraser Rivers, all function to constrain the physical development of the City. The natural landscape forms a topographic "bowl" at the confluence of the Fraser and Nechako Rivers. The microclimate in the bowl favoured early settlement, particularly for agriculture, and was a benefit to Prince George in the first half of this century. More recently, however, it is becoming a problem by both constraining the physical growth of the City and trapping air pollution at certain times of the year when there is little or no wind to carry it away.

Finally, a proportion of the Prince George population has always lived outside of City boundaries. Estimates suggest that in 1991 between 25 and 30 percent of the Prince George urban market population lived in the rural areas outside the City's legal boundaries (BC Stats, 1993). Such boundaries on a map are at once both real and imaginary. On one side they can be a source of management and jurisdictional limits, providing benefits or hardships. On the other side they often do not conform to the natural environment nor the distribution of people's activities. Measuring population growth outside the boundaries of a city is important in understanding the influence the rural population has on regional demands of services, fiscal balance, and boundary growth. However, while the rural population around a city can play a role in its growth and development, this portion of the population is very difficult to analyse. As a result, while some discussion of this "ex-urban" population is included in this chapter, the remainder of the book concentrates upon the population within Prince George itself.

HISTORICAL DEVELOPMENT OF PRINCE GEORGE

Prince George has always been a place of opportunity. The reasons for coming to Prince George have changed and each new change has brought with it a growth in local population. Early business people recognized the potential of the area and began promotional campaigns to attract people from as far away as the British Isles. Advertisements boasted of vast expanses of agricultural land and endless forests to serve as timber resources for the frontier city (Hak, 1990; Runnals,

1946).

Prince George has developed as a resource-based town, highly dependent on the forest industry. Like other forest dependent communities, much of the industrial development in and around the City has been in the primary industry sector and local economic fortunes rise and fall with global markets for local forest products (Hayter, 1976; Marchak, 1989; Mullins, 1967). With this resource development came supporting service and commercial sector employment. Such spinoff growth in supporting industries is generally termed a "multiplier effect" from the basic resource industry. These forces led to a rapid increase in population from the mid 1960s to the early 1980s. This period could be considered Prince George's modern boom years, when economic development led to an influx of people to fill a growing demand for labour. Important events in the recent growth and development of Prince George are listed in Table 1.1 and are portrayed in Figure 1.1. With each of these key events, there has been an impact upon population growth and the development of the City. Beginning first with the forest industry and then later with the College of New Caledonia and the University of Northern British Columbia, many linkages were created with other service, support, and supplier agencies such that growth now extends well beyond employment in any particular mill or institution.

Table 1.1
IMPORTANT HISTORICAL EVENTS

1914	Grand Trunk Pacific Railway connection completed
1915	Incorporation of Fort George (name soon changed to Prince George)
1920s-1950s	Forestry, logging, and sawmills
1952	Pacific Great Eastern (BCR) connection completed
1966	PG Pulp and Paper Mill / Northwood Pulp Mill
1968	Intercontinental Pulp and Paper Mill
1975	Major City boundary expansion
1990	Announcement on founding UNBC

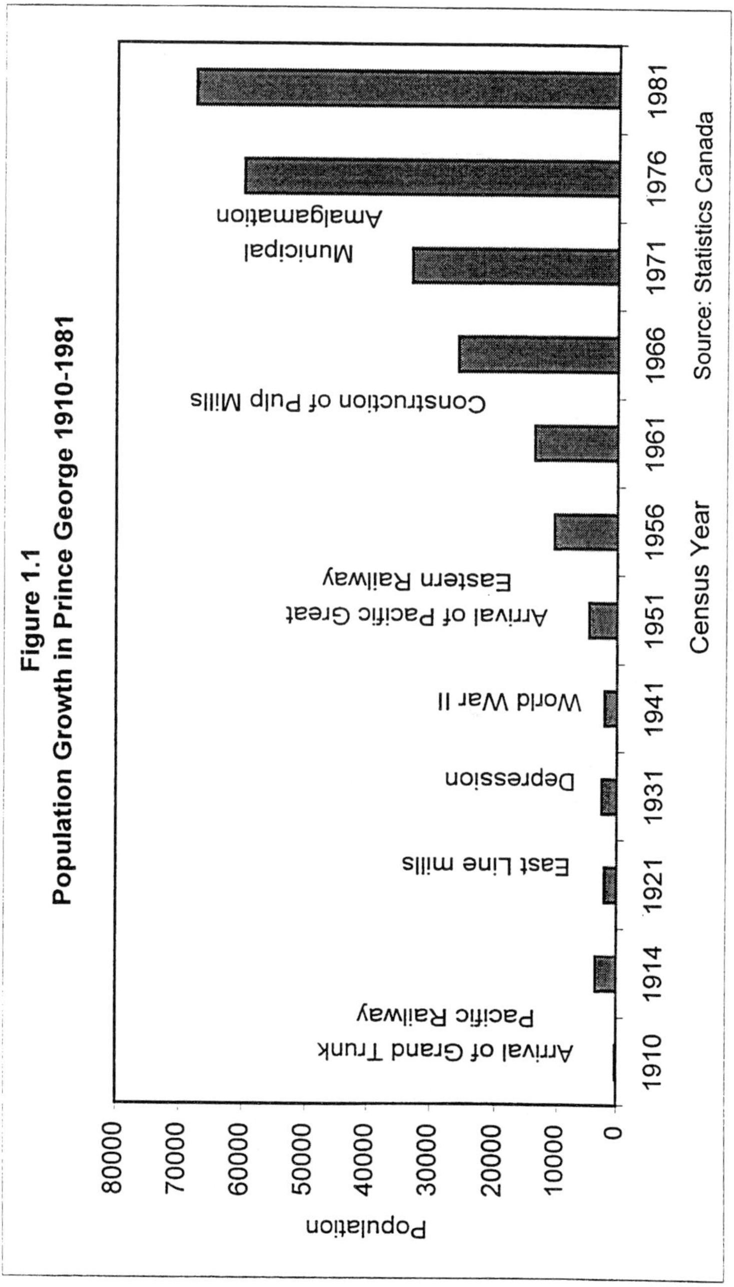

Figure 1.1
Population Growth in Prince George 1910-1981

The first impetus for growth in the 20th Century came with early railway connections to markets in eastern Canada. The Grand Trunk Pacific Railway, later amalgamated with other rail lines to form the Canadian National Railway, was constructed past Fort George in 1914 (Leonard, 1984). The native reserve which included much of the present downtown area, was purchased by the Grand Trunk Pacific in order to build a townsite (Prince George Directory, 1954). The native community was displaced further upstream on the Fraser River to the community of Shelley. On March 6, 1915, an application by the railroad and local government for incorporation of Fort George was passed in the British Columbia Legislature (Government of British Columbia, 1915). The first civic election was held on May 20, 1915, and a proclamation to have the name changed to Prince George was made June 14, 1915 (Smelts, 1915).

Between 1915 and the mid 1950s, immigration to the City was relatively slow. Economic opportunities in the area were connected with logging and the sawmills. Many of the people employed in the sawmills around the City were young men, many of whom were recent immigrants to Canada who had come to the area intending to make their fortunes. During this period there were about 500 small sawmills operating within a forty mile radius around Prince George, as well as fifteen planer mills in the immediate vicinity of the City itself (Prince George Directory, 1954). Many of these saw mills were found in the "East Line" communities such as Hansard, Longworth, and Penny, which were spread eastward along the Grand Trunk Pacific Railway line between Prince George and McBride. The rough lumber or logs would be brought into the City for processing and shipment. In 1964, the forest industry employed about 10,400 people in the region (BC Research Council, 1965) with Prince George emerging as a main supply and services point for a large part of the Central Interior.

The importance for local economic development of access to external markets had been clearly demonstrated with the Grand Trunk Pacific rail line. In the 1950s, a second rail connection initiated a renewed upswing in economic activity in Prince George. On November 1, 1952, the first Pacific Great

Eastern Railway (PGE) train rolled into Prince George from North Vancouver. Started in 1912, the Pacific Great Eastern line to Prince George took 40 years to construct and was plagued with financial problems, threats of abandonment, and other difficulties which earned it the local nickname of the "Prince George Eventually" railway. The extension of the PGE north to Prince George was a critical part of recent City growth as it provided a key transportation link for the developing pulp and paper industry. It was, and still is, a vital link to the Lower Mainland and the rest of the world for the industries of the Prince George region. This major infrastructure link transports the industrial output of the region and brings in needed goods for a rapidly growing community.

One of the most significant events in the City's recent history was the construction of the Northwood Pulp Mill and the Prince George Pulp and Paper Mill in 1966. Encouraged by government legislation and public policy developed by former resident and then Provincial Cabinet Minister Ray Williston (Williston and Keller, 1997), the pulp mills transformed Prince George from a small service community into one of the province's major industrial centres (Bernsohn, 1981). During the construction phase, the mills brought skilled trades people to the City, some of whom later stayed on as operations and maintenance people:

> As an indication of the direct effects on the population of the construction of a pulp mill, the Prince George Pulp and Paper Company plant alone has been employing 1,200 men during the current construction period. Permanent production employees after startup will be scarcely more than a third this number. The three mills slated for the environs of Prince George will create about 1,100 new permanent jobs by the end of 1967 (BC Research Council, 1965, p. 8).

Many new employees brought their families with them, or married and started families, making Prince George their home. The construction in 1968 of a third mill, the Intercontinental Pulp and Paper Mill, next to Prince George Pulp and Paper continued the City's industrial development. About 400 permanent full time jobs were created with this new mill.

With industrial and economic growth came population growth, and with rapid urban development proceeding apace with rapid population growth, urban management problems were encountered. In 1973, the City of Prince George conducted a study to try and find solutions to some of the growth pressures facing the City. One of the important issues of the day concerned the question of whether to expand the City boundaries to include adjacent areas with increasing populations. There was some question as to whether South Fort George, the Nechako Improvement District, and the College Heights Improvement District actually wanted to become part of Prince George. While some rural residents voiced opposition to being included in redrawn city boundaries, the City argued that "the proposed amalgamation of greater Prince George offers rural people an opportunity for services, orderly growth and planning" (Nixon, 1974, p.1). In their submission to the District Municipality Committee, the City continued this argument that expansion was a solution to the service problems of rural life:

> If the present City of Prince George considered only the financial aspects of the problem, they would only look into the expansion of the Municipality in the area now lying in the bowl. The present City still has many problems but a substantial number have been solved over the past decade and the City services have dramatically improved. Its finances are in excellent shape and the foreseeable assessment increases are excellent. Many of our problems are caused by the surrounding fringe who are without many of the services such as recreational facilities, parks, fire protection, bus service, dog control, public housing, etc. (Prince George, 1974, not paginated).

During this period, the population of the greater Prince George area was growing very rapidly. While the national population growth rate was averaging less than 2 percent per year and the provincial average was about 4 percent, the greater Prince George area, which included the rural and unincorporated areas around the City, had a growth rate between 6.5 percent and 7.5 percent per annum. This rate of growth was taken as an indication that Prince George needed to be prepared for a significantly larger population in the near future. The population of the greater Prince George area at the time was approximately 66,000, with 40,000 people living within the existing City boundaries (Regional District of Fraser-Fort George, 1974). An application for municipal amalgamation was made to the Province and in 1975 Prince George expanded its boundaries to encompass most of the surrounding population. As shown on Map 1.3, while the 1975 amalgamation was the largest territorial addition to the City of Prince George, it was only one of a series of jurisdictional boundary changes which have occurred in the area as the City administration tried to keep pace with the rapid population growth in and around Prince George.

Since Prince George is primarily a resource industry town, it is very susceptible to economic market fluctuations. During the early 1980s, an economic recession in the forest industry had a noticeable impact on the Prince George population. Economic development in the community slowed considerably and the City's population remained virtually unchanged between 1981 and 1986.

By the early 1990s the forest industry had recovered from the recession and the population stagnation of the early 1980s was ended. As well, in June of 1990, the creation of the University of Northern British Columbia (UNBC) was announced. By 1992, the university began limited operations and in August 1994, Her Majesty Queen Elizabeth II officially opened UNBC at its main campus in Prince George. The opening of UNBC is a further milestone in the history of Prince George in that it signifies the emergence of a more cosmopolitan city and is in many respects a visible symbol of a longer-term process which has seen the emergence of the City as British Columbia's "Northern Capital". As Prince George has seen an increasing number of federal and provincial government offices and retail services move into the City, now UNBC and an expanded College of New Caledonia (CNC), allows young people from northern BC to remain "at home" while

Map 1.3
Historical Growth of Prince George Boundaries

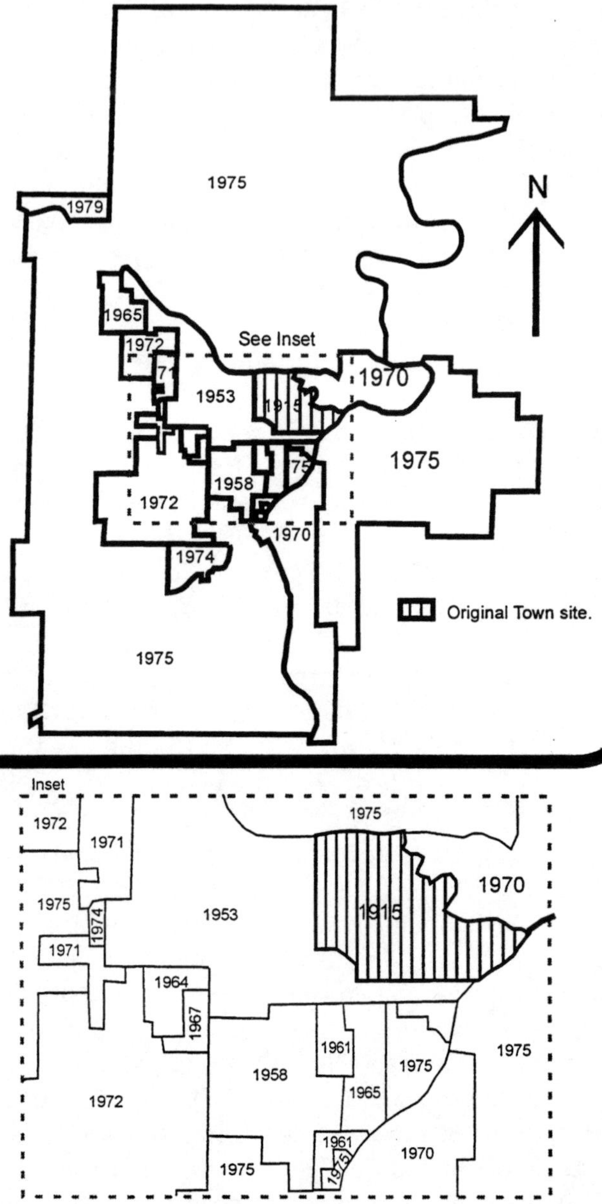

pursuing post-secondary education. While the hiring of faculty and support staff at both CNC and UNBC has brought additional population and economic growth to the City, there is speculation that the growing educational sector may have additional impacts as research and other spin-off activities develop.

POPULATION CHANGE

Recent population changes for the City of Prince George are shown in Table 1.2. The table uses census data for the years 1921 to 1996. Two background points are worth noting. First is that between 1921 and 1951 the census was conducted at 10 year intervals while after 1951 the census was conducted at 5 year intervals. A second point is that it takes two to three years following each census for detailed data to be published by Statistics Canada. As a result, in this chapter and others in this collection, only the 1996 "total population count" for Prince George was available.

Table 1.2
Summary of Population Growth 1921-1996

Census Dates	Population	% Change From Prev. Census	Annual Avg. Pop. Change
1921	2,053	n/a	n/a
1931	2,479	20.8	2.08
1941	2,027	-18.2	-1.82
1951	4,703	132.0	13.20
1956	10,563	124.6	24.92
1961	13,877	31.4	6.28
1966	24,471	76.3	15.26
1971	33,100	35.3	7.06
1976	59,929	81.0	16.20
1981	67,559	12.7	2.54
1986	67,621	0.1	0.02
1991	69,655	3.0	0.60

Source: Statistics Canada, Census

As suggested in the discussion of the historical development of Prince George, certain key events marked significant changes in the City's growth. The post World War II boom period saw a large percentage growth in area population as the forestry industry expanded rapidly with many small operations in the Central Interior. The construction of the pulp and paper mills during the 1960s led into a sustained 15 year period of population growth and urban development. The growth rate for the 5 year period leading into 1981 was nearly 13 percent, marking the later stages of the pulp mill development effects in the City. The growth rate for the 5 year period leading into 1991 was, by contrast, only 3 percent. Recession and slowdowns through the 1980s contributed to the stagnant population growth.

To introduce issues of population into this study of the social geography of Prince George, Table 1.3 includes information on gender, age and marital status. For comparative purposes, information for the 1981 and 1991 censuses are included to highlight recent patterns of change. While there

Table 1.3
Prince George Population
1981 and 1991 Census

Variable	1981	1991
Population	67,559	69,655
Percent females	48.8	49.4
Percent males	51.2	50.6
Avg. Age (for pop. 15 and over)	25.6	30.8
Percent Single	26.3	31.2
Percent Married	67.6	54.1
Percent Divorced/Separated	3.1	11.0
Percent Widowed	2.7	3.7
Average Persons per Family	3.4	3.2

Source: Statistics Canada, Census

was little change in the relative shares of men and women in the City, the average age of residents increased by nearly 5 years. The maturing of the workforce and the slow growth of the 1980s no doubt played a part in this pattern of aging. The data on marital status is difficult to interpret as the census included "separated" as an additional category in the 1991 census. Such changes in the way data are defined, collected, and presented is always a concern in trying to develop meaningful comparisons over time. Lastly, the average number of persons per family declined only slightly between 1981 and 1991, and this result likely represents the general North American trend towards smaller families rather than any Prince George specific events.

RURAL-URBAN DIFFERENCES

A key problem in trying to interpret patterns of population growth and change in communities involves jurisdictional boundaries. Population data collection agencies such as Statistics Canada and BC Stats usually use established municipal boundaries to collect population data. The reason for this is that the primary function of most such statistical agencies is to provide the population count information which forms the basis for inter-governmental transfers of monies. While this may serve the accounting needs of senior government, the difficulty for social geography research comes in trying to interpret the "functional" population of communities beyond their legal jurisdictional boundaries. A functional community includes all those people/households who normally interact with the services/businesses/institutions of the city on a daily basis. For Prince George, this includes not only the population within City boundaries but also the population living in rural communities just outside of these boundaries. The recent growth along Chief Lake Road north of the City, and in the Beaverly area south of the City, are examples of population growth occurring outside of Prince George's boundaries which is not readily captured in census and other statistical information.

Table 1.4 is included to try to illustrate some of the rural-urban differences in the population around Prince George. As a surrogate for the "functional" Prince George community, the boundaries of the Fraser Fort George Regional District, which includes the City of Prince George, are used. While the fit between the Fraser Fort George Regional District and the functional area of the City of Prince George is not perfect, it does illustrate the importance of this rural population component. As seen in Table 1.4, the rural area outside of Prince George adds approximately 21,000 people to the Region's population.

TABLE 1.4
Population Comparison
1991 Census

	Prince George	Fraser Fort George Regional District
Population	69,653	90,739
Pop. growth rate over previous 5 years	3.0%	1.6%
Pop. Density (people per km^2)	220.6	1.77

Source: BC Stats.

POPULATION DISTRIBUTION

The following two sections review specific aspects of Prince George's population. The first section employs population pyramids as a visual tool to portray the age and gender characteristics of the City population over time. The second section employs a set of maps to demonstrate the varying population densities across the City. The purpose of these sections is to highlight some of the outcomes of the City's recent and rapid population growth.

Population Pyramids

Population pyramids are graphical representations which show the distribution of age groups within a population. Four population pyramids for the census years from 1961 to 1991 have been developed. These pyramids show the changing structure of the Prince George population during the period of its greatest growth. Each of the population pyramids is divided by gender, then into 10 year age categories (also called "cohorts"). Ages beyond either 70 or 75 years (depending on which census was used) are typically grouped together due to the small relative numbers of people involved. The census defines the age of respondents as being the age at last birthday prior to the census being conducted (Statistics Canada, 1991). For example, the 1986 census was conducted on June 3, 1986. Changes in the shape of the population pyramid over time can be insightful into highlighting changes which may be occurring in a population.

In 1961, the population of Prince George was 13,877. As shown in Figure 1.2, this was a relatively young population: that is, a large share of the population is clustered in the younger age cohorts. By looking at the proportion of the population in the 20-29 and 30-39 year age groups we can also suggest that much of the population of Prince George is comprised of young families with children. As is common in developing resource-based communities where industrial employment activity creates male employment opportunities, the age groups from 20 onward are all slightly skewed towards having more males than females.

By 1971, the population of Prince George had increased to 33,100. While there were still a large number of children within the population, some of the differences in the relative distribution of men and women had levelled out (Figure 1.3). The growth in the 40-49 year age group demonstrates the aging of the 1961 workforce. With this exception, the population structure of the City remained very much one of young families with children.

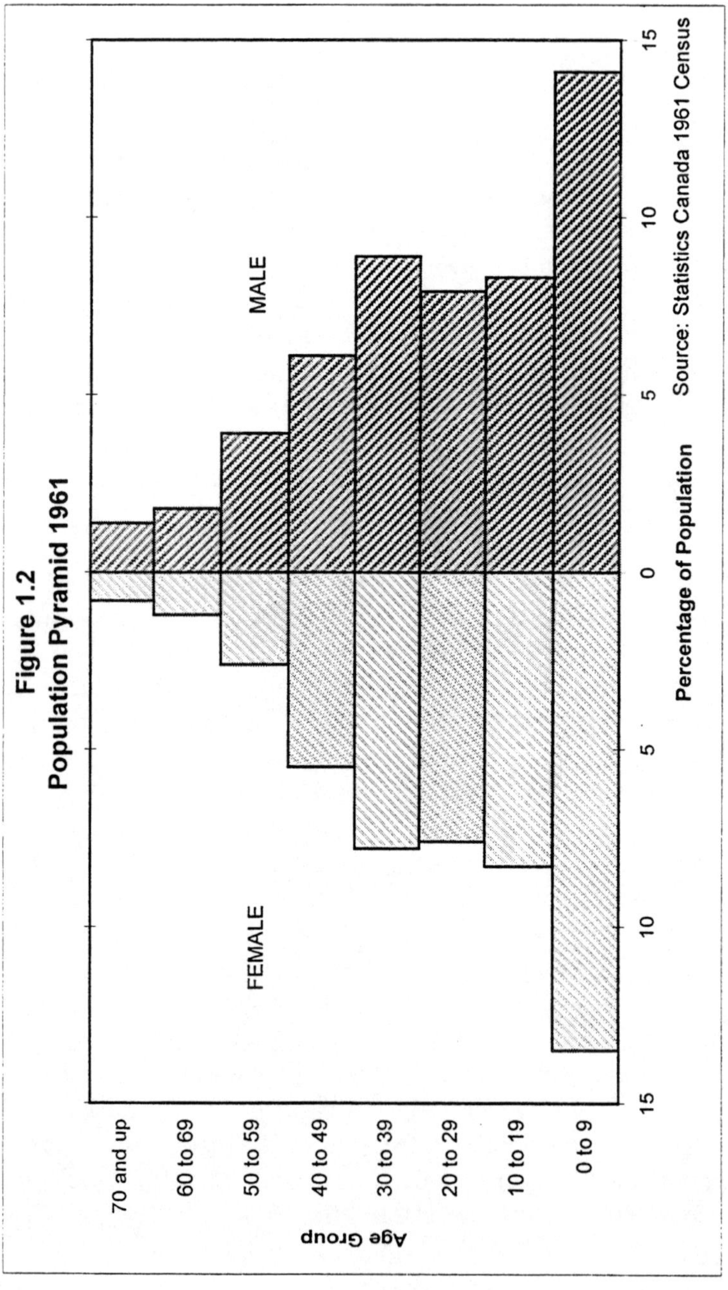

Figure 1.2
Population Pyramid 1961

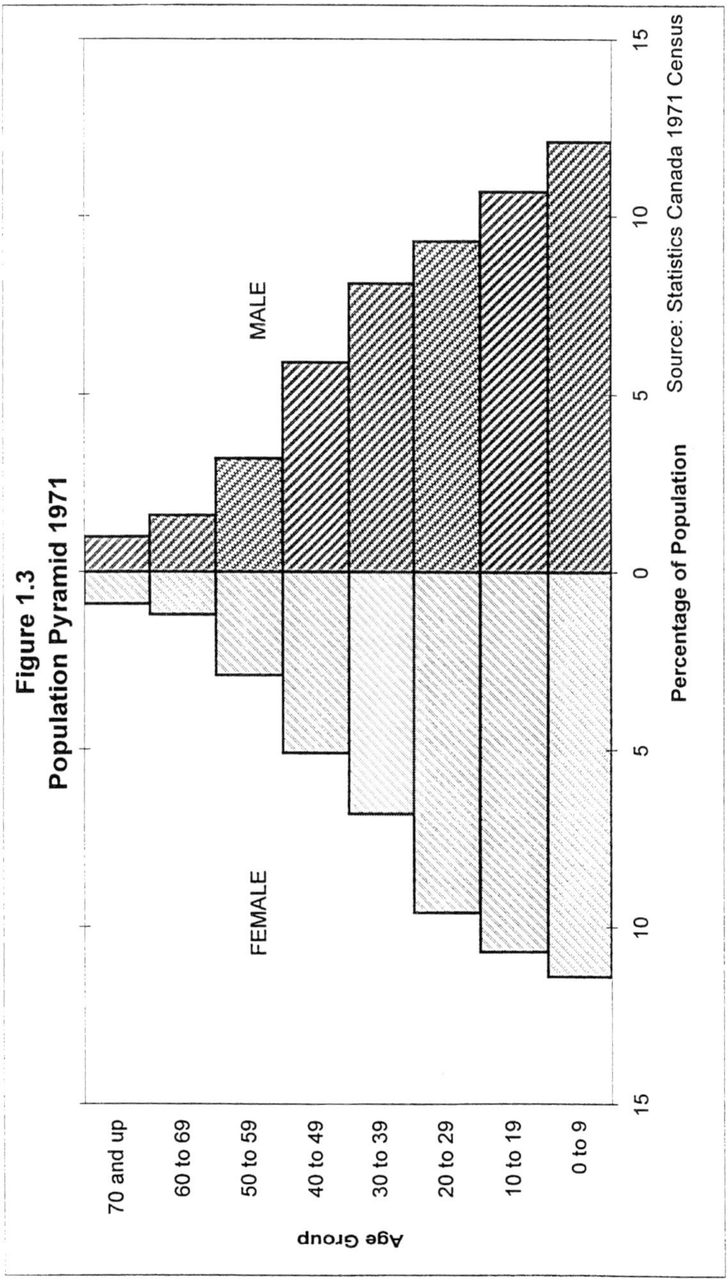
Figure 1.3
Population Pyramid 1971
MALE
FEMALE
Age Group
70 and up
60 to 69
50 to 59
40 to 49
30 to 39
20 to 29
10 to 19
0 to 9
15
10
5
0
5
10
15
Percentage of Population
Source: Statistics Canada 1971 Census

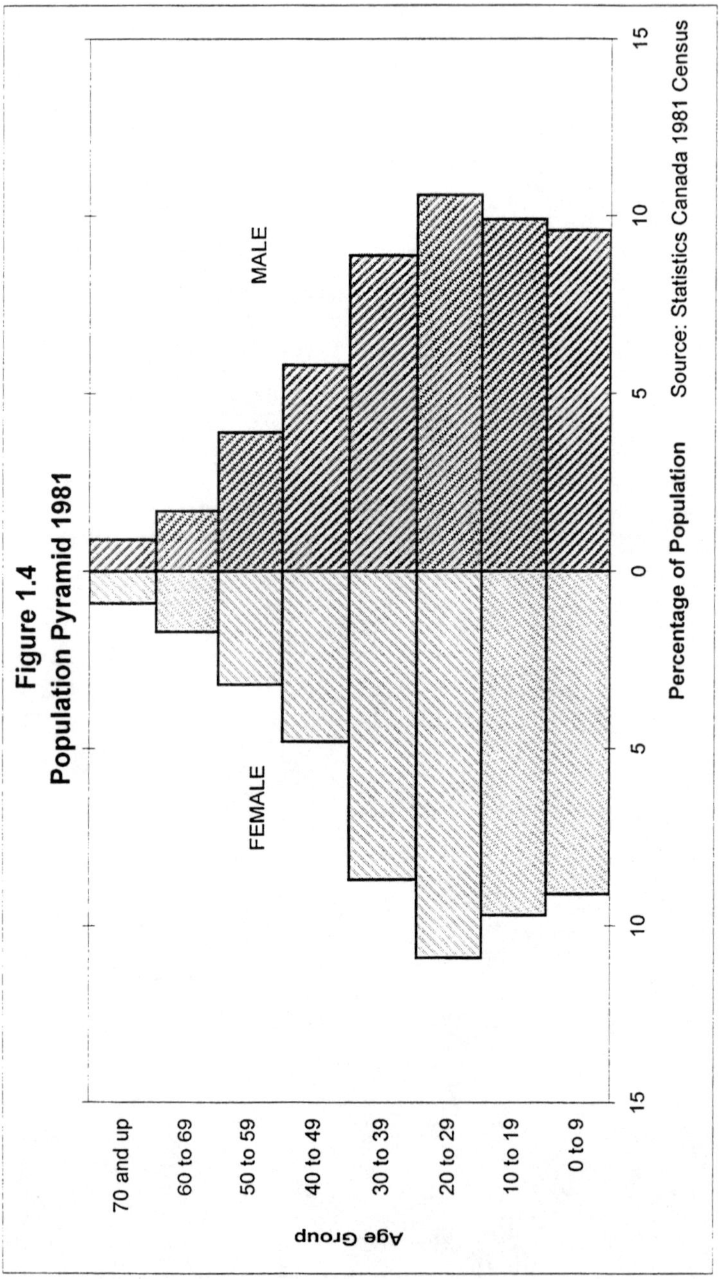

Figure 1.4
Population Pyramid 1981

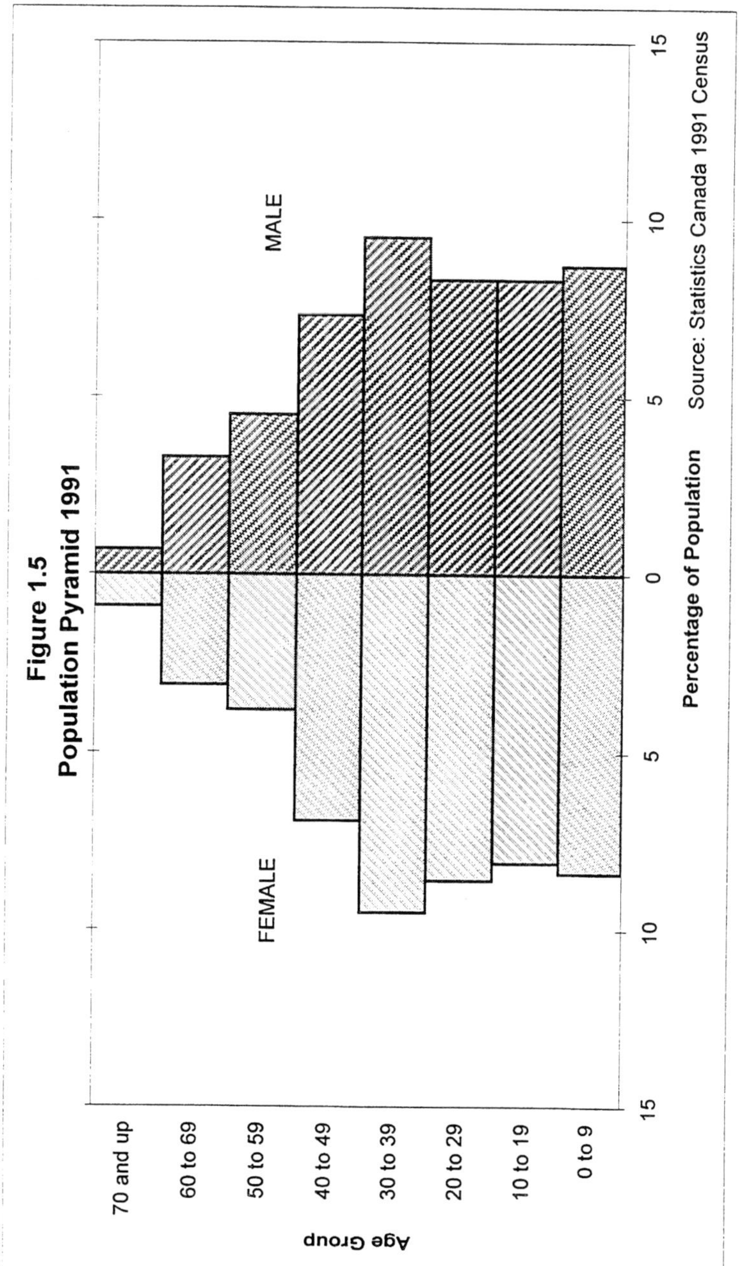

Figure 1.5
Population Pyramid 1991

While Prince George continues to be a city of young families some real changes were occurring by 1981. With a population of over 67,000, for the first time the 20-29 year age cohort replaces the youngest children as the largest age group in the City (Figure 1.4). Continuing with earlier trends concerning the aging of the local workforce, the 50 and older age categories now have larger shares of the local population than they did in 1971 or 1961.

Previous trends are confirmed in the final population pyramid (Figure 1.5). In 1991, Prince George's population had reached 69,655. It should be noted that there is a slight change in the age group scales for the 60 to 74 and 75+ categories compared to the previous population pyramids. The majority of the Prince George population still involves young families with young children. The 0-9 and 30-39 age group categories continue to be the largest. Also, the local population continues to age and this shows up with larger shares of the population who are now over 60 years of age.

Models of resource or single-industry town growth and development suggest that early boom periods will be characterized by a predominately male workforce and a predominance of young families with young children (Lucas, 1971). Over time, as the community matures and additional development of services, industries, etc., occurs, the population structure will slowly even out. Prince George, thus far, appears to be following this type of population change model. In 1961 the population pyramid shows few older residents and many young families. By 1991, however, there were larger shares of the population in the middle and older age categories. A number of issues from services provision, to amenities, to economic opportunities, to local weather and climate may affect a population's structure and it will be interesting to see how Prince George's population pyramid looks in a further 20 years.

Beyond simple tables which list the total population for Prince George, social geographers are interested in how this population is distributed across the neighbourhoods which make up our communiuty. Maps showing population distribution and density employ thematic cartography

Map 1.4
Population Distribution, 1991

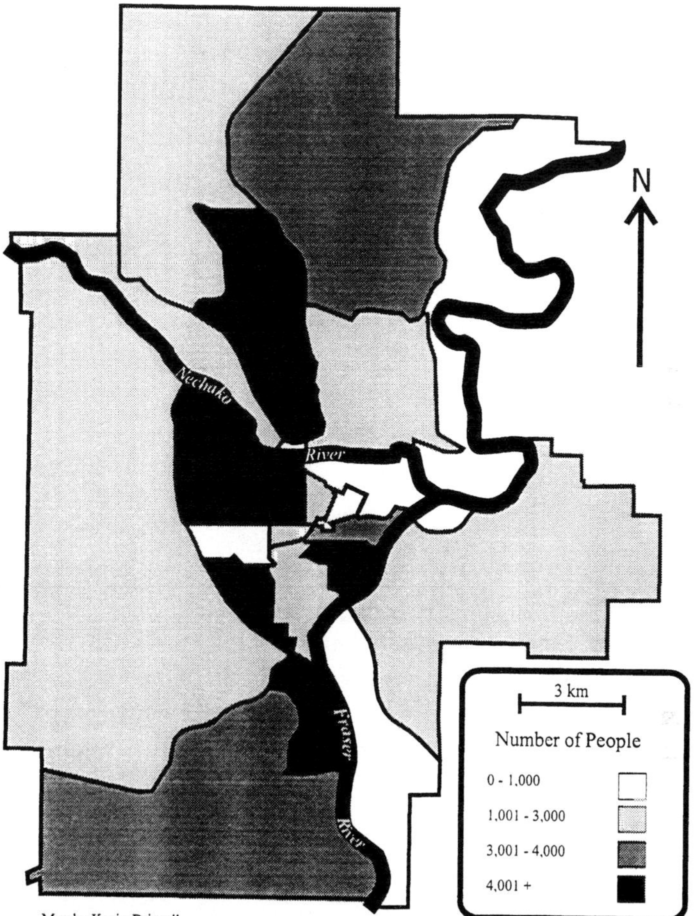

Map by Kevin Driscoll

techniques to show concentrations of people across the City. Census boundaries from 1991 form the base for the following maps in which each of the 23 census tracts in Prince George were "shaded-in" according to which category (population numbers, population density, etc.) they fit under. The result is a set of maps which provide quick visual demonstrations of population characteristics. This mapping technique is used extensively in subsequent chapters of this book.

Map 1.4 shows the population distribution within Prince George for 1991. Maps of such population distributions can show where people live across the community, and may point to areas that need relatively more residential services. The information included is based simply on the total number of people living within each census tract area.

In terms of population distribution (Map 1.4), much of the Prince George population lives within those census tracts which are commonly referred to as the "Bowl". This includes neighbourhoods close to the downtown core such as the Carney Hill area, as well as other "suburban" neighbourhoods such as Foothills/Lakewood and Peden Hill areas. Outside of the Bowl, the suburban landscapes of College Heights and the Hart Highlands areas contain large shares of the City's population.

To examine areas of relative "crowding" within communities, population density maps are commonly used. The density of a population can give clues to aspects of neighbourhood character such as expectations with respect to living conditions, the demand on residential and community services, and the types of housing available. Map 1.5 is a population density map, and the difference between this map and Map 1.4 is that a population density map shows the number of people per square kilometre within each census tract boundary.

A population density map (1.5) was developed for the City of Prince George based upon 1991 census data. The scale of population densities used in Map 1.5 is a relative one; comparing areas of the community on the basis of whether they are more or less dense than other areas. As seen on this map, there is a relatively high concentration of population living within the Bowl area. Exceptions to this pattern are the Central Business District and the Carter light industrial / Prince George Exhibition grounds area. Unlike the distribution map (Map 1.4), outside of the Bowl area, only College Heights shows up as a relatively high density residential neighbourhood. However, since density maps are based on both population numbers and the size of the land area included, some areas of

Map 1.5
Population Density, 1991

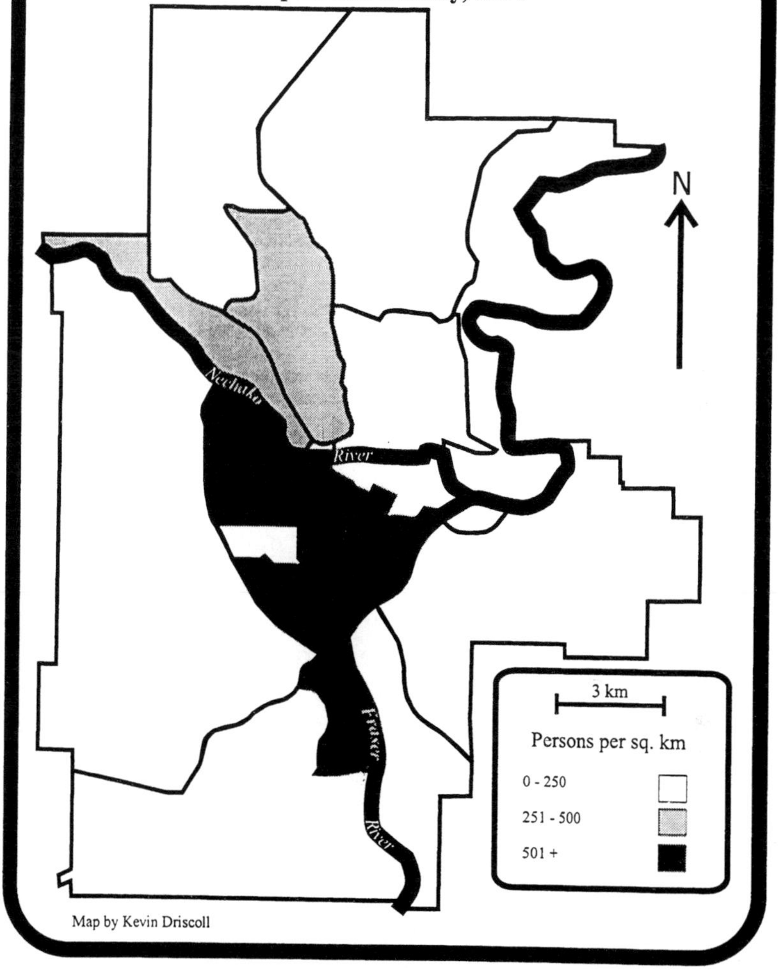

relatively dense residential settlement may not show clearly on the map. For example, the Parkridge and St. Lawrence Heights areas are identified on Map 1.5 as having middle to low residential densities. This is largely a consequence of the large rural land area within which these suburban neighbourhoods are set. Given recent growth in Prince George, it will be interesting to see how the population densities of census tracts in the Hart Highlands and North Nechako areas will change.

Map 1.6 shows the percentage change in population levels in each of the City's 23 census tracts from 1986 to 1991. A population change map can highlight areas of population decline or rapid growth. As with the other maps in this section, information on patterns of population change highlight the dynamics of both the local population and the local community.

Population change within an area is a relative measure, that is, the scale of growth within any census tract depends on the size of the original population in that area and the number of people who move into/move out of the area. As a result, Map 1.6 may at first appear confusing. For example, the census tract which includes the BCR Industrial Site shows a large increase simply because there were very few people living in that area initially. Generally, however, Map 1.6 shows a pattern of recent population increase in areas outside of the Bowl. The Hart Highlands and Parkridge areas show the largest increases, while the College Heights and Pineview areas also show population growth. This result fits well with popular impressions of recent growth in Prince George as new suburban areas are being built outside of the urban core. Overall, if the trends identified in Map 1.6 continue, instead of the previous concentrated pattern, the population of Prince George will become increasingly dispersed outside of the Bowl area. Implications of this transformation will include increased local government expenditures on residential services and infrastructure. Should this development pattern continue, the efficiencies of a compact urban design will not be realized in Prince George.

Taken together, the maps of population distribution, population density, and population change can provide a clearer sense of the dynamics of the City's population. Such maps also provide a foundation for interpreting other social geography issues across the community such as housing, where the type of housing found within neighbourhoods is directly related to population numbers and densities.

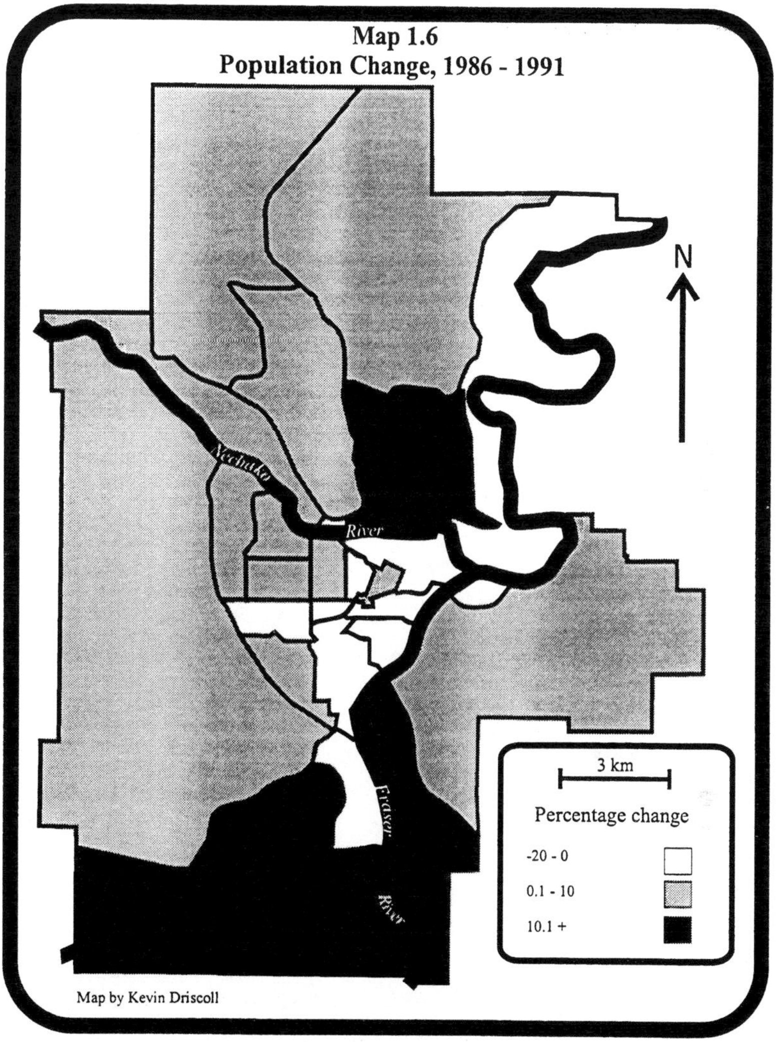

GROWTH RATE AND PROJECTIONS

Growth rate projections enable a city to plan for its future. They are important for determining budgets and the future demand for various types of services. To give some idea of the population projections that have been made in the past, a study from 1965 forecast that "based on the forgoing assumptions, trends, and indications, it is forecast that the population of urban Prince George area should reach about 46,000 by 1970 and 60,000 by 1975" (BC Research Council, 1965, p. 18). These forecasts were based on a 90 percent increase between 1965 and 1975. The actual population of Prince George reached 33,100 in 1971 and 59,929 in 1976.

More recent population forecasts have been developed for the 1993 Official Community Plan for Prince George (Prince George, 1993). Assessing the impact of the University and other large construction projects on local population change, the 1993 Official Community Plan forecasts growth rates of about 1 to 1.5 percent per year. Such growth rates, which are not out of line with recent experience, suggest that by the year 2000, Prince George may have a local population estimated at over 80,000 people.

CONCLUSION

Population growth in Prince George has been shaped by key historical events in its recent development. The Grand Trunk Pacific Railway, and later the Pacific Great Eastern Railway, formed contemporary counterpoints to the historic transportation routes of the Fraser and Nechako Rivers and allowed for the large scale development of the Central Interior lumber industry. Population growth resulted from the influx of workers into this expanding forest industry. The construction of three major pulp mills in Prince George resulted in a surge in population growth and established a strong resource based economy in the City. The 1960s and 1970s were the boom years for Prince George and the City developed significantly. Many young families moved to the community to take advantage of its increasing employment opportunities. Some were also attracted by the affordable housing opportunities within the City, while still others were attracted to the rural lifestyle and lived just outside the City boundaries. During the 1980s recession, growth stagnated. With economic restructuring and investment in the early 1990s, Prince George began to see growth again. The construction of UNBC, the Civic Centre, Multiplex, and Courthouse among other projects, signalled an upturn in the growth and development of Prince George.

The population of Prince George is largely concentrated in the Bowl area. This is mostly due to the physiographic barriers of Cranbrook Hill and the Fraser and Nechako Rivers. Recent population growth, however, is now away from the Bowl area into subdivisions in the surrounding College Heights and Hart Highland areas. Prince George's population is "spilling over" from the core into the less densely developed areas surrounding the City.

The population structure should continue to age as more people retire in the City. Young people will be able to stay, attend college and university, and perhaps make British Columbia's Northern Capital their home. Many service sector growth industries, like technology and communications, are likely to develop along with the University. At present, Prince George is the major centre in the central and northern interior, and if past trends are an indication, it is likely to continue to develop and continue to expand its role in northern British Columbia.

REFERENCES

BC Research Council. (1965). *Population Growth in the Prince George area to 1975*. Vancouver: BC Research Council.

BC Statistics. (1993). *Community Profile for the Fraser Fort George Regional District*. Victoria: Central Statistics Bureau.

_______. (1996). "Total Population Estimates: Municipal and Regional District 1976-1995". Internet document at http://www.bcstats.gov.bc/data/pop/popstart.htm#pop.

Bernsohn, K. (1981). *Cutting up the North*. Vancouver: Hancock Press.

Government of British Columbia (1915). *Fort George Incorporation Act*. Victoria: March 6, 1915, Chapter 29, p. 145.

Hak, G. (1990). "Prairie Capital, Prairie Markets, and Prairie Labour: The Forest Products Industry in the Prince George District, 1910-1930". *Prairie Forum*, 14 (2), 9-22.

Hayter, R. (1976). "Corporate Strategies and Industrial Change in the Canadian Forest Products Industries". *Geographical Review*, 66, 209-228.

Leonard, F. (1984). "Grand Trunk Pacific and the establishment of the City of Prince George". *BC Studies*, 63, pp. 29-54.

Lucas, R. (1971). *Minetown, Milltown, Railtown: Life in Canadian communities of single industries*. Toronto: University of Toronto Press.

Marchak, P. (1989). "History of a Resource Industry". In *A History of British Columbia*, ed. P. Roy. Toronto: Copp Clark, p. 108-128.

Mullins, D.K. (1967). *Changes in Location and Structure in the Forest Industry of North Central BC, 1909-1966*. Vancouver: University of British Columbia, unpublished MA Thesis.

Nixon, T. (1974). "Time has come to share 'rural' residents told". *The Prince George Citizen*. October 25, p. 1.

Prince George (1954). *Prince George City Directory, 1954*. Vancouver: BC Directories.

_______. (1974). *Report of the District Municipality Committee*. Prince George: City of Prince George District Municipality Committee.

_______. (1993). *Prince George Official Community Plan Supplement.* Prince George: City of Prince George Department of Development Services.

_______ . (n.d.). *Map - Boundary Expansions Since 1915.* Prince George: Prince George: City of Prince George Department of Development Services.

Regional District of Fraser-Fort George. (1974). *The City of Prince George - Statistics - 1974.* Prince George: Regional District of Fraser-Fort George, Regional Development Commission.

Runnalls, Rev. F.E. (1946). *The History of Prince George.* Vancouver: Wrigley Printing Co.

Smelts, D. (1915). *Issues in Townsite Development: Government and Railway Involvement in the Incorporation of Prince George, 1914-1915.* Prince George: Local History Document No. 1, College of New Caledonia Archives.

Statistics Canada (1991). *1991 Census Catalogue No. 95-384: Profiles.* Ottawa: Statistics Canada.

_______. (1986). *1986 Census Catalogue No. 95-139: Profiles.* Ottawa: Statistics Canada.

_______. (1981). *1981 Census Catalogue No. 95-964: Profiles.* Ottawa: Statistics Canada.

_______. (1976). *1976 Census Catalogue No. 92-810: General Population.* Ottawa: Statistics Canada.

_______. (1971). *1971 General Population Statistics.* Ottawa: Statistics Canada.

_______. (1961). *Census Summary 1901-1961: Population by Census Subdivisions.* Ottawa. Statistics Canada.

Williston, E and Keller, B. (1997). *Forests, Power and Policy: The legacy of Ray Williston.* Prince George: Caitlin Press.

Chapter 2

EMPLOYMENT IN PRINCE GEORGE

Brannon Rennie and Greg Halseth

INTRODUCTION

This chapter examines issues of work and employment in a northern community. This is an important topic for the social geography of Prince George as the economy remains primarily dependent upon one major sector, the forestry industry. As a result, fluctuations in the fortunes of the forestry sector through boom and bust cycles in product demand can have large effects on the local economy. In other words, if the value of pulp or timber drops, the economy of the Prince George area suffers. Not only do such drops affect forest industry jobs, but they also affect many other industries and economic sectors as well. For example, service and retail sectors will suffer as many households no longer have disposable income to spend. After an outline of the issue of employment, this chapter examines a number of indicators as to the status of work and employment participation in Prince George.

EMPLOYMENT

Employment is a major underlying framework to determining how our society is organized and structured. It is one of the most significant elements in the lives of Canadians. As a result, the topic is of great importance in social geography. Even before a form of currency was used for buying or trading goods, people had to work in order to live and prosper. Today, paid work through employment activity is one basis upon which society is divided. Western society is centred around the ability to consume material goods and, when seen this way, there is a clear connection between employment and such social issues as poverty, housing, gender relations and others in a community.

The workplace is a major starting point for any study of inequality in a society. One's life chances, and her/his ability to buy needed goods and services, is highly dependent on where they are situated in the division of labour (Cater and Jones, 1989). Employers take risks and create opportunities for paid employment in order to gain potential profits in return. Workers contribute their labour, in exchange for a wage or salary, to producing the goods and services that create these profits. Depending upon a number of factors including the level of skill, training, and expertise, workers earn a range of salary/wage returns from minimum wage to very substantial salaries.

There is an emerging consensus that the organization of work and the structure of employment is undergoing a process of change or "restructuring" (Cater and Jones, 1989). Previously, industrial organization was modelled around what has been labelled a "Fordist Regime" of production. Under this model, the organization of work revolved around single, repetitive, tasks that promoted a deskilling of the labour force. The organization of production was based on an isolated shop floor where workers did not have input into production practices or the design of finished products. Industrial workers were simply told what their task was and they followed these instructions. Things even got to the point where "scientific management", or "Taylorism", conceptualized worker movements as similar to that of a robot and then went on to organize all employee activities and body movements on the production line. The Fordist Regime was well suited for large scale production runs with little product differentiation.

Currently, an alternative model of industrial organization commonly referred to as the "Flexible Regime of Production", is suggested as becoming more common (Cater and Jones, 1989). A Flexible Regime model centres upon both the retraining of workers so that they can undertake multiple production tasks and the re-organization of work in order for the industry to produce a greater variety of specialized products. In a Flexible Regime, the workers on the shop floor are not isolated from decision-making but are invited to provide input to firm management with a goal of making workers feel like they are part of the whole process of production. The industrial operations of many large forestry firms now embody Flexible Regime principles that promote a united team of workers and management. Operating under the philosophy that a satisfied worker will contribute to a happier and more productive workplace, firms convey a real sense of concern for their employees and strive to offer a range of services and social benefits like counseling and leaves of absence for various personal or family reasons.

The Flexible Regime model of industrial organization has proved to be increasingly appealing for firms for a variety of reasons. Important among these reasons are global competition and rising production costs. Global competition in most resource and manufacturing industries has meant that large production runs of single products cannot survive against constantly changing consumer demands, adaptive competitors, and a rapidly changing marketplace. Instead, niche marketing and product differentiation, characteristic of the Flexible Regime model, are increasingly important and allow for rapid changes in types of goods produced. This helps a firm remain competitive. A second motivation for firms is the possibility of a net savings in labour costs. By increasing the use of automation and computers, more and more manual labour can be replaced with a smaller but more highly skilled work force. As well, some functions within the firm can be eliminated and replaced by contracting work out to consultants. Benefits to the firm derived from the contracting out of work include the paying of consultants only when the firm needs their specific expertise, and the replacing of large on-going benefits packages for employees with set contract fees for consultants and contractors. Recent studies looking at the process of restructuring to a Flexible Regime of production in a set of pulp and paper towns from across Canada clearly demonstrate that significant job losses were a universal community impact (Mackenzie and Norcliffe, 1997).

Technology and Restructuring

As suggested above, the increasing use of technology in production processes has been an integral part of restructuring to a Flexible Regime. As the economy of Prince George has become more diversified over the past 30 years, service sector jobs have formed an increasingly important part of our economy. Technology is, however, rapidly changing service sector employment as well. As O'Reilly (1995, p. 2) has put it, "nothing can replace the human touch. However, the human touch is not as essential as had been thought. People are willing to pump their own gas, talk to voice mail recordings, and do their banking at an instant teller". It is expected that the service sector will undergo further changes and job eliminations through the increased application of technologies. O'Reilly (1996, p. 17) suggests examples where:

> restaurants will have laser cookers and information systems that allow customers to press buttons to get a hamburger just the way they want. Cashiers may be traded with robot cashiers where shoppers simply run their groceries through an optical scanner and touch the screen command box to signal readiness to pay with a bank card or cash.

Technology also has an enormous impact upon women. Females have traditionally made up a large percentage of those employed in clerical and service sector jobs, and it is in these jobs that replacement through technology is particularly common. O'Reilly (1995, p. 16) suggests that:

> Technology had its first impact on clerical workers in the 1980's. With the introduction of the personal computer, all workers were able to produce their own documents, memos, and letters, thus eliminating many clerical jobs. The second wave of technology, in the form of electronic data interchange, which is the computer to computer exchange of information, is now positioned to move beyond the banking sector where it originated. In order for women to keep their clerical jobs, they must develop strong technical skills, including advanced word processing, spreadsheet capabilities as well as other software programs.

Restructuring impacts and technological change, it seems, are widespread in the contemporary economy. To keep pace with the changing nature of workplace technology, issues such as retraining, skills upgrading, and the process of "life-long learning" are now more important than ever.

FORESTRY-BASED COMMUNITIES

It has been suggested that over the past decade the forestry industry in British Columbia has undergone a sea-change of sorts as it moves from a Fordist to a Flexible Regime of production (Hayter, Barnes and Grass, 1992). Along with this transformation, new products, technologies, and labour practices were introduced. As a result of such changes, many jobs were lost and numbers of mills and facilities have been shut down. In part, this continues a longer pattern of job loss and firm consolidation through the introduction of automation and the need for major capital financing in the industry. While these changes have had an effect upon the British Columbia economy, the most affected economies are those in the province's small, forestry-dependent, communities. Hayter, Barnes, and Grass (1992, p. 1) argue that the coastal forest resource base has dwindled partly as a result of "inadequate reforestation, earlier clear cutting, and most recently environmental and native aboriginal concerns. These particular difficulties are "part of a general problem endemic to industrial capitalism. Historically there has always been a potential tension between the fluidity of the market and the rootedness of place. While capital is mobile, the community is not" (Hayter, Barnes and Grass, 1992, p. 1).

Since the late 1970s, a growing disjuncture between market forces and community dependence upon single industries has created considerable uncertainty for residents in resource-dependent communities across North America. As Hayter, Barnes and Grass (1992) point out, the problem for many resource-dependent communities is that critical corporate decision-making is often based outside of the community. If resources become exhausted, commodity prices fall, or demand dwindles, the historical evidence is that while the firms often survive by moving to other areas, the fate for most single-industry towns is eventual abandonment. Large international corporations can relocate, having taken many years worth of profits out of a local area. The community, however, cannot so easily relocate. While Prince George is not a single industry town, the City would face economic uncertainty if the major mills were to close down.

Because Prince George is the focal point of a regional forestry industry, it is important to raise the issue of "regional" employment impacts. Cater and Jones (1989) suggest that specific communities may suffer or prosper due to the unique characteristics of the region within which they are set. The hypothesis is that all regions in any given economic system are competing for a share of the total economic activity generated within that system. By virtue of their location, some regions possess relative advantages and disadvantages. The result is that "competitive" regions will be able to attract large scale economic development at the expense of other regions (Cater and Jones, 1989). Being a "northern" community, Prince George does not have some of the advantages of a large population or inexpensive transportation costs to markets. The city is also relatively isolated from other major urban and manufacturing centres. As economies become more global, northern cities such as Prince George face a struggle as large firms are increasingly drawn to warmer, low cost, production sites closer to major world markets. Balancing this, Prince George is developing as a government and service centre for northern British Columbia and is blessed with a range of natural resources.

Prince George's economy has, and is continuing to experience, a snowball growth effect; that is, regional growth has been steady and cumulative (see Chapter 1 by Stauffer and Halseth, 1998). The establishment of the Grand Trunk Pacific and later the BC Rail railway lines, provided major boosts to area development. Establishment of sawmills, and later the three pulp mills, also encouraged growth by creating opportunities for steady, well-paid, employment. This in turn brought an increase in demands for other services. Schools, a hospital, government services, medical specialists, and the like developed or increased in Prince George as a result of population growth from resource industry development. These effects continue as the City grows, diversifies, and matures. Further diversity in the City's economy can provide a counterbalance to the boom and bust cycles of resource industries.

PRINCE GEORGE

This discussion begins with an introduction to the major employers in Prince George and is followed by three sections examining local employment issues that describe first, the size of the Prince George labour force, second its occupational structure, and third the relative share of employment versus other income sources in the community. Taken together, the issues raised in these sections form a foundation for interpreting other social geography issues in the City.

Major Employers

Despite local diversification, the forestry sector continues to play a vital role in the Prince George economy. An article in the newspaper supplement "Prince George: City of Opportunity" (Prince George Citizen, March 21, 1996, p. 32) noted that:

> Prince George is extremely dependent on the revenue created throughout the logging industry. Employees in the Central Interior produce 2.9 billion board feet of lumber - enough wood to girdle the globe at the equator two feet wide, one inch thick, plus 900,000 metric tons of pulp and paper, specialty forest products, and 175 million square feet of plywood. Highly dependent on the abundance of natural resources in and around the Northern Interior, the area produced 395 million dollars that accounted for 8,500 direct jobs. This capital meant that the average pay was 46,470 dollars for people in the industry in 1993. If these jobs were to be eliminated, plus those jobs supplying the industry and jobs which were created because there were people in town making those wages, and Prince George would shrink from 75,000 people to 31,500. This prediction in the rate of population decrease derives from the fact that forty-two per cent of the present employment in the Prince George and surrounding area is directly related to the forest industry.

The largest forestry sector employers in the Prince George region are Northwood Pulp and Timber, and Canadian Forest Products Limited (Canfor). As of 1997, Northwood employed approximately 2,000 people locally (personal communication). This includes approximately 670 people in the pulp mill and 1,380 people in their forestry and sawmills divisions. Northwood has a number of local operations including four sawmills, a treated wood plant, a plywood plant, and a tree nursery operation. Canfor employed a total of approximately 1,650 people in the Prince George area (personal communication). Local operations include the two pulp and paper mills together with the Netherlands and Clear Lake forestry divisions. Both companies have either experienced, or are presently going through, a process of employment reduction brought about by the pressure to reduce costs as a result of global competition, increased use of technology, and replacement of older production processes for more flexible product lines. Along with job reductions, the nature of employment with firms such as Canfor and Northwood has changed as well. Gone are the times when a person with only a grade 12 education could get a good job in the mills (personal communication). These jobs are becoming highly skilled with the companies being strongly committed to in-house education and training programs to keep employees up-to-date on new technologies.

Besides absolute job losses, the impacts of temporary shut downs or "curtailments" at both Northwood and Canfor operations can be significant for the local economy. Scheduled curtailments in 1996 and economic disruption in 1997 mean less income is available to be spent at local stores, and support industries will also have less work and income.

The largest single employer in the City is School District 57. Employing approximately 2,700 people, the School District operates administrative offices, 53 elementary schools, and 11 secondary schools (personal communication). While the School District extends beyond the boundaries of Prince George, most schools and most of the employment occurs within the City. Like Northwood and Canfor, School District 57 has faced a changing economic climate. In recent years, cutbacks in provincial funding has resulted in the loss of employment positions. In 1996 alone, the School District faced a decision on how to cut an additional $2 million from its already reduced budget. Under this scenario:

> the school district has plans to cut eight administrative officer positions by consolidating management of several smaller schools under one principal, consolidating the management of adjacent schools under one principal, increasing enrolment qualification levels for vice-principals, or relocating administrative resources from elementary schools to secondary schools. They also plan to shorten the lunch hour from forty-five minutes to half an hour in order to reduce supervisory costs, and decrease the administrative positions within the district. Other services being looked at are to centralize services, such as library

resources (The Free Press, 1996, p. A7).

The development of the University of Northern British Columbia (UNBC), and the expansion of the College of New Caledonia (CNC), are expected to have a number of employment related effects in Prince George. In terms of employees, UNBC presently employs approximately 130 faculty and 200 staff while CNC employs approximately 700 people (Personal communication; Prince George Region Development Corporation, 1993). Beyond direct employment, both institutions are expected to contribute to the training and development of the local population and workforce. For example, CNC has expanded its training and career-vocational programs to better fit the needs of the industry, community, business, government and residents of Prince George. Additional spinoff growth in support services and the innovation of new economic opportunities are expected benefits from having two large post-secondary educational institutions in the City.

The Prince George Regional Hospital is another important employer in Prince George. Presently employing approximately 1,350 people in various jobs from doctors and nurses to food services staff and custodians, the hospital is also feeling the effects of government cutbacks (personal communication). Budget cutbacks caused lay-offs in a number of nursing and other occupational areas. For the local hospital, moves toward community based health care will also cause some shifts in employment. The Prince George Regional Hospital also has access to a pool of nurses available on a casual basis. Given present labour conditions, a Bachelor of nursing degree is now a valuable part of being selected for a job (Labour Market Information Unit, 1995).

Finally, small business and "self-employed" business growth is an important part of the Prince George economy. Agencies such as the Community Futures Development Corporation, Human Resources Development Canada, and the Development Bank of Canada work to support such business growth to promote local economic development and employment. Even organizations such as the Prince George Native Friendship

Centre and others are looking at establishing "lending circles" and other mechanisms to promote economic and employment growth (Prince George Citizen, 1996b). While definitions of small businesses vary, they play a significant role in local communities. As O'Reilly (1995) suggests, there are distinct advantages and disadvantages to employment with small businesses. Among the disadvantages are usually lower pay and benefits, together with less opportunity for advancement. Among the advantages are opportunities to "learn the ropes" and to gain a broad range of skills. Self-employment is an increasingly common option in Prince George.

Labour Force

The Prince George labour force is presently experiencing some of the employment impacts described earlier in the chapter. As a result, sets of changes are starting to show up in the aggregate employment statistics. In Table 2.1, the size of the Prince George labour force is shown together with a comparison of the labour force relative to the local population. In the 10 year period since 1981, the City's population increased by approximately 3.1 percent (or about 2,100 people). Over that same period the local labour force increased approximately 9.2 percent (or about 3,300 positions). In part, this growth must take into account the fact that the forestry industry was in a recession at the start of the 1980s and there

Table 2.1
Labour Force Size in Prince George

	Total Labour Force	Labour Force as a % of Population
1981	35,595	52.7
1986	36,045	53.3
1991	38,870	55.8

Source: Statistics Canada

were fewer jobs in the local economy. A second item of note is that the size of the labour force as a percentage of the local population increased over this same period from approximately 53 percent to nearly 56 percent. The increasing need for two-adult households to have two incomes no doubt also plays some role in these changes.

A further element in the growth of the Prince George labour force from 1981 to 1991 includes the increasing participation of women in paid employment. Figure 2.1 shows this increasing labour force participation. In 1981, approximately 14,000 women in Prince George were active in the paid employment force. By 1996, this number had growth to just under 17,000 women. These types of changes not only have implications in the work place with respect to occupational structure and issues such as pay equity, they also affect other social issues in the community such as the provision of safe and affordable daycare.

Figure 2.1
Number of Females in Prince George Labour Force
1981-1991

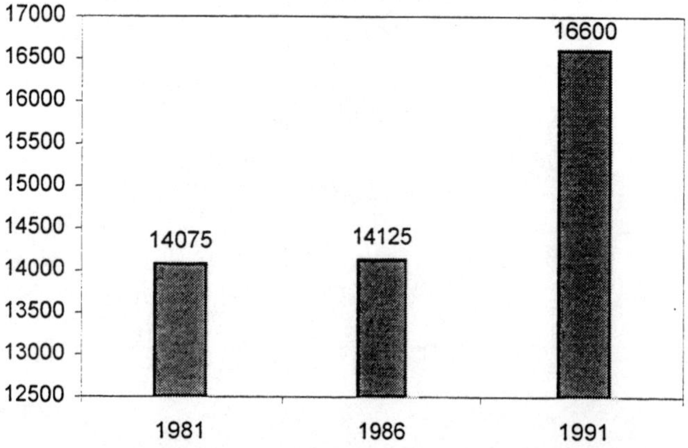

Source: Statistics Canada 1981/86/91

In Table 2.2, the increasing labour force participation of women in Prince George is further explored. In this case, the local labour force from 1981 to 1991 is compared in terms of the percentage who are male and the percentage who are female. In 1981, females accounted for 39.6 percent of the Prince George labour force, yet by 1991 they accounted for 44.6 percent. This pattern of an increasing participation of women in the paid labour force mirrors Canada-wide trends.

Table 2.2
Prince George Labour Force,
by Gender

	Percent Male	Percent Female
1981	60.4	39.6
1986	58.7	41.3
1991	55.4	44.6

Source: Statistics Canada

Occupation Structure

In this section, the structure of the Prince George labour force is examined using information on "Occupations". As noted in Chapter 1 (Stauffer and Halseth, 1998), any time we use aggregated statistical data we need to be cautious in its interpretation and aware of the constraints imposed by the data collection agencies. In the case of occupational classifications recorded in the Census, we are not able to disaggregate the information by economic sector. For example, within the pulp and paper sector there are employees working in a wide range of occupational areas. A further problem with occupation data is that it combines workers across some very large skill, training, and income gaps. Take for example Medicine and Health, where hospital orderlies are grouped with surgeons. With these cautionary notes in mind, the review of occupational structure in Prince George examines both the total labour force and the labour force divided by males and females.

In Table 2.3, the percentage share of the Prince George labour force within each of the census' occupational categories is shown for the years 1981, 1986, and 1991. The largest single occupational category is Clerical, accounting for approximately 17 percent of the Prince George labour force in 1991. The next most common occupational groupings are in the Service, Sales, and Managerial/Administrative categories. In 1991, these next three occupational groups accounted for approximately 14, 10, and 8 percent respectively of the Prince George labour force. Interestingly, some of the occupational sectors commonly associated with resource-dependent employment such as Primary, Processing, and Transportation each accounted for only approximately 5 percent of the Prince George labour force in 1991.

Table 2.3
Occupational Structure
Prince George Labour Force

	1981		1986		1991	
	#	%	#	%	#	%
Total Labour Force	35,595		36,045		38,870	
Manager/Administrative	2,625	7.4	2,970	8.6	3,085	8.1
Teaching	1,510	4.2	1,435	4.1	1,765	4.6
Medical/Health	1,350	3.8	1,325	3.8	1,680	4.4
Tech./Art.	1,810	5.1	2,000	5.8	2,405	6.3
Clerical	6,740	18.9	6,025	17.4	6,610	17.3
Sales	3,445	9.7	3,200	9.2	3,640	9.5
Service	4,270	12.0	5,015	14.5	5,320	13.9
Primary	1,210	3.4	2,045	5.9	2,045	5.3
Processing	1,930	5.4	1,875	5.4	2,100	5.5
Machinery	3,105	8.7	2,955	8.5	2,990	7.8
Construction	3,335	9.4	2,445	7.1	2,675	6.9
Transportation	1,780	5.0	2,690	7.8	1,980	5.2
Other	2,020	5.7	1,705	4.9	1,750	4.6

Source: Statistics Canada.

If we re-examine Table 2.3 by looking for changes over time, it is clear that over the recent past the occupational structure has remained relatively static. A few particular occupations have experienced small shifts from 1981 to 1991.

Clerical and Construction have seen their relative shares of the Prince George labour force decline, while the Service and Primary occupational categories have seen their share increase.

In Figures 2.2 and 2.3, the number of people employed within each of the census' occupational categories is shown for 1981 and 1991 respectively. The figures break down the data from Table 2.3 to show the separate distributions for males and females. In looking at both figures, it is clear that there is considerable occupation segregation in the Prince George labour force, a segregation which in many respects also reflects occupational segregation patterns which persist in Canadian society as a whole.

As shown in Figures 2.2 and 2.3, females are over-represented in the Clerical and Medicine and Health occupational categories. In both cases, the number of women employed is four to six times the number of men. The occupational categories of Service and Teaching also have an over-representation of women. In these two cases, nearly twice as many women are employed as are men.

Next, we can identify the occupational categories within which men are over-represented. Figures 2.2 and 2.3 identify Primary, Processing, Machining, Construction, and Transportation as male dominated occupations. Given the importance of the resource sector in the Prince George economy this result is not especially surprising. In all five of these categories very few women are employed. As well, all five of these categories are often associated with the historic label of "mens' work". The category of Managerial and Administration is the only one which shows some significant change between 1981 and 1991. While still dominated by men, a much larger number of women are employed in Managerial and Administration occupations in 1991 as compared to 1981.

Self-employment is becoming more common for both men and women in Prince George. In 1986, census data reported that 440 females out of a total female labour force of 14,140 were self-employed. In 1991 this changed to 790 in a female labour force of 16,700. This represents a change from 3.0 to 4.7 percent of employed women who are self-employed. This pattern of growth is seen for males as well. In 1986 there were

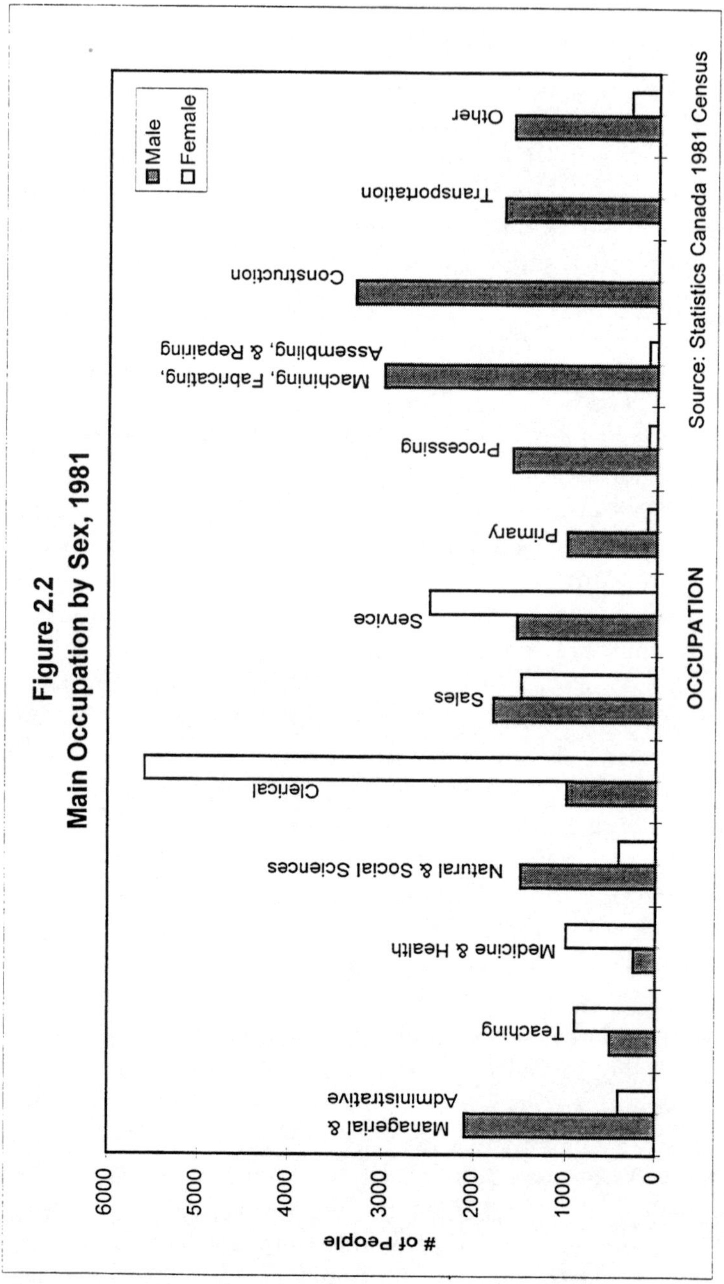

Figure 2.2
Main Occupation by Sex, 1981

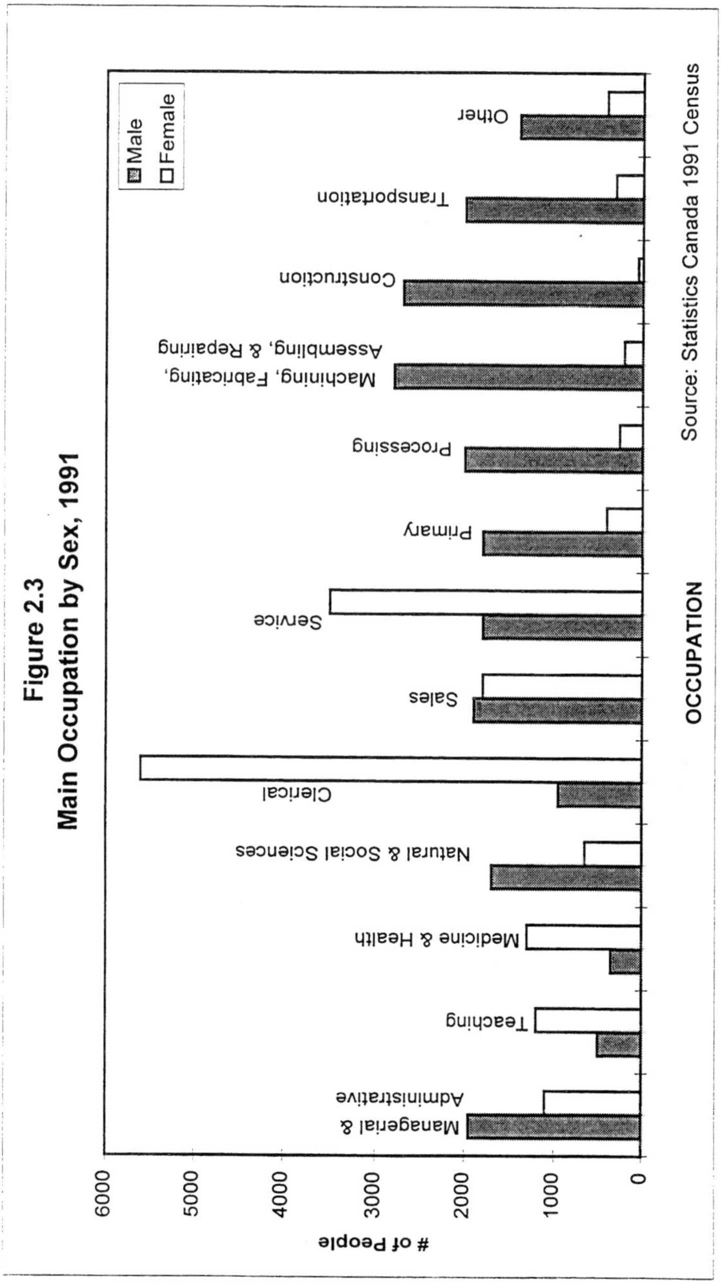

Figure 2.3
Main Occupation by Sex, 1991

1,190 self-employed men in a labour force of 20,545 (5.7 percent of labour force). By 1991 this had increased to nearly 2,000 out of a labour force of 21,540 (9.2 percent of labour force).

Employment Income

Newspaper reports and other accounts suggest that income levels in the City of Prince George are high relative to other communities. Table 2.4 includes one such income comparison. Many issues are involved in "income" and many factors contribute to whether local income levels are relatively high or relatively low. One of the first such issues is the type of employment opportunities in a community and whether they are in high or low wage sectors. As seen in an earlier section, the forestry and educational sectors are significant local employers. Both such sectors could be characterized as involving high wage paying jobs with good benefits plans. Certainly across Canada, resource industry communities often have high wage characteristics (Lucas, 1971; Marchak, 1983). The employment profile for Prince George suggests that high average local income levels can be expected, but that there is an uncertainty of employment over the long run through demand cycles and resource availability.

Table 2.4
Median Family Income Comparison

City	Median Family Income
Prince George	$49,405
Vancouver	$57,100
Victoria	$46,255
Kamloops	$46,387
Kelowna	$39,209

Source: Statistics Canada, 1991 Census.

Table 2.5
Employment Income

	Composition of Total Income		
	Percent Employment Income	Percent Government Transfer Income	Percent Other Income
1986	87.0	8.8	4.2
1991	85.5	9.2	5.3

Source: Statistics Canada, 1986 and 1991 Census.

However, "income" includes components beyond employment wages. In Table 2.5, information from the 1986 and 1991 census is included to compare the percentage of local income derived from employment, government transfers, and other sources. In Prince George, employment income dominates. If however, the community being studied was a large retirement destination, for example, we would expect that this pattern would look quite different. In Prince George, government transfers account for approximately 9 percent of total income. Government transfer income includes funds delivered from a government body, program, or agency, to the individual. Such transfers include Canada Pension Plan, Old Age Supplement, Employment Insurance, Child Benefits and the like. In Prince George, "other" sources of income account for between 4 and 5 percent of total income and can include such things as private pension or insurance plans, as well as income from property investments.

CONSIDERING THE FUTURE

To conclude this chapter on employment, it is important to note that Prince George, like many other communities, is changing. Technology has had an important impact on employment and will continue to do so. Gone are the days when a student could drop out of high-school and obtain a full-

Figure 2.4
General Employment Characteristics

	PAST	FUTURE
ECONOMY	- Competitive advantages based on resource endowments	- Competitive advantage based on knowledge, skills, and attitudes of workers
	- Rapid economic growth	- Slower economic growth
LABOUR MARKET	- High-wage resource jobs	- Fewer high-wage, secure resource jobs; more service jobs
	- Most jobs in large firms or institutions	- Many more small business jobs
	- Relatively secure full-time jobs	- Many jobs contingent
	- Little upgrading required	- Need for continual upgrading
DIVERSITY	-Focus on Baby Boomers and women	- Much greater diversity - existing work force - emerging - transitional - aboriginal peoples and members of equity groups
NATURE OF WORK/SKILLS NEEDED	- Narrow skill sets	- Complex, job-ready skill sets
	- Little training to qualify for intermediate skill level jobs	- Most intermediate skill level jobs require training
	- "Work Force"	- "Learning Force"
EDUCATION/ TRAINING	- Time-based credentials	- Skill-based credentials
	- Steady increase in public resources	- Reduced public resources
	- System largely Public	- More balanced integrated learning systems - public institutions - private, community-based - workplace, non-formal

Source: adapted from British Columbia Labour Force Development Board, 1995.

time, high-paying, job in an industrial mill. Figure 2.4 attempts to capture some of these future implications for work and employment. Given the present importance of the forestry industry in Prince George, these implications will likely play a large role in changing the local social geography of work.

Whether in goods, services, or the industrial sector, most firms in Prince George are adapting to a new working environment brought on by a number of factors. Global competition, increased use of technology, and international trade treaties are reinforcing the need to remain competitive - a need often satisfied through leaner operations, flexible production, increased use of technologies, and development of both new products and processes. These factors are bringing permanent changes to the economy. Restructuring has already resulted in job losses in resource industries, traditional areas of low and medium skilled employment opportunities. In Prince George, such pressures create perhaps as many opportunities as they do losses. It will be interesting to see what the City's social geography of work and employment looks like 10 or 20 years into the future. At present, indications are for continued diversification and growth as the City's role as British Columbia's "Northern Capital" continues to develop.

REFERENCES

British Columbia Labour Force Development Board. (1995). *Training for What?* Victoria: British Columbia Labour Force Development Board.

Carson, R. and Carson, A. (1991). *Statistical Review of the British Columbia Labour Market.* Associated Economic Consultants Ltd..

Cater, J. and Jones, T. (1989). *Social Geography: An Introduction to Contemporary Issues.* London: Edward Arnold.

Free Press, The (1996). "School Board Pushes on With Budget", March 21, p. A7.

Hayter, R., Barnes, T., and Grass, E. (1994). *Single Industry Towns and Local Development: Three Coastal British Columbia Forest Product Communities.* Thunder Bay: Lakehead University Centre for Northern Studies.

Labour Market Information Unit. (1993). *Labour Market Bulletin - Prince George and Area, May 1993.* Prince George: Labour Market Information Unit.

Lucas, R. (1971). *Minetown, Milltown, Railtown: Life in Canadian communities of single industry.* Toronto: University of Toronto Press.

Mackenzie, S. and Norcliffe, G. (1997). Restructuring in the Canadian Newsprint Industry. *The Canadian Geographer*, 41 (1) pp. 2-6.

Marchak, P. (1983). *Green Gold: The Forest Industry in British Columbia.* Vancouver: University of British Columbia Press, pp. 213-248.

O'Reilly, E. (1995). *Making Career Sense of Labour Market Information.* Ottawa: Canadian Guidance and Counseling Foundation.

Prince George. (1996). "Forest Firms remain major players here", in *Prince George: City of Opportunity* supplement to The Prince George Citizen, March 21, p. 32.

________. (1996). "Just Watch us Keep Growing", in *Prince George: City of Opportunity* supplement to The Prince George Citizen, March 21, p. 3.

Prince George Citizen, The. (1996). "Lending Circle Helps Budding Entrepreneurs", March 18, pp. 13.

Prince George Region Development Corporation. (1993). *Prince George, British Columbia: Profile.* Prince George, Prince George Region Development Corporation.

Chapter 3

SOCIAL GEOGRAPHY OF HOUSING

Kathy Marchuk

INTRODUCTION

The topic of housing is extremely important within social geography. Housing is "not only shelter, and a major capital good, it is the largest component in an average household's expenditures and wealth, as well as a visible status symbol" (Bourne and Bunting, 1993, p. 175). The term "housing" is often used synonymously with the term "home". They do, however, have very different meanings. The first is more of a physical structure while the second encompasses a sense of emotion. This chapter will examine housing issues in Prince George, and through mapping the social landscape of housing across the City, will provide a sense of how communities and neighbourhoods are organizing themselves within the housing sub-markets. A social geography framework of housing theories will set the stage for a discussion of issues such as housing types, tenure, values, the state of the market, and some special housing needs.

DEFINITIONS OF HOUSING

A house is more "than a place to eat, sleep and procreate ... it is required to provide privacy, security, warmth and comfort together with ample facilities for leisure, family life, storage of possessions, entertainment of visitors and maintenance of hygiene..." (Cater and Jones, 1989, p. 38). Housing is considered a shelter that most people strive for, require to remain healthy and satisfy demands, and as a place for reproduction. Cater and Jones suggest that to understand housing, three levels of satisfaction - material utility, cultural norms, and externalities - need to be considered (Table 3.1). Material utility is determined by whether the house meets our individual needs and wants, with "needs" being defined as that which enables a person to remain well and survive whereas "wants" are culturally determined (Cater and Jones, 1989).

Cultural norms, a second level of housing satisfaction, focus on the ways we collectively value different types and styles of housing. In North America, it is strongly suggested that we judge housing with middle-class values. While everyone should be entitled to decent housing conditions, cultural norms set a framework for subjectively judging each other's housing. These culturally defined frameworks for judging what is and what is not adequate does vary around the world. What North American culture determines are good conditions will vary from that of say a third world country. Houses, therefore, function not just as shelter but as culturally defined symbols and displays of status.

A third level of housing satisfaction involves "externalities", which are described in Table 3.1 as being made up of such residential location features as neighbourhoods and community amenities. Within this context, the house is seen not just as a single unit, but rather as part of a neighbourhood. External amenities such as the house's proximity to employment, and distance from certain types of social environments, are thus important factors in both the price and desirability of the house, and will affect an individual's decision whether or not to make a purchase. Collectively, the set of features which includes both the characteristics of the house as well as the characteristics of the neighbourhood is considered the "housing bundle". The house is now a dwelling in "geographical space which in itself exerts a profound influence on the well-being and life chances of its occupants" (Cater and Jones, 1989, p. 42). Different neighbourhoods can place their residents in varying degrees of danger, and pose varying health hazards and social disadvantages. As an example of this concept, think about an inner-city housing slum compared to a high status housing area - there is a segregation of residential areas which in general terms marks both social differentiation (at a collective level) and life chances (at an individual level). From this example, a community's housing landscape can be thought of as a "product of inequality, conflict and injustice" (Cater and Jones, 1989, p. 44).

TABLE 3.1
LEVELS OF HOUSING SATISFACTION

Material Utility	Needs/Wants ie: family size
Cultural Norms	Value judgements ie: status symbol
Externalities	Neighbourhood/community ie: close to schools

Adapted from Cater and Jones (1989).

THE MEANING OF HOME

Home is not just a place where one resides. It has taken on a much more complex and broader meaning. The Canadian view of home has been evolving as society has changed. Harris and Pratt, in an article entitled "The Meaning of Home, Homeownership, and Public Policy" argue that this change has occurred in three ways (Table 3.2). The first was produced by a shift in paid employment away from the house. Rarely were houses considered as a supplemental source of income. For example, in 18th century Montreal, "working-class families supplemented their wages by keeping pigs, tending vegetable gardens, and renting to boarders" (Harris and Pratt, 1993, p. 282). Since the 1930s the number of households keeping boarders has declined and this has altered the meaning of the term "home".

The second area of change is that there is an increased separation between home and work. Earlier this century, one's workplace was in close proximity to the home. As we near the twenty-first century, this has changed. People are now moving further away from their place of employment as transportation routes have improved and the average work day has been shortened. These factors have resulted in an increase in the number of commuters and a boom in the development of suburbs. As homes became more private, distance and a lack of boarders allow the home to take on the role of a 'third parent'. Harris and Pratt (1993, p. 282) draw out one 1950s view of the home:

> The house in which children grow up is almost as much a parent to them as a father or mother. With its all-pervading influences - good and bad - a house helps shape values and set standards for the younger generation. In this respect a house is really a third parent.

Children are considered to be sheltered from the assumed harmful influences of urban society.

The third area of change is that the home has increasingly become a status symbol. Harris and Pratt discuss ideas of homeownership, neighbourhood, style, and decoration. The home can be moulded to fit individual tastes and preferences, therefore, setting oneself apart from others. A beautifully landscaped yard in a well kept neighbourhood reflects on the owner's wealth and social status. This can be contrasted with rundown inner-city areas which might have garbage littering public and private properties. The assumption here is generally made that the occupiers are poorer and of a lower social class. Interior decorations also denote social class. As trends change, only elite populations with disposable income can afford to furnish their homes to meet the changing trends. House exteriors are the visible part of the home and are, therefore, the first recognizable feature used to distinguish class and status opinions. Cater and Jones (1989, p. 40) agree that housing represents a status symbol, using the example that "the rich family's mansion is not simply a place of habitation ....

It is a visible monument to opulence, success and worthiness .... By the same token, to live in a slum is a public admission of poverty". They are saying that the idea of a home is no longer just an individual accomplishment and private matter but that of a public issue that must be proclaimed to all.

TABLE 3.2
CHANGING MEANING OF HOME

Less Important as Supplemental Source of Income
Increasing Separation of Workplace and Home
Increasing Role as Status Symbol

(adapted from Harris and Pratt, 1993).

In recent years, the appearance of new social and economic realities have generated pressures to create changed meanings for home and housing. This includes a return to the historic linkage between home and employment through the creation of home/work spaces. Tele-commuting via personal computer from a home office may be a way to reduce the stress and cost of commuting. As well, domestic and employment responsibilities may be more easily fulfilled when everything is in one place. Such restructuring of the meaning of home does vary depending on individual experiences and location. New pressures may continue to force change in the social meaning of housing, and this in turn will result in changing the social geography of housing landscapes.

HOME OWNERSHIP

In North America, the idea of a home as a status symbol has developed mainly on the ideal of ownership of a single-family dwelling. In this way, homeownership is linked to the idea of social class distinction or status. There is a certain amount of pride that comes along with owning your own home. Forrest (1983, p. 429) suggests that "homeownership encourages social stability and pride, reflects natural instincts, and that its growth is historically inevitable". As well, privacy is a concern in today's society and the home satisfies this need. A single detached dwelling is considered more private than dwellings within apartment complexes. Together, the ideal of homeownership, and the North American preference for the single detached house, shape most housing landscapes.

Home ownership is also an important economic issue. Generally, a house is a valuable investment and only in "explosive" boom and bust housing markets is there a chance of significant value loss after purchase. As a result of the combined pressures of increasing construction costs and increasing land prices, there is an *almost* certain guarantee that housing prices will continue to rise above the rate of inflation (Harris and Pratt, 1993). In Canada, home ownership is valued for both image sake and as a reliable investment.

Affordability is another factor that comes into play with homeownership. Recently the growth of home-ownership rates has been slowing. While affordability is linked with income, and therefore individual cases are different, two general trends are evident across Canada. Over the past four decades, rising incomes has meant that houses became more affordable to a broader range of households and this has allowed many more people to purchase their own home. More recently, however, house prices have been increasing faster than incomes and this has worked to slow the growth of home ownership. There are, of course, regional and local differences to these general trends. Homes in rural areas are often less expensive than homes in growing urban centres with the result that rural areas often report a higher percentage of ownership than urban centres. Affordability remains an issue and many households still cannot own their own home and must seek "only the cheapest of accommodation. Of these, the most numerous are single-parent, usually female-led families" (Harris and Pratt, 1993, p. 292).

PUBLIC POLICY & HOMEOWNERSHIP

In Canada, government plays a small but central role in the housing market. Policies implemented by the federal government have given new meaning to the term homeownership by increasing the attraction to its benefits:

> Government has helped create homogeneous residential environments which make the home a retreat, a status symbol, and a focus for a family-centred life-style. The federal government has done this by targeting mortgage funding and insurance to suburban areas and to large developers who were prepared to construct 'appropriate' suburban environments (Harris and Pratt, 1993, p. 294).

The federal government's role is assisting individuals with housing affordability problems has also been important. Canada Mortgage and Housing Corporation (CMHC) offers "second mortgages" which often fill the gap between what a household can afford as a down payment on a house and the 20 percent which most banks require as a downpayment before they will lend their mortgage funds. Over the past decade, CMHC has increased the amount of assistance it will provide in this regard in order to assist more households with housing purchases.

Provincial and local governments are also active in the housing market. Beyond issues such as taxation and licensing, provincial governments also set "building codes" which specify minimum requirements and standards. As such standards and requirements change, so too do the costs of house construction. In jurisdictions such as Prince George, it is the City building inspectors who are charged with enforcing the provincial building code. Local governments also lend a hand in forming the social homogeneity of suburban areas through community plans and zoning bylaws. In many "suburban" settings, zoning is used to exclude some types of housing (mobile homes, row houses, duplexes, etc.) and exclude types of households (large homes on large lots exclude many low- and moderate-income households).

HISTORICAL AND CURRENT PRINCE GEORGE DATA

In order to get an overall picture of housing issues in Prince George it was essential to collect data from many sources. Six information sources are extremely helpful when searching for local housing information. These include: Statistics Canada, Prince George Home Builders Association, CMHC, the City of Prince George Planning Department, the Prince George Native Friendship Centre, and the local newspapers. By using these sources, the remainder of this chapter develops a comparison between the historical housing data and the current housing data for the City of Prince George. It has been suggested that Prince George has essentially three different housing markets:

> Modest housing includes the smaller, older homes in the city. Middle-of-the-road housing includes average modern suburban single-family homes and makes up the major part of the market in Prince George. Housing at the upper end of the real estate market includes the bigger homes built on speculation, executive two-storey homes and the like. (Strickland, 1994, p. 1).

Housing Types

Housing in Prince George is predominantly composed of detached single-family dwellings. This has always been the trend in the City and it is unlikely to change in the near future. The amount of land available for development, the general affordability of single detached homes relative to household incomes in the City, and the general social imagery and prestige associated with single detached houses on a large piece of private property likely account for this pattern. Although there has been a recent increase in townhouse and condominium construction, it will not be large enough to overtake single-family dwellings.

As of the 1991 Census, approximately two-thirds of the housing in Prince George consisted of single-detached homes (Table 3.3). The next largest component involved low-rise apartment buildings (approximately 13% of the City's housing stock). Other types of housing were less common.

TABLE 3.3
Housing Structure Types in Prince George

Structure Type	Number of Dwelling Units	Percent
Single-Detached House	15,930	66.0
Apt. building, less than 5 storeys	3,265	13.5
Semi-Detached House	1,470	6.1
Movable Dwelling	1,410	5.8
Row House	900	3.7
Apt., detached duplex	695	2.9
Apt. building, 5 or more storeys	445	1.8
Other single attached house	25	0.01

Source: Statistics Canada, 1991 Census.

The Prince George Home Builders Association and the City's Development Services Department report that this pattern continues in new housing construction in the City. In Table 3.4, a comparison of recent residential construction starts shows a continuing emphasis upon single detached dwellings. In most recent years, single detached houses account for approximately 70 to 80 percent of the dwelling units being added in Prince George.

Predominantly, four different material types for house construction are used in Prince George. The four groups of exterior siding materials include vinyl siding, wood, stucco, and brick. City builders report the most common siding material at present is vinyl siding, which is the most inexpensive of the four (personal communication, 1996). Stucco ranks second while wood ranks third, and brick, the most expensive type of building material, is least common.

TABLE 3.4
Housing Structure - New Residential Construction Starts

Year	Single Detached Starts (dwellings)	Multi-Family Starts (dwellings)	Total Residential Starts	Single Detached as Percent of Total Starts
1990	217	42	259	83.8
1991	273	89	362	75.4
1992	371	89	460	80.7
1993	307	93	400	76.8
1994	253	115	369	68.6
1995	205	79	284	72.2

Source: CMHC, 1996a.

Construction of dwellings over the last 45 years has fluctuated (Table 3.5). Construction boomed during the 1971-1980 period. This is most likely due to the increase in employment opportunities in the local pulp and paper industries, and in the associated support and service industries. The areas with the highest construction increases were College Heights (Census Tract 002), The Westwood area (Census Tract 005), and the area behind Tabor Boulevard (Census Tract 016), between 15th Avenue and the Nechako River. These "suburban" subdivisions were being built to accommodate the influx of population, and also feature primarily single detached houses. It was also during this time frame that Foothills Boulevard was built, opening up more areas for development and giving better access to other parts of the City.

TABLE 3.5
Historic Summary
Age of Dwellings in Prince George

Time Period House was built	Number of Dwellings
Before 1946	800
1946-1960	2,570
1961-1970	6,840
1971-1980	10,475
1981-1985	2,350
1986-1991	1,090

Source: Statistics Canada, 1991 Census.

Figure 3.1 shows the pattern of housing starts activity within Prince George for the period 1972 to 1995. The tail end of the early 1970s boom period is clearly shown. Also clearly shown is the impact of the mid-1980s economic recession. Recent building growth has been associated with economic prosperity in the forestry sectors, the continued growth of Prince George as the major service and government centre in the central interior, and with the establishment of new institutions such as the University of Northern British Columbia.

Building permit data for the 1990-1994 period shows that the recent "boom" in housing starts has involved single family dwellings in primarily the College Heights/Southridge and the Hart Highland's areas (Table 3.6). As suggested earlier, house types other than single detached continue to be less common. As well, the number and distribution of mobile homes is relatively restricted. The zoning bylaw does not permit manufactured homes in the bowl area except in manufactured home parks and in only one subdivision (personal communication, 1996).

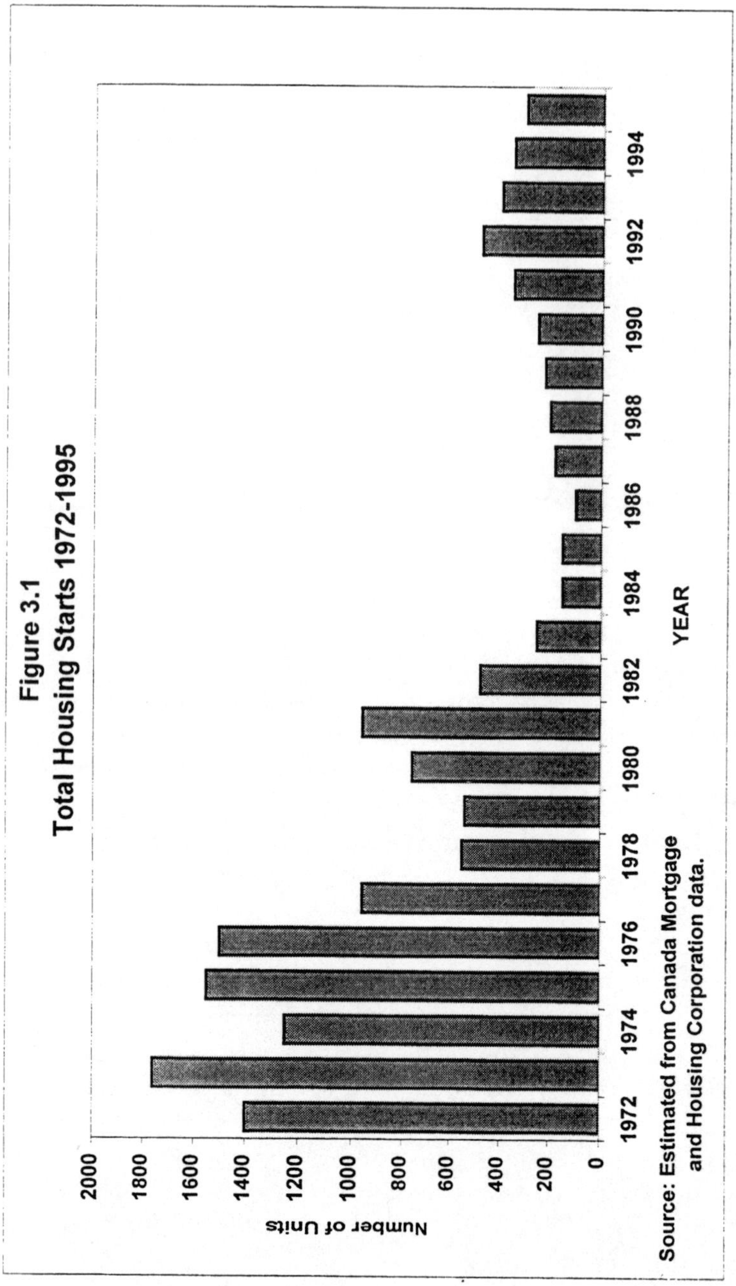

Figure 3.1
Total Housing Starts 1972-1995

Source: Estimated from Canada Mortgage and Housing Corporation data.

TABLE 3.6
Single Family Dwelling Building Permits By Area - 1994

YEAR	BOWL		NORTH		SOUTH-WEST		CRANBK. HILL		EAST		TOTAL
	SFD	MH	SFD	MH	SFD	MH	SFD	MH	SFD	MH	
1990	56	0	93	12	70	3	1	0	4	8	247
1991	62	0	112	10	89	2	5	1	10	2	293
1992	68	0	200	41	101	4	1	0	18	6	439
1993	46	0	149	33	106	6	5	0	21	17	367
1994	20	0	91	58	112	4	2	0	15	23	325

SFD = Single Family Dwelling.
MH = Manufactured Home.
Source: Prince George Development Services Department, 1995.

As Prince George's population expands, especially with the influx of students and academics, housing construction will continue. Single-family dwellings will remain the preference for housing structures but more affordable housing such as townhouses and condominiums will be on the rise.

Tenure

A common dream for many individuals or families is to own their own home. The term "Housing Tenure" refers to the ownership structure of accommodation, such as whether it is owned, rented or leased, or is some type of strata-title condominium. The Prince George housing market is dominated by "owned" accommodation (Figure 3.2). In 1991, 68 percent of the 24,130 occupied private dwellings in the City were owned, while the remaining 32 percent (7,730 units) were rented or leased (Statistics Canada, 1991 Census).

Figure 3.2
Housing Tenure in Prince George

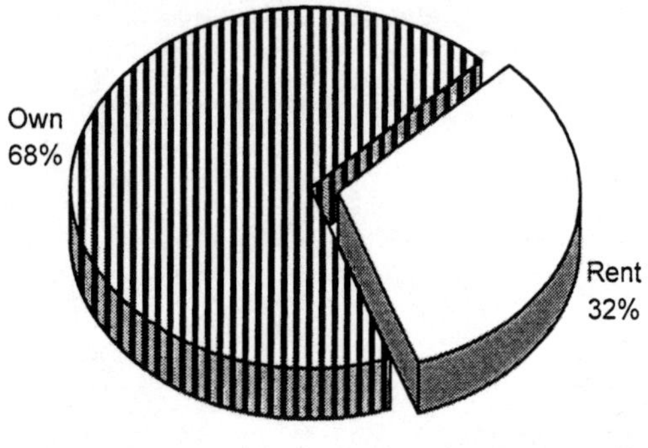

Source: CMHC, 1993, p.6

The spatial distribution of owned versus rented housing across Prince George in 1991 is seen on Maps 3.1 and 3.2. Areas where the majority of the housing is "rented" are highlighted with shading and are focussed on the downtown

Map 3.1
"Owned" Versus "Rented" Housing, 1991

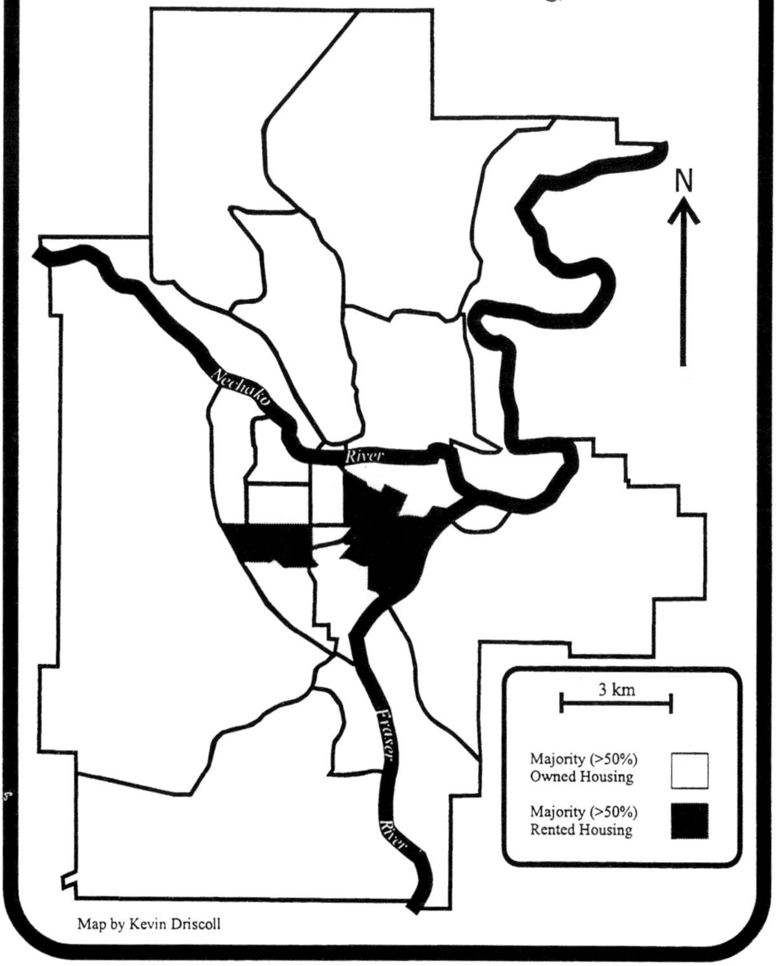

core. Map 3.2 clarifies this pattern by using the City average of 32 percent rental housing as a baseline, and highlighting all areas where more than 32 percent of the housing is rented accommodation. Noting that Census Tract 006 reported 31 percent rental housing, the pattern is of a clear concentration of rental accommodation in the City core. This finding corresponds to social geography notions that more low cost

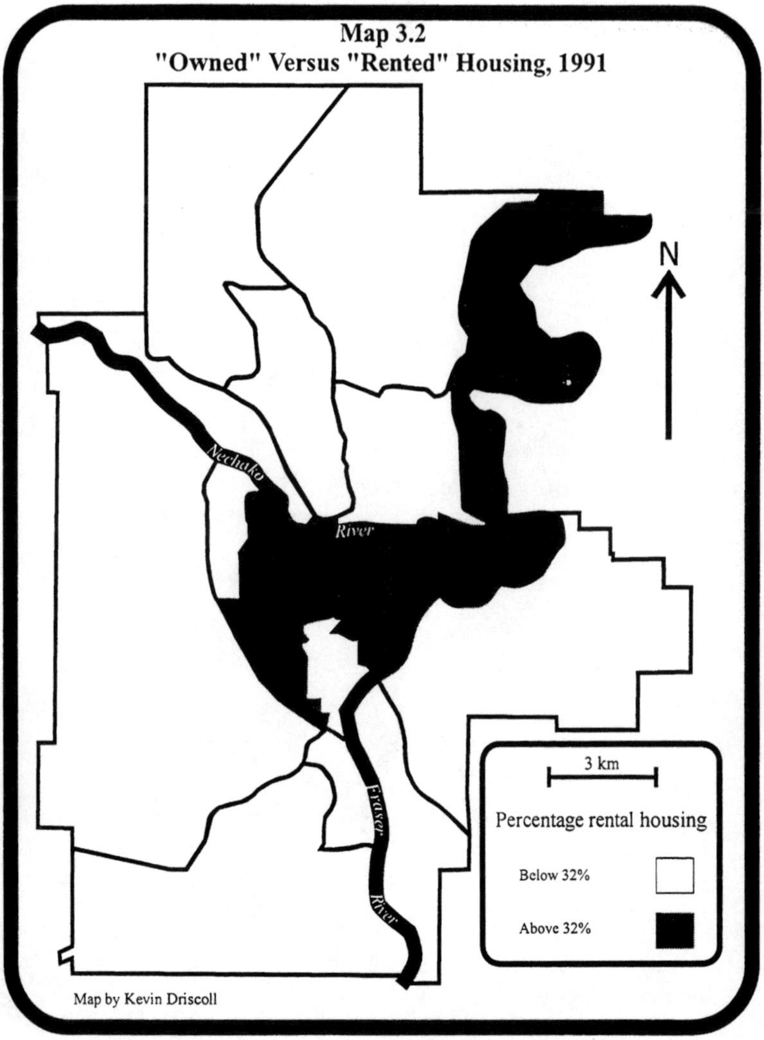

Map 3.2
"Owned" Versus "Rented" Housing, 1991

rental accommodation is found in the downtown core, city areas which usually have higher density housing (apartment style), older housing, are close to a wide range of employment opportunities for low income persons, are close to a range of social service and support agencies, and are generally well served by public transit. Apartment complexes with rental accommodation are common in Prince George's bowl area, with the area between 22nd Avenue and 15th Avenue just west of Central Avenue having a conglomeration of rental apartment complexes.

Home-Ownership

In Prince George, "residents have higher than average family and household incomes than either the provincial and national averages as-a-whole" (Prince George, 1993, Chapter 4-6). However, it is important to keep in mind that annual income figures are not the sole determinant of ownership affordability. For households with low to moderate incomes, it is often very difficult to save enough for a down-payment as much of their income would be needed for food, rent, utilities, clothing and transportation. Changes in the required percentage (from 10% to 5%) of the sale price which must be put as downpayment before qualifying for a CMHC second mortgage on a home has led to more first-time buyers entering the homeownership market. In Prince George, the number of first-time home buyers is seen in the comparison of data from 1993 and 1995 (Figure 3.3). In 1995, only 45 percent of these first-time buyers were

Figure 3.3
First-time Home Buyers

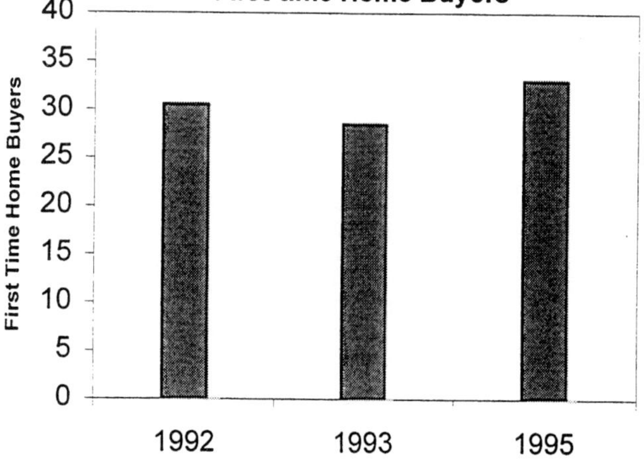

Source: Cariboo Real Estate

able to pay the full 10 percent downpayment, compared to 85 percent of first time-buyers in 1993 (Prince George Citizen, 1996).

Rental accommodations can provide a more affordable housing option. In Prince George there seems to be an abundance of rental properties. However, the vacancy rates in the rental market have been quite low over the period from 1993 to 1995. In April of 1995, "there were 81 vacant rental units in Prince George, from a survey of 3,915 units in privately initiated apartment buildings and townhouse structures" (CMHC, 1995a, p. 10). The overall vacancy rates for Prince George from 1989 to 1995 are shown in Figure 3.4.

Figure 3.4
Vacancy Rates by Area 1990-1995

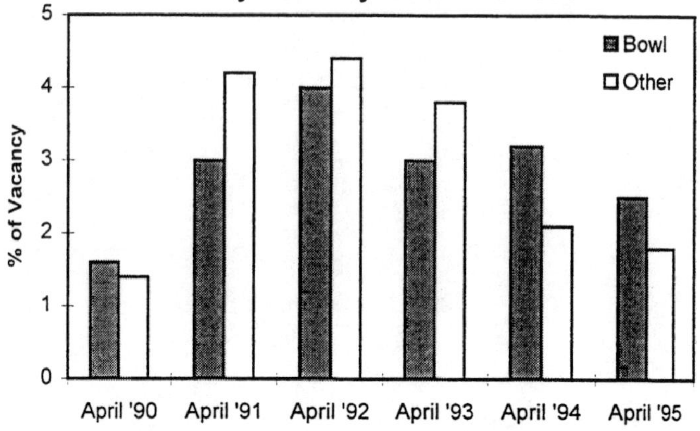

Source: CMHC

There are more vacancies in the bowl area than any other area of the City. In this data, the bowl area encompasses a space between the Fraser River, 1st Avenue, Highway 97, and 20th Avenue (CMHC, 1995a). As apartments and townhouses were built outside of the Bowl, renters moved out of the downtown core. We can only speculate on why renters have made moves out of the core, with possible factors including perceptions of crime, noise, health concerns, and the quality of units available in older central City buildings.

The outlook for the Prince George rental market is for continuing low vacancy rates and higher rent increases. The future vacancy rates are forecasted to rise slightly but still fall below the 3% benchmark which Canada Mortgage and Housing Corporation considers to be a "balanced" rental market (CMHC, 1995a). The University of Northern British Columbia now plays a role in the rental market as students come into Prince George looking for accommodations. The "additional demand for student housing has been partly alleviated by alternated accommodations such as boarding, accessory suites, rented houses, and student residences" (CMHC, 1995b, p. 4). A low vacancy rate often points to a need for increased construction of rental accommodations, however, the seasonal variations of the student population often make builders hesitant to invest (CMHC, 1995b). Regardless, the amount of rental properties will need to increase for Prince George's expanding population. Further discussion of affordable housing issues is included in Chapter 4, "Poverty and Homelessness", and Chapter 5, "A Gender Study of Prince George".

Occupied Dwellings

Prince George has an uneven distribution of occupied dwellings, be they rented or owned. Maps 3.3 and 3.4 allow for comparison of the distribution of occupied dwellings between 1986 and 1991. This uneven distribution is easily seen and the changes over the five year period are quite apparent. Only seven of the 23 census areas in the City remained unchanged - and five of these seven are either entirely or partially located within the Bowl area. One of the reasons these central areas remained relatively unchanged is because of a lack of space and available building lots.

New subdivisions outside of the Bowl area are changing the City's social landscape. College Heights and its surrounding areas, and parts of the Hart Highway area, are growing quickly. Subdivisions such as Hart Highlands, Nechako Heights, Valleyview, St. Lawrence Heights, and St. Dennis Heights,

Map 3.3
Number of Occupied Dwellings, 1986

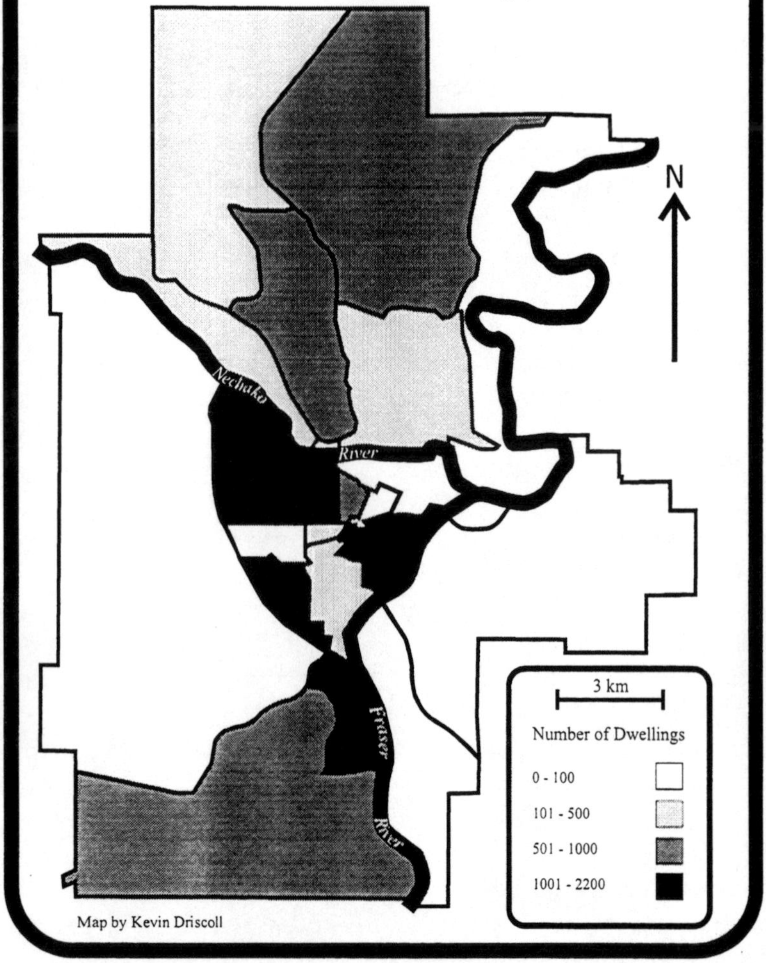

together with some more rural outlying areas, have experienced tremendous growth in recent years. The two maps also point out, indirectly, the changing population distribution of Prince George as areas outside of the Bowl develop as residential areas. This in turn can suggest areas where new types of services and needs will have to be addressed.

Map 3.4
Number of Occupied Dwellings, 1991

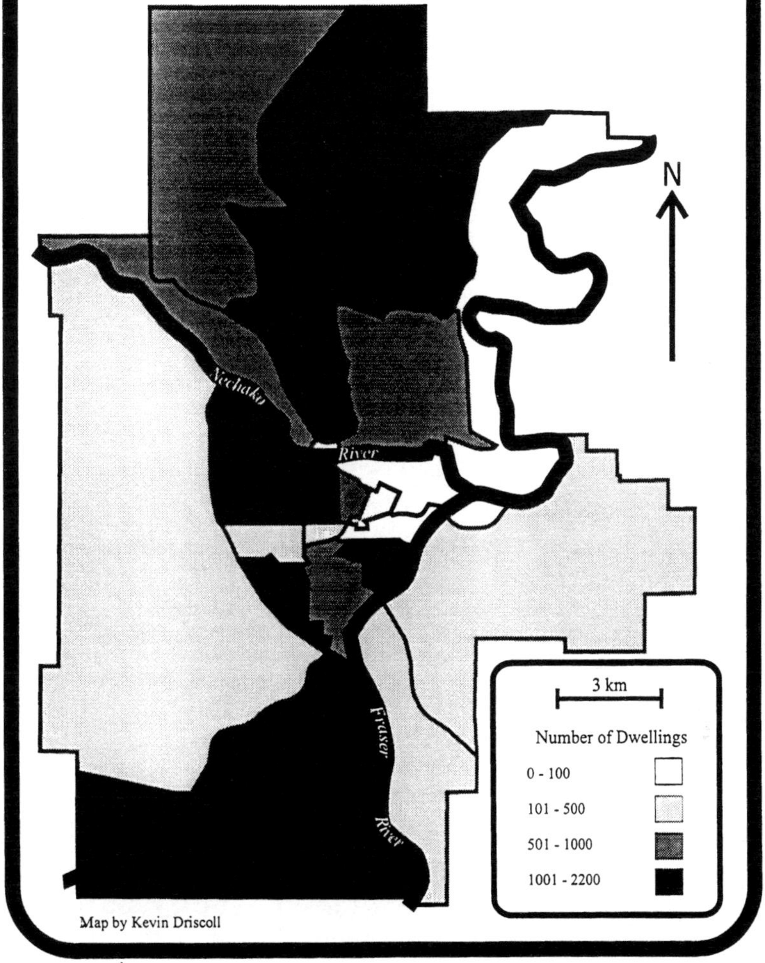

House Values

Housing prices in Prince George have increased quite dramatically in the last ten years. The average house price in the local market in 1988 was approximately $60,000 while in 1996 it was approximately $130,000. Table 3.7 includes a comparison of average house price information for the City of Prince George from 1986 to 1991. Comparing "Current Dollar Value", the average value of dwellings recorded in the 1986 Census is $63,698 while by 1991 that value had increased to $84,448. While this suggests a large increase in house values in the City, we must also take into account the effects of inflation over the intervening five year period. Comparing "Constant Dollar Values" is one way to control for (or eliminate) the effects of inflation. In Table 3.7, the average house values for Prince George are expressed in 1986 dollars. When inflation effects are deleted, it is clear that across the City house values increased a small amount between 1986 and 1991.

TABLE 3.7
Average House Values in Prince George

Year	Current Dollar Value	Constant* Dollar Value (1986$)
1986	63,698	63,698
1991	84,448	66,916

* see note at end on calculating
Source: Statistics Canada census data.

Using a different set of data, average prices for single detached houses listed on the real estate Multiple Listings Service (MLS), there is a strong suggestion that Prince George house values are continuing to rise into the 1990s. In 1991, average prices for single detached houses on the MLS was approximately $76,000. By 1995, this average price had increased to approximately $130,000 (Strickland, 1996a, p. 21).

Housing values vary significantly across Prince George. Maps 3.5 and 3.6 show Average House Value data for Census Tracts across Prince George for the years 1986 and 1991 respectively. Census Tracts 004, 020, 021, and 018 have high average values. This is not a surprising finding when looking at the subdivisions contained within them. Census

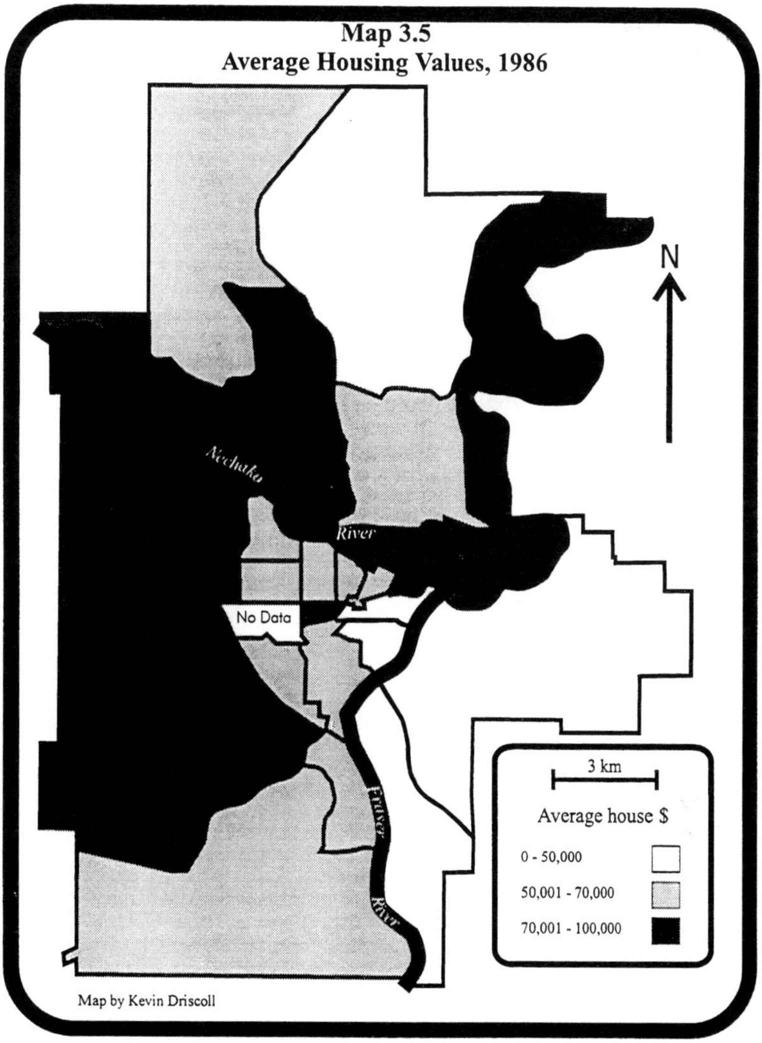

Tract 004 is mainly the Cranbrook Hill region. The houses in that area are fairly large, situated on generally larger lots with plenty of acreage - features which will boost the value. Census Tract 021 is the North Nechako subdivision. While there are two mobile home parks in this area, there are also many very large homes on the benches along the Nechako River. These homes may range anywhere from $70,000 to $350-400,000.

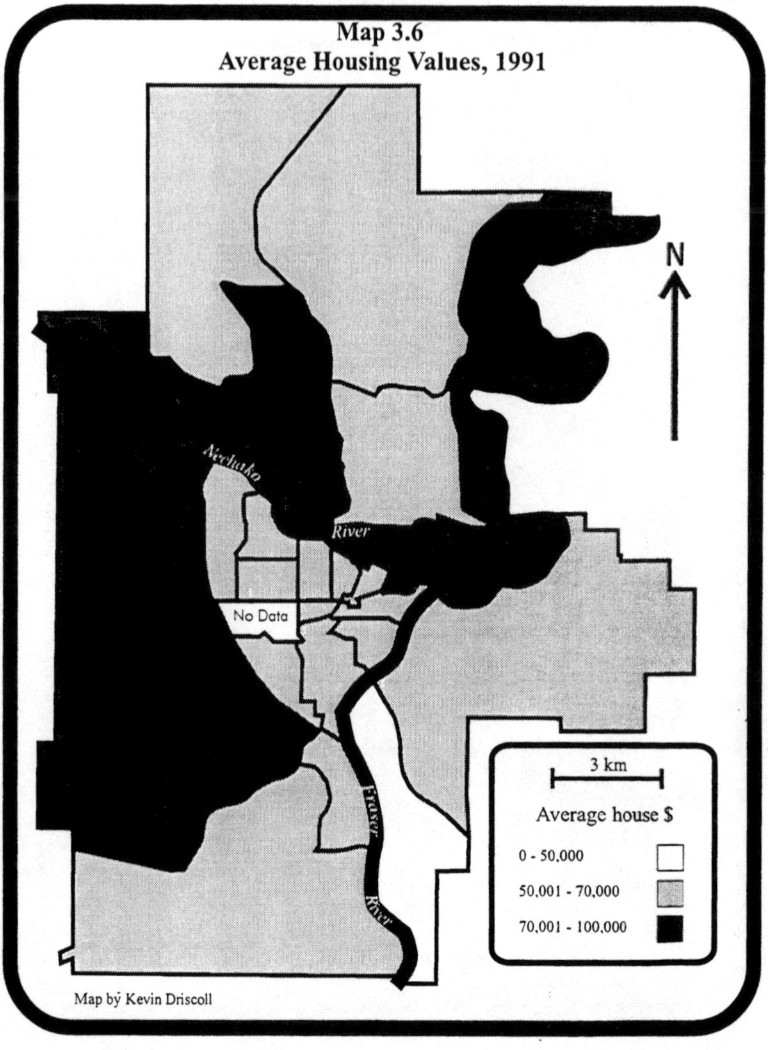

When looking at the 1991 values, 14 out of the 23 Census Tracts have average housing values of between $70,000 and $95,000. There was only one decrease in housing values across these Census Tracts between 1986 and 1991. This occurred in Census Tract 001, which is primarily the BCR Industrial Site and where the data must be read with caution as there are few houses.

Some of the subdivisions now being developed across Prince George are building and selling new homes up into the $350,000 range. St. Lawrence Heights, located between Highway 16 West and Domano Boulevard, has been among the most active construction centres in Prince George (Seymour, 1996a). Most of the building has taken place over the last five to seven years and today this new neighbourhood comes complete with a new elementary school. In 1996, the starting price for an entry-level, single-detached home in this area was $120,000. This of course increased with the size of the house or the unique features included in the housing bundle. The most expensive homes in the area range to $350,000. In St. Dennis Heights, a neighbourhood adjacent to St. Lawrence Heights, houses start at $175,000 and increase from there (Seymour, 1996a). Nechako Heights is a new subdivision in the Hart Highlands area, located between Foothills Boulevard and Highland Drive. The first phase of development began around 1983, while a second phase is presently under development. The homes start at around $160,000 and can range up to $280,000 (Seymour, 1996b). While Valleyview Park along the east side of the Hart Highway is not a new subdivision, it still has building lots available. These lots are quite large, ranging from one half acre to a full acre, and the house prices are also high, valued from $190,000 to $320,000. While many subdivisions around Prince George are expanding, and building homes aimed at the high end of the market (250,000 - $350 000 range), housing prices are forecasted to stabilize over the short term as new construction slows down slightly (compared to previous years) and the market levels off.

Current State of the Housing Market

From all indications, the Prince George housing market is expected to stabilize in 1996 and for the next couple of years. The market has fluctuated over time with a boom in the seventies, a stagnation period in the 1980s and then an increase in the late 80s and early 1990s. The housing data suggests that the "strong economic growth of the first half of this decade has fuelled the housing recovery and created another small housing boom" (CMHC, 1996b, p. 21). Housing prices in Prince George have "reached a new plateau, following double digit price appreciation in the early 1990s" (CMHC, 1995b, p. 4). In the future, "a steady turnover of properties ... will lead to slow, but continued price growth in coming years" (CMHC, 1995b, p. 4).

Special Issues - Needs of the Elderly

In 1991, there were 3,255 persons 65 years or older in the City of Prince George (Statistics Canada, 1991 Census). This works out to approximately 5 percent of the total population, compared to a national average of approximately 10 percent. In the City, there is a limited housing market for seniors. The options are much more limited than areas in the Okanagan and Victoria (Prince George, 1993). In a Seniors' Housing Survey conducted in Prince George by CMHC, 22 percent of seniors contacted responded that they were currently waiting for accommodations in a Senior's Housing Unit (CMHC, 1994). Of those on the waiting list, 12 percent were elderly homeowners, 33 percent were living with relatives, and 55 percent were renting their housing (CMHC, 1994). This demonstrates the strong demand for elderly housing which will only increase as the Prince George population ages.

There are very definite price considerations for seniors wishing to purchase a home. Most seniors have limited incomes so affordability is an issue. The CMHC survey found that 68 percent of respondents desired a unit between $60,000 and $75,000, 26 percent wanted a unit in the $76,000 to $100,000 range, and only 6 percent wanted a unit priced over $100,000 (CMHC, 1994).

For seniors', security also plays an important role when choosing housing. The survey results indicated that there was a strong demand for "increased protection services (e.g. community policing, neighbourhood watch programs etc...), security alarms, and an increased awareness of how to protect themselves and their belongings from burglary" (CMHC, 1994, p. 8). In a study done by the City's Housing Needs Research Project Steering Committee, it was recognized that on-site support services could enhance the safety and security of seniors. Such services include transportation (especially public transportation) networks, recreation, personal grooming, personal laundry, medication reminders, etc.. The City's study, however, found that there were not enough of these on-site support services available at present. The demand for such services is growing stronger due to the "increasing numbers of psycho-geriatric clients, complexity of cases, dementia, frailty, [and] Alzheimer's Disease" (Prince George, 1993, Chapter 2-4).

The demand for easily maintained and accessible housing is starting to gain recognition. One case of a housing project that included the needs of the elderly was in the Hart Highlands area. Built by Kim Forrest, co-executive member of the Prince George Home Builders Association, these homes are 1,000 square foot grade-level ranchers priced at $110,000 which are considered barrier free in that they are "designed for people with accessibility problems" (Free Press, 1996, p. C6). Among their features are wider hallways, bathrooms and kitchens designed for wheelchair access, lower light switches, raised plug-ins, and outside grading considerations. The homes are designed to fit an individuals budget and provide building options to accommodate this.

CONCLUSION

The study of housing across Prince George can assist with our understanding of the social landscapes of communities and neighbourhoods. Within the City, new subdivisions are being built and more people are purchasing homes. In recent years, this has been partially fuelled by lower mortgage rates, but longer term rationales such as housing as an investment and as a status symbol remain important. In terms of the social geography of the City, patterns can be seen with respect to where people are buying and the types of housing being built in particular areas. Rental housing, which makes up a significant portion of the housing market and provides inexpensive housing options, is found in most neighbourhoods but is concentrated in one part of the City. Other affordable housing options such as townhouses and condominiums will increase in sales as first-time buyers enter the market and the prices of single detached houses rise. The housing market in Prince George is used to change and periods of rapid growth, first with the pulp mills, and now with the increasing diversity of the City's economic base. The housing landscape will continue to reflect the changing social geography of Prince George.

There are special needs within the Prince George housing market which do require attention. Elderly or senior's housing needs are high, and with the stabilizing of market construction, it is not certain if new projects will meet the present and coming demands. Another type of housing which has become increasingly important as a local housing option over the last few years has been manufactured homes. Across Canada numbers are increasing as the quality rises and the prices stay competitive. In Prince George, new manufactured home neighbourhoods may provide a possible affordable option for those not able to purchase a single detached house.

At this time, the indications from analysts at CMHC, the City of Prince George, the British Columbia Real Estate Association, and the Prince George Home Builders Association, point to a favourable housing market for Prince George (Strickland, 1996b and 1996c). The market continues to grow at a low to moderate pace, and this slow growth has allowed housing prices to stabilize. As the Prince George economy strengthens, grows, and diversifies, so too will the social mix and social landscape of the community continue to change. Attention to the geography of housing over such periods of change will be important as the social geography of the City is reflected in its neighbourhoods.

NOTE:
The calculation of house values data into constant 1986 dollars uses conversion factors from Statistics Canada's Consumer Price Index. The conversion formula is: [(current Year $) * 100] / (conversion factor) = constant 1986 $. Conversion factors are: 1981=74.1, 1986=100, 1991=126.2

REFERENCES

Bourne, L.S. and Bunting T. (1993). Housing Markets, Community Development, and Neighbourhood Change. In *The Changing Social Geography of Canadian Cities*, L. Bourne and D. Ley eds.. Montreal: McGill-Queen's University Press. pp. 175-198.

Cater, J. and Jones, T. (1989). *Social Geography*. London: Edward Arnold.

Canada Mortgage and Housing Corporation. (1994). *Seniors' Housing Needs Survey*. Prince George: CMHC and the Prince George Council of Seniors.

_______. (1995a). *Rental Market Report*. Prince George: CMHC.

_______. (1995b). *Prince George Housing Forecast Fall 1995*. Prince George: CMHC.

_______. (1996a). *New Housing Market Report - Northern British Columbia - Third Quarter, 1996*. Prince George: CMHC.

_______. (1996b). "Untitled Pamphlet". Prince George: CMHC.

Forrest R. (1983). *The Meaning of Homeownership*. Great Britain: Pion Publishers.

Harris, R. And Pratt, G.J. (1993). The Meaning of Home ownership and Public Policy. In *The Changing Social Geography of Canadian Cities*. L. Bourne and D. Ley eds.. Montreal: McGill-Queen's University Press. pp. 281-297.

Prince George. (1993). *Prince George Housing Needs Research Project: Final Report*. Prince George: City of Prince George Housing Needs Research Project Steering Committee.

Prince George Citizen, The. (1996). "More first-time buyers entered market in 1995". February 24, p. 31.

Prince George Development Services Department. (1995). *Annual Housing Circular for 1994*. Prince George: City of Prince George Development Services Department.

Prince George Free Press, The. (1996). "Homes that meet special needs". March 10, p. C6.

Seymour, B. (1996a). "Builders busy in St. Lawrence Heights". *The Prince George Citizen*. February 17, p. 27.

_______. (1996b). "Nechako Heights in its Second Phase". *The Prince George Citizen*. February 3, p. 25.

Strickland, P. (1994). "City's housing market in midst of change". *The Prince George Citizen*. December, p. 1.

_______. (1996a). "Improved housing market seen here". *The Prince George Citizen*. April 6, p. 21.

_______. (1996b). "Building permits office busy here". *The Prince George Citizen*. March 9, p. 25.

_______. (1996c). "Improved housing market seen here". *The Prince George Citizen*. April 6, p. 21.

APPENDIX

Statistics Canada Data For:

(1) "Owned" versus "Rented" Properties - 1991 - Maps 3.1 and 3.2.
Source: 1991 Census, 100% Data Tables.

(2) Number of Occupied Dwellings - 1986 and 1991 - Maps 3.3 and 3.4.
Source: 1986 and 1991 Census, 20% Data Tables.

(3) Average Housing Values - 1986 and 1991 - Maps 3.5 and 3.6
Source: 1986 and 1991 Census, 20% Data Tables.

	MAPS 3.1 and 3.2		MAPS 3.3 and 3.4		MAPS 3.5 and 3.6	
Census	Owned	Rented	1986	1991	1986	1991 Area
001	120	5	60	125	30665	23028
002	1620	165	1740	1785	69437	92177
003	1085	120	1040	1200	52034	80179
004	360	40	350	400	85904	98368
005	1480	665	1980	2145	65894	94898
006	665	205	845	865	57701	73618
007	330	60	325	390	49362	60483
008	745	1020	1705	1765	49691	62933
009	5	120	120	135	350000	no data
010	295	205	510	505	70196	90911
011	535	865	1355	1400	57520	73210
012	15	55	100	70	56636	74727
013	405	555	980	955	60187	77307
014	1075	860	1780	1930	55807	73639
015	965	930	1750	1875	65435	89946
016	1675	480	2060	2150	72348	92408
017	1140	785	1805	1935	68404	88381
018	20	10	30	30	82622	121882
019	520	115	545	635	52845	73507
020	1145	135	1155	1275	71166	95008
021	755	65	745	825	70927	111375
022	585	125	670	710	57573	76463
023	865	165	975	1030	48257	63197

Chapter 4

POVERTY AND HOMELESSNESS IN PRINCE GEORGE

Kerry Kilden and Leon Geisler

INTRODUCTION

This chapter is a survey of the issues of poverty and homelessness. Examples drawn from the City of Prince George are used to illustrate some of the more general social geography patterns associated with both of these issues. It is important at the outset to explain that the issue of poverty is both complex and difficult to define - it is not simply a question of being unemployed, but in many cases of being under-employed or working for wages that do not cover your household costs-of-living. The issue of homelessness is closely related to that of poverty. In many cases, homelessness is the most visible consequence of poverty. In Prince George, the social geography of both poverty and homelessness is an important part of the story of the City's downtown district.

DEFINING POVERTY

Poverty is a very important issue and a continuing social problem in our communities. However, the concept of poverty is very complex and involves many interrelated issues. In its most simple form, we can understand poverty as involving conditions whereby people lack the means to satisfy their most basic needs of food, shelter, clothing, etc.. As it is most often understood in Canadian society, poverty involves individuals or households living below accepted thresholds of income and consumption. Exactly where these threshold levels should be set relative to Canadian society has, however, been the subject of much contentious debate.

Measures of poverty are most often based on a dollar amount calculation which is connected in some way with household costs-of-living. Very often in popular and political debates these dollar value measures become labelled the "poverty line" (Hoeven and Anker, 1994, p. 3). Such labelling must, however, be done with caution. For example, Statistics Canada generates a measure which it calls the "Low Income Cut Off" (LICO). This is an artificial measure which attempts to establish an income level at which families will be spending more than a set percentage of their incomes just for the basic necessities of food, shelter and clothing. In 1968, it was established that Canadian families spent an average of 50 percent of their income on these necessities. Based on this, the LICO was arbitrarily established at 70 percent of average household income; that is, the average costs of the basic necessities of food, shelter, and clothing are calculated and all households whose income levels are such that 70 percent or more would need to be spent on these basic necessities are considered to be below the LICO (Statistics Canada, 1992). Statistics Canada LICOs differentiate by family size and degree of urbanization. Revised LICOs, based on national family expenditure patterns, were established in 1969, 1978, and 1986. Between revision dates, the LICOs are updated according to changes in the Canadian consumer price index. The purpose of this measure, therefore, is to be a relative gauge for counting, or comparing counts, of lower income households across the country and from one time period to the next. It is, therefore, a comparative statistic *not* a definitive calculation of poverty. Yet, too often in popular debate the LICO line is mislabelled as Canada's "poverty line".

Focussing upon the dollar value calculation of low-income thresholds, there is a good deal of debate about how to calculate and where to set such thresholds. Spector has argued that there are at least four broad approaches to the calculation of low-income levels (Spector, 1992). He labels the first, the "budget standard approach" and suggests that this calculation is based on the minimum income required to purchase a specified 'basket' of goods and services. A second broad approach, which he labels the "subjective approach", is based on public perceptions of the threshold levels that constitute low-income and poverty. A third broad approach, which Spector labels as the "expenditure patterns approach", involves a calculation based on a percentage of income which is required to be spent on a selected set of household necessities (food, clothing, shelter). In this sense, Statistics Canada's LICO is an example of an expenditure patterns approach. The final approach, which Spector identifies as the "relative income approach", estimates low-incomes relative to the incomes of all people in the data set. In each of these calculations there are many hidden and subjective decisions which must first be made; what goods and services are in the 'basket', what constitutes a household necessity, and where to place the relative percentage cutoff points?

Table 4.1 is an adaptation of "poverty line" data from Sheila Baxter's work on women and poverty (Baxter, 1995). In the table, three sets of poverty line calculations commonly used in Canada are compared. Even though the number of variables is kept simple, "family size" and "community size", it is important to note the range of values presented. Values vary for each family size unit across the three agencies and only two make some effort to distinguish different costs-of-living by community size. Further, this comparison does not take into account the many additional important factors which affect cost-of-living, such as region within Canada and ages of family members. These concerns reinforce the need for caution in the use of terms like "*the* poverty line".

Poverty, Work, and People

Today in the 1990s, job security seems to be a non-existent ideal. The issues of poverty cannot be divorced from recent processes of economic restructuring. Since the mid 1970s, high paying industrial jobs have been decreasing due to declining demands or the substitution of automation and technology for human labour. These high paying (primary and manufacturing sector) jobs have increasingly been replaced by service (tertiary

TABLE 4.1
Poverty Lines in Canada

Sample Family Sizes	Statistics Canada Low Income Cut-off (LICO) for 1994		National Council of Welfare Low Income Cut-off: 1995 estimates		Canadian Council on Social Development Poverty Lines: 1994 estimates
	Rural	City, 500,000 or more	Rural	City, 500,000 or more	
	$	$	$	$	$
1	10,538	15,479	10,728	15,758	13,770
2	14,286	20,981	14,543	21,359	22,950
3	18,157	26,670	18,484	27,150	27,540
4	20,905	30,708	21,281	31,261	32,130
5	22,841	33,550	23,252	34,154	36,720

Adapted from Baxter, 1995.

sector) jobs, and such service sector jobs often pay low wages or are part-time with little job security (Baldwin and Gorecki, 1990). In Prince George, as elsewhere, these kinds of jobs are going to increase. One result from economic restructuring pressures is that an increasing number of people will be earning lower wages in the future relative to wage levels over the past 20 years. A second result from economic restructuring is that the distribution of wage earnings will be unequal; that is, many of the people employed in the service sector will be women (a traditional sector for women's employment) and many of them will be earning relatively low wages. The net result is that more households may be living in poverty or in circumstances in which they are unable to meet their basic costs-of-living.

Part-time work is a hallmark of service sector employment (Cater and Jones, 1989). The problem is that many part-time jobs pay lower hourly wages than do full time jobs. Vacations, statutory holidays, pensions, health and life insurance, sick leave, maternity leave and various other benefits are not commonly available to those who participate in part-time employment and such jobs frequently provide limited opportunities for advancement or additional educational or skills-training upgrades. Traditionally, such part time service sector employment has functioned as an area of "women's work" in the wage economy, and women continue to make up a large proportion of part-time workers. Sometimes this is by choice, other times not. The duties of raising children and caring for a family often preclude women's abilities to work full time. Part-time work allows some women the flexibility to make the choice to both earn a wage and to carry out their family commitments. Mothers, and women in general, do however suffer the benefit disadvantages listed above when they work in part-time jobs.

In Canada, there is an increasing number of women, and women with families, who are living in poverty (Baxter, 1995). There is an increasing awareness that these situations for women are the by-products of a "feminization of poverty" that comes from the historic relationship between women's employment and part-time service sector jobs, and the new pressures of economic restructuring which are focussing more employment within the service sector. As well, family breakdowns through divorce, desertion, or abuse, can leave women without the financial resources or credit records necessary to avoid mortgage foreclosures or evictions. For some women, to leave a relationship may mean becoming homeless (Baxter, 1995). Faced with this prospect, some women choose to remain in an abusive relationship because they do not have any place to go and believe their children's lives would be better by remaining in the relationship (Baxter, 1995). In Prince George, a number of services are available to low-income or homeless women.

Poverty in Prince George

Tables 4.2 and 4.3 introduce the issue of poverty in Prince George. Table 4.2 compares low-income levels (as measured by Statistics Canada) for "economic families" in the City. According to Statistics Canada, an economic family refers to a group of two or more persons living in the same dwelling who are related to one another by blood, marriage, common law or adoption. According to Statistics Canada. in 1981 approximately 11 percent of economic families in Prince George were considered to be low-income households. In 1986 this level was 14.9 percent, while in 1991 it was approximately 12 percent. Compared to the Canadian national average, Prince George consistently has a lower proportion of economic families who are classified low-income.

The incidence of low-incomes among individuals living outside of family units was much higher. In Table 4.3, the level of low-incomes among "unattached" individuals in Prince George ranged between approximately 28 and 36 percent. Both Tables 4.2 and 4.3 suggest that there is a continuing level of need in the community and pressure to address the issue of poverty in Prince George.

TABLE 4.2
Low-Income Families in Prince George

Year	All Economic Families	Low-Income Economic Families	% Low-Income	Canadian National % Low-Income
1981	17,520	1,925	11.0	13.0
1986	17,975	2,675	14.9	15.9
1991	18,850	2,277	12.1	13.2

Source: Statistics Canada Census Data, 1981, 1986, 1991.

TABLE 4.3
Low-Income Individuals in Prince George

Year	All Unattached Individuals	All Unattached Low-Income Individuals	% Low-Income
1981	6,185	1,735	28.1
1986	6,455	2,360	36.5
1991	7,260	2,435	33.5

Source: Census Data, British Columbia, 1981, 1986, 1991.

Table 4.4 concludes the presentation of poverty statistics for Prince George. Tracking income assistance from 1990 to 1993, we can see a clear pattern of increasing numbers of cases, increasing numbers of individuals affected, and increasing dollar values spent. Poverty is an important issue in Prince George - it is an issue which affects thousands in the community (Mills, 1995). The geographic pattern of these impacts within the community is, however, rather more limited.

TABLE 4.4
Income Assistance Statistics - Prince George

Date	Total Cases	Income Assistance ($millions)	Total Recipients
February 1990	3,698	$2.1	7,037
August 1990	3,777	$2.4	7,352
February 1991	4,365	$2.6	8,158
August 1991	4,704	$3.0	8,816
February 1992	5,355	$3.5	9,626
August 1992	5,496	$3.7	10,101
February 1993	6,072	$4.2	10,862

Source: Prince George (1993), Housing Needs Research Project. (Chapter 4 - 4).

Map 4.1
Percentage Low Income Households in Census Tracts, 1991

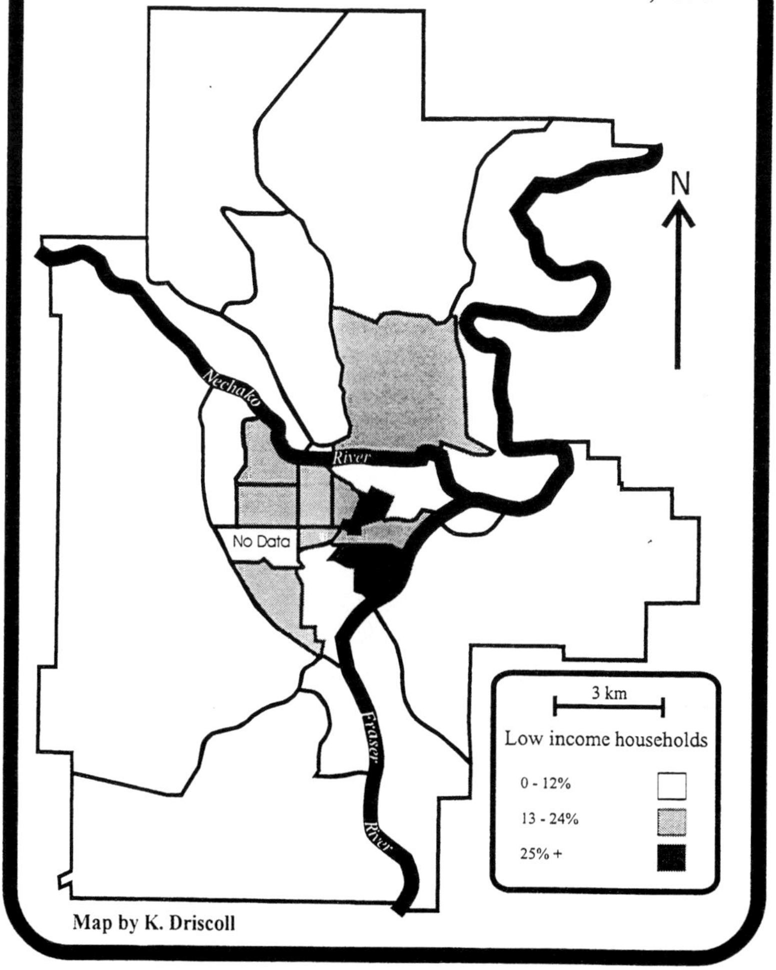

Map 4.1 shows a very distinct clustering of low-income households in Prince George. Census Tracts 008 and 012, in the City's downtown core, record an incidence of low-income families of approximately 25 and 36 percent respectively. A ring of Census Tracts around the downtown core could also be said to be "over-represented" in terms of their share of low-income families; that is, these areas have more than the 12

percent City average share of lower income families. In contrast, the Cranbrook Hill, College Heights, and Hart Highway areas have fewer than the city average share of low-income families. A further discussion of this link between low income households and central city locations is found in Chapter 7, "Social Services", by Allen.

HOMELESSNESS

Homelessness is the most visible form of poverty. Since the early 1980s, the public has become increasingly aware that many people cannot house themselves and the phenomenon of homelessness has become generally recognized (Oberlander and Fallick, 1988). The term homelessness first came into prominence during the recession of 1981 and 1982. Before this, the homeless were often referred to as bums, hoboes, drunks, or tramps. Most were recognized as male. Today, however, the homeless population has changed and can include people who are male or female, elderly or young, in families or single, temporarily unemployed or underemployed. It can also include the socially marginalized such as the mentally ill, disabled, and chronically ill (Baxter, 1993). These groups of people may not always have been homeless; but what now separates them from the rest of the community is the lack of a home.

Homelessness is an ambiguous term that is often difficult to define. At a general level most would define homelessness "as the absence of a stable residence of place where one can sleep and receive mail" (Baxter, 1993, p. 11). But definitions of homelessness can also be broken down into two specific categories, "absolute" and "relative". Absolute homelessness refers to those individuals living on the street who do not have physical shelter. Relative homelessness refers to people living in housing that does not meet basic health and safety standards (Hulchanski, 1991). The five basic housing requirements that determine whether a house is adequate for inhabitance are identified in Table 4.5. If a person is living in a place in which these basic needs are not being met, they may be considered to be "relatively" homeless.

TABLE 4.5
Basic Housing Requirements

1) Protection from the weather
2) Access to safe water/sanitation
3) Security of tenure
4) Proximity to employment opportunities, education facilities, and health services
5) affordability

adapted from Hulchanski, 1991.

There are varying times in which a person may find himself/herself homeless. There are three basic categories in which we can divide homelessness: chronic, periodic, and temporary. Chronic homelessness is experienced repeatedly or continuously over an extended period of time and is "generally experienced by socially marginal people, including some with alcohol, drug or solvent abuse problems and current or former psychiatric patients" (Begin, 1994, p. 3). In most cities, these people occupy approximately twenty to thirty percent of the available beds in emergency shelters and hostels.

Periodic homelessness "does not involve the loss of shelter per se; rather it involves any number of temporary departures from the home when pressures or tensions become intense" (Begin, 1994, p. 3). The people placed in this category are very often victims of abuse within the walls of their own home. These victims include women and children who are looking for a temporary escape from the violence that occurs in their family.

The temporarily homeless are often victims of a crisis resulting from a natural disaster, fire, hospitalization, or financial difficulty. They may have been faced with the expiration of their Employment Insurance, eviction, or a foreclosed mortgage. A sudden change in personal or economic situation for the working poor could cause the loss of permanent shelter (Begin, 1994).

Where are the Homeless?

Homeless people are not usually distributed uniformly throughout the City. They are not usually found in suburban residential areas, but rather they live in that part of town which is close to the kinds of support services they require. Their "spatial distribution tends to reflect the location of institutions that serve their needs, such as shelters and soup kitchens and outreach services" (Bentley, 1995, p. 7). It would probably be safe to say that most homeless people do not own their own vehicle and, therefore, it would be difficult for them to commute to the area of town in which required services are located. In Prince George, most of the homeless people are found in the downtown core and it is in this vicinity that the services that aid them can be found. They appear to make very good use of the hostels and services that are provided. Some of the homeless, however, cannot be 'squeezed into' a shelter or make the choice to sleep under the stars. The people who must brave the elements can be found in areas such as Rainbow Park, Fort George Park, in a tent at the bottom of Foothills Boulevard and 15th Avenue, and in alleys behind businesses in the Central Business District. Evidence of a concentration of homeless people at this time can sometimes be found under the truck trailers parked on the corner of Ottawa Street and 2nd Avenue adjacent to downtown. Under the trailers are blankets, water bottles and clothing.

As in many communities dealing with the issue of homelessness, there is an on-going debate in Prince George over services provision to the poor and homeless (Seymour, 1996; Trick, 1995a). Some Prince George business owners do not want more services located in the downtown area. In a study looking at these issues, however, people believed that it is the poor people themselves who should be consulted as to what services are needed and where they should be located (Trick, 1995b). In a survey of 37 people, all 37 identified that more low-cost housing should be built downtown and all wanted public washrooms with shower facilities. There was a strong feeling in that survey that the poor deserve the same quality of life as everyone else, but because they are poor they are too often ignored, negated or hidden away (Trick, 1995a).

SERVICES FOR THE POOR AND HOMELESS IN PRINCE GEORGE

There are many services in Prince George to aid those in need of food, shelter, and clothing. A sampling of such services as were available in 1996 is described in Table 4.6 and mapped on Map 4.2 (see also Chapter 7 in this book by Allen).

Map 4.2
Services for the Poor and Homeless

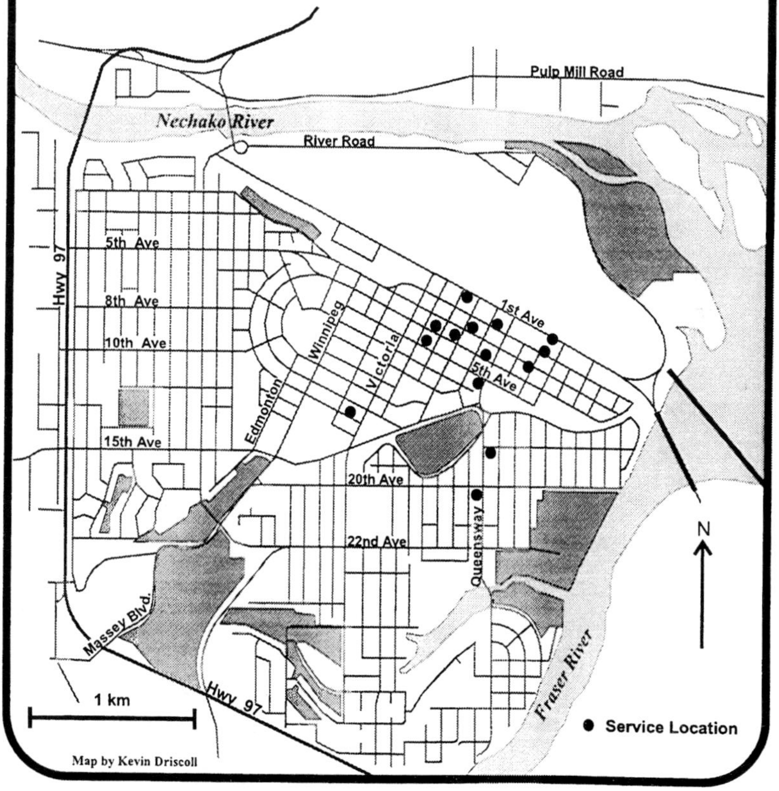

TABLE 4.6
Food, Shelter, and Treatment in Downtown Prince George 1996

AAKRON 160 Quebec Street
- single male only; will provide a place to sleep and meals

NATIVE FRIENDSHIP CENTRE [now 657 Douglas Street]
- education and treatment programs (drug, alcohol, abuse, etc.)
- many services including men's hostel, health programs, AIDS awareness.

CHRISTIAN LIFE CENTRE 270 Dominion Street
- breakfast, ministry services

ST. VINCENT DE PAULS 1130-3rd Avenue
- food, clothing, entertainment

PRINCE GEORGE GOSPEL MISSION 1130-4th Avenue
- food and clothing, connection of people to church

SALVATION ARMY FAMILY SERVICES 1088-4th Avenue
- food and clothing, programs for kids, new mothers
- emergency social services (aid in the event of a disaster)

PRINCE GEORGE GOSPEL MISSION 1153-4th Avenue
- emergency shelter and life counselling

SALVATION ARMY ADDICTION TREATMENT CENTRE 835-3rd Ave
- offers treatment for alcohol and drug addictions
- Harbour Lights (sandwich bus) also run out of the same building.

ACTIVE SUPPORT AGAINST POVERTY #306-1268 5th Avenue
- counselling and reference to various services

MINISTRY OF SOCIAL SERVICES 585 Queensway
- aids in finding accommodation, food, and clothing

PRINCE GEORGE CRISIS & INFORMATION CENTRE 1306-7th Ave
- sets up programs for those who have a lack of housing, food, clothing, etc..

THE ELIZABETH FRY SOCIETY #204-2666 Queensway
- for women and children; will provide place to sleep and meals, clothing etc...

SEVENTH DAY ADVENTIST 4388-15th Avenue
- food hampers, soup line across from P.G. Native Friendship Centre, clothing.

ST. PATRICKS HOUSE 1735 Yew Street
- for male alcoholics in need of treatment, will provide place to sleep and meals

PHOENIX TRANSITION 1770-11th Avenue
- place to sleep and meals for women and children; also gives other support

According to the people who help provide these services, there should be no one in this city who has to do without food, clothing, or shelter (even if such shelter is not permanent). The spatial locations of these services are directly related to the location of the people who require their assistance. For those familiar with Prince George, there is usually no problem in finding these services, as they are clustered in the downtown area so those requiring assistance do not have far to go from one type of service to another. Many of these services also offer some type of counseling service for those who need to talk about their situations. Further, low-income and homeless people develop their own form of community and social network where useful information can be learned and shared. This sense of community is reinforced by the clustering of service providers in the downtown core, and by the atmosphere for socializing which many of these services provide in their facilities.

The Salvation Army

One of the most familiar and recognizable agencies across Canada providing services for the poor or homeless is the Salvation Army. This organization provides people in need with emergency food, clothing, and furniture as well as numerous other services. The Salvation Army Family Services Centre in Prince George is staffed by volunteers who donate their time, energy, and services. These volunteers help run a Coffee House from Monday to Friday from 1:00 p.m. to 3:00 p.m. in which they serve coffee and cake, and provide a comfortable atmosphere in which people can come in and feel free to socialize. A Day Camp is organized once a year for children to give them "a camp-like experience without having to leave Prince George" (Salvation Army pamphlet, p. 1). The Family Services centre also provides baby starter packages for mothers and provides courses on how to properly care for their newborn children. The Centre will soon be starting up a program in conjunction with the Prince George Regional Hospital and the Healthiest Babies Program known as the Infant Formula Milk Bank. Local businesses will be donating baby formula to the Salvation Army, and they in turn will distribute it to mothers with newborns along with training in how to care for their new baby (Personal communication, 1995). The Salvation Army also runs a thrift store above Family Services to raise money for all of the programs and services that they provide.

At Christmas time the Salvation Army pays particular attention to the children. Christmas dinners are cooked, toys are given out, and food hampers are created. Last year (1994), food hampers were given to 715 families ($35,750.00), toys were given to 1,182 children ($11,820.00), and 215 people attended a Seniors Dinner ($2,150.00). Throughout the year $154,891.33 was spent on clothing, furniture, and food for needy families and individuals (Salvation Army Family Services, p. 3). The money is raised from sales in the thrift store, Christmas Kettles, private donations, and local companies such as Costco donate bakery goods and grocery items at the end of each working day.

The Salvation Army also operates an Addictions Treatment Centre in the City. This is primarily a facility for those dependent on drugs and alcohol. Harbour Lights sandwich bus is also run from this location and serves soup and sandwiches Monday to Friday at 12:30 p.m.

St. Vincent de Paul's

The Society of St. Vincent de Paul is an international organization run by the Catholic Church. Founded in 1833 in Paris, it was established in Canada by Dr. Painchaud in 1846. Its goal is to try and alleviate the pain and suffering of mankind and promote self-dignity and integrity (St. Vincent's pamphlet). St. Vincent's was established in Prince George approximately twenty years ago as a sandwich truck that drove around downtown. Today they have a drop-in centre for people to come in and get food, warm-up, and socialize with the staff and each other. In the room there is a couch, a television and VCR, books, picnic tables, cards, games, a telephone, and people willing to listen and talk. There is no smoking or consumption of alcohol permitted in the building.

St. Vincent de Paul is a very "low key" service provider in the downtown core as they do not wish to publicly expose their clientele. Everything is kept private to let the users of the service keep their pride and dignity. The service includes the space of two buildings side by side. One side is a thrift store that sells donated clothing at a very low cost. People can generally come in and pick out clothing, paying for it whatever they can afford.

The drop-in centre and thrift store are run by four paid staff and approximately one hundred and fifty volunteers. Their main focus is making sure the under-privileged in this city have enough to eat. There is a vegetable line every Thursday at 9:30 a.m. in which families are given bags of vegetables, bread, fruit, cheese, etc.. Approximately one hundred and thirty families line up every Thursday morning. Soup is served on Wednesdays and Sundays. Sandwiches are served every other day, and approximately 400 cups of coffee are served every day. Most of the food used is donated by individuals and by businesses such as Tim Horton's. Extra Foods donates vegetables, cheese, canned goods, bulk foods, and other items which may be slightly damaged and cannot be put out on the shelf for sale purposes. All of the left over bakery buns at the end of the day are also given to St. Vincent's. St. Vincent's holds a supper for families three times a year (Christmas, Easter, and Thanksgiving) and puts together two hundred food hampers each year at Christmas time. Finally, St. Vincent de Paul also provides the logistical support base for the "Soup Bus", a mobile kitchen staffed by area churches who take turns providing a meal service that has become "an essential part of the lives of low income families and street people" in Prince George (Peebles, 1994, p. 1).

The Native Friendship Centre

The Prince George Native Friendship Centre (PGNFC) was established in the community twenty-three years ago. It is a non-profit organization that is "dedicated to servicing the needs of native people residing in the urban area and improving the quality of life in the community as a whole" (PGNFC pamphlet,

p. 2). It was developed primarily to assist native people in their adjustment to life in an urban centre. Beyond a number of social services such as education and alcohol and drug treatment counseling, the PGNFC facilities include a halfway house and a single men's hostel. The objective is to "provide temporary living facilities for single transient men in need. The program provides beds, meals, bedding, towels, and toiletries" (PGNFC pamphlet, p. 4). The Centre provides an option to life on the streets for people.

ASSISTED HOUSING

Traditionally, senior levels of government have taken the lead role in providing or sponsoring assisted housing for low-income households and people with special housing needs that would not normally be available in the private market (Prince George, 1993). However, during the past 13 years, the federal government has modified its role significantly in the housing field by reducing or withdrawing funding from programs. In the recent past, most direct federal government involvement in the creation of new assisted housing has been terminated, and for the foreseeable future the "cupboard is bare" for capital financing of new socially-assisted housing (Prince George, 1993, p. 2). However, at the present time the British Columbia provincial government is taking a much more pro-active approach in addressing unmet housing needs. The Provincial Government has been participating financially in the Federal-Provincial Non-Profit Program Families and Seniors and has earmarked $22.5 million over three years to a "Homeless Initiative" (Prince George, 1993).

Local Context

There is a very limited supply of low-income and assisted housing in the Prince George area. During 1993, approximately 6,100 income assistance cases were handled by the Ministry of Social Services from their two main offices serving the Prince George area (Prince George, 1993). These cases represented a total of almost 10,900 people - including individuals and families with little or no employment income and people with health-related disabilities. Over the preceding six year period, the ministry estimated that applications for low-cost housing in Prince George had increased 60 percent.

Map 4.3
B.C. Housing in Prince George

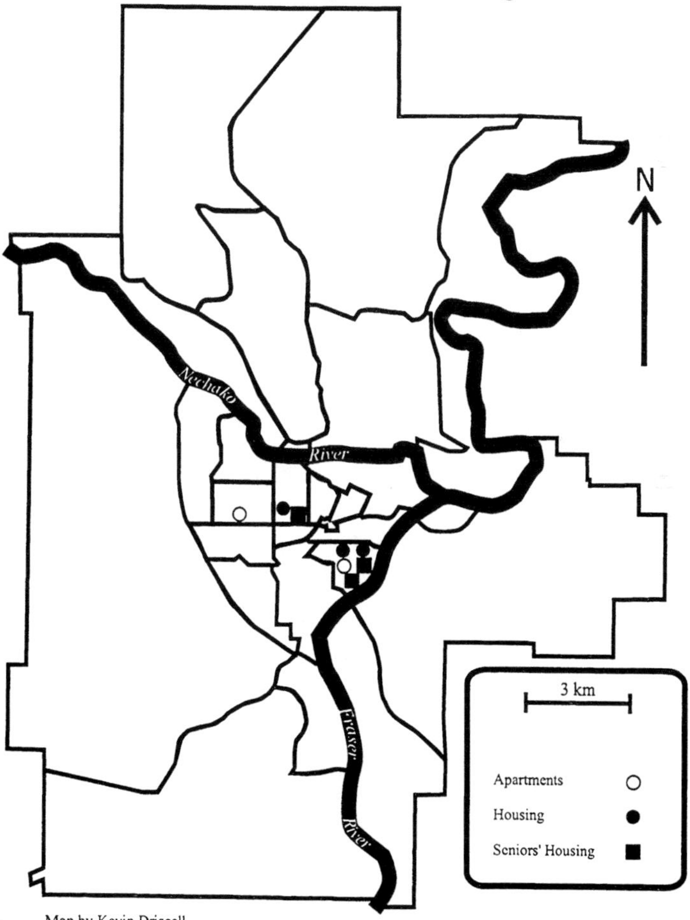

Map by Kevin Driscoll

As with other small urban centres, Prince George has achieved limited success in establishing non-profit housing societies and co-operative housing projects (Prince George, 1993). Two groups, the British Columbia Housing Management Commission (BC Housing) and the Prince George Metis Housing Society, were responsible for providing most available assisted housing in the City. Together, they have 260 units, made up of both houses and apartments. There are lengthy waiting lists for both agencies. As shown on Map 4.3, the BC Housing managed facilities tend to be strongly concentrated either in the Carney Hill area or along the 15th Avenue corridor. However, there are also a few organizations now working to create new non-profit housing options (Heyman, 1996).

In 1995 and 1996 some progress was made in creating new assisted and non-profit housing. Local MLA and then Health Minister Paul Ramsey announced that the Active Support Against Poverty would receive $2 million to build a 20-unit apartment building for the homeless in the downtown area (Horth, 1995) While this initiative has stalled, it is presently being reworked with the assistance of BC Housing. It was also announced that the Elizabeth Fry Society would receive $4 million to construct approximately 40 units for low and middle income families. These new housing projects will be up to four-bedroom houses for families with children, and some of the units are specifically designed to be wheelchair accessible. The "Irwin House" project was officially opened by the Elizabeth Fry Society in September 1997 (Trick, 1997). The Elizabeth Fry Society is also proceeding with construction of an 11 unit low-cost housing facility for women fleeing abuse or for teenage mothers seeking a safe shelter.

In Prince George, the vast majority of housing for low-income people will continue to be provided by the private sector through rental accommodation; including apartments, basement suites, and sleeping rooms. Private sector rental accommodation suited to the special needs of the physically disabled is generally limited (Prince George, 1993). Further, there is a sense of discrimination by some private sector landlords and this appears to be a concern to renters in Prince George. This discrimination is targeted by age (too young), "race" (Native), and financial circumstances (low-income or on income assistance).

There is a growing concern for the middle aged and older people living on, or near the streets of downtown Prince George. Some live in hotels, rooming houses, and motels. However, the supply of low-cost housing facilities for them is low and is declining. With the continuing revitalization activity in downtown Prince George, some low-cost housing is being lost. The demolition of the MacDonald and Canada Hotels to make way for a new courthouse complex forced many older low-income individuals to find new low-cost housing, an already scarce commodity. It seems with revitalization, the poor and the homeless are often forgotten. The continuing loss of sleeping rooms in single occupancy residential hotels in the downtown core is increasing pressure for more affordable housing options in the downtown. An inventory undertaken by the City identified about 350 units of affordable housing, most of which were usually shared facilities, in or near the downtown core (Prince George, 1993). The new courthouse is expected to spur further revitalization in the downtown as lawyers and support services likely will desire new offices nearby. As a result, more low-cost housing in the downtown core may be lost, with little likelihood that it will be replaced.

CONCLUSION

Cities do not stand still, they are vibrant and constantly changing. During a period of change it is important that the needs of those least able to speak for themselves be considered. There are many services offered in Prince George to aid those in need of food, shelter, and clothing. The spatial locations of these services are directly related to the location of the people who require them. Many of the available services also offer some type of counseling service for those who need to talk about their situation. In our society "the dwelling place assumes immense significance as a public badge of worth, a means of status affirmation" (Cater and Jones, 1989, p. 40). It would therefore be a fair assumption that many homeless people feel a lack of self-esteem and do not feel much in the way of self-worth. They are also exposed to the psychological and physical elements that accompany life on the street. As the most visible component of the poor, the homeless are a part of downtown Prince George, and their social geography represents a key issue which must be addressed. As a final note, without the hard work of the people who volunteer and work in the various service and support centres the general well being of our community would be much lower than it presently is.

REFERENCES

Baldwin, J.R. and Gorecki, P.K. (1990). *Structural Change and the Adjustment Process: Perspectives on firm growth and worker turnover.* Ottawa: Statistics Canada and the Economic Council of Canada.

Baxter, S. (1993). *A Child is Not a Toy.* Vancouver: New Star Books.

________. (1995). *No Way to Live: poor women speak out.* Vancouver: New Star Books.

Begin, P. (1994). *Homelessness in Canada.* Ottawa: Canada Communication Group.

Bentley, D. (1995). *Measuring Homelessness: A Review of Recent Research.* Winnipeg: Institute of Urban Studies.

Cater, J. and Jones, T. (1989). *Social Geography: An Introduction to Contemporary Issues.* New York: Edward Arnold.

Heyman, D. (1996). "Gospel Mission's New Home Won't be Flophouse". *The Prince George Citizen.* February 28, p. 15.

Hoeven, R. and Anker, R. (1994). *Poverty Monitoring: An International Concern.* Britain: St. Martin's.

Horth, D. (1995). "$6 Million for Housing Projects". *Prince George This Week*, November 5, p. 10.

Hulchanski, D.J. (1991). *Solutions to Homelessness.* Vancouver: University of British Columbia Centre for Human Settlements.

Mills, S. (1995). "Project Aimed at Poor". *Prince George Free Press*, November 2, p. 1.

Oberlander, P.H. and Fallick, A.L. (1988). *Homelessness and the Homeless: Responses and Innovations.* Vancouver: University of British Columbia Press.

Peebles, F. (1994). "Soup Bus meeting an ever-increasing demand". *Prince George Free Press.* December 22, p. 1.

Prince George. (1993). *Housing Needs Research Project.* Prince George: City of Prince George Housing Needs Research Project Steering Committee.

Prince George Native Friendship Centre. (n.d.). *Prince George Native Friendship Centre.* Prince George: Prince George Native Friendship Centre, pamphlet.

Salvation Army. (n.d.). *Salvation Army.* Prince George: Salvation Army, pamphlet.

Salvation Army Family Services. (n.d.). *Salvation Army Family Services.* Prince George: Salvation Army, pamphlet.

Seymour, B. (1996). "Downtown Housing Proposal Moves Step Closer to Reality". *The Prince George Citizen*. February 22, p. 3.

Spector, A. (1992). Measuring Low Incomes in Canada. *Canadian Social Trends*. Summer, pp. 9-10.

St. Vincent de Paul. (n.d.). *St. Vincent de Paul Services*. Prince George: St. Vincent de Paul, pamphlet.

Statistics Canada. (1992). *1991 Census Dictionary*. Ottawa: Statistics Canada.

Trick, B. (1997). "Irwin Place housing project has something for everyone". *The Prince George Citizen*. September 20, p. 3.

_______. (1995a). "Downtown Facilities Sought for the Poor". *The Prince George Citizen*. June 6, p. 3.

_______. (1995b). "Users of Drop-in Centre Resent 'Transient' Label". *The Prince George Citizen*. April 6, p. 3.

APPENDIX
Meals Available - Downtown Prince George - 1996

Monday	Breakfast	9:30-11:30	Christian Life Centre, 270 Dominion Street
	Soup & Sandwiches	12:30	Salvation Army, 835-3rd Avenue
	Soup & Sandwiches	1:00-2:00	Gospel Mission, 1130-4th Avenue
	Coffee & Sandwiches	7:00	Gospel Mission
	Coffee & Sandwiches	7:30	St. Vincent de Paul, 1180-3rd Avenue
	Coffee	1:00-3:00	Salvation Army, 1088-4th Avenue
	Coffee	10:00-3:00	St. Vincent de Paul
Tuesday	Soup & Sandwiches	12:30	Salvation Army, 835-3rd Avenue
	Soup & Sandwiches	1:00-2:00	Gospel Mission
	Coffee & Sandwiches	7:00	Gospel Mission
	Coffee & Sandwiches	7:30	St. Vincent de Paul
	Coffee	1:00-3:00	Salvation Army, 1088- 4th Avenue
	Coffee	10:00-3:00	St. Vincent de Paul
Wed.	Soup & Sandwiches	12:30	Salvation Army, 835-3rd Avenue
	Soup & Sandwiches	1:00-2:00	Gospel Mission
	Coffee & Sandwiches	7:00	Gospel Mission
	Soup & Sandwiches	7:30	Soup Bus (group of churches)
	Coffee	1:00-3:00	Salvation Army, 1088-4th Avenue
	Coffee	10:00-3:00	St. Vincent de Paul
Thursday	Soup & Sandwiches	12:30	Salvation Army, 835-3rd Avenue
	Soup & Sandwiches	1:00-2:00	Gospel Mission
	Coffee & Sandwiches	7:00	Gospel Mission
	Coffee & Sandwiches	7:30	St. Vincent de Paul
	Coffee	1:00-3:00	Salvation Army, 1088-4th Avenue
	Coffee	10:00-3:00	St. Vincent de Paul
Friday	Breakfast/or Meal	8:30-11:30	Christian Life Centre
	Soup & Sandwiches	12:30	Salvation Army, 835-3rd Avenue
	Soup & Sandwiches	1:00-2:00	Gospel Mission
	Coffee & Sandwiches	7:00	Gospel Mission
	Coffee & Sandwiches	7:30	St. Vincent de Paul
	Coffee	1:00-3:00	Salvation Army, 1088-4th Avenue
	Coffee	10:00-3:00	St. Vincent de Paul
Saturday	Soup/Chili or similar every other week	3:00	By Seventh Day Adventists - across from Native Friendship Centre
	Coffee & Sandwiches	4:00	St. Vincent de Paul
	Soup & Sandwiches	7:00	Gospel Mission
	Chili/Sandwiches occasionally	7:30-11:30	Christian Life Centre
Sunday	Soup & Sandwiches	3:30	Soup Bus (group of churches)
	Soup & Sandwiches	6:30	Salvation Army, 835-3rd Avenue
	Soup & Sandwiches	7:00	Gospel Mission

Chapter 5

A GENDER STUDY OF PRINCE GEORGE

Kerry Kilden

INTRODUCTION

Gender is a very important issue to consider when examining the social structure of a community. Throughout this chapter we will be looking at a number of gender issues in the City of Prince George. While gender issues apply to men and women, most of the focus will be placed on women in the community. We will investigate the various services that are offered to women for financial support, emotional support, and for interaction with other women in the community. As part of this study, it will also be important to examine the role that the single parent plays in our society. As we will discover, more often than not, it is the mother who takes responsibility for the children in a single parent family, an arrangement which often proves to be economically strenuous. Therefore, we will conclude by examining the services available for the lone parent family as well as assistance that is provided for the traditional family in their struggle to keep up with the pace of today's hectic world.

CONSTRAINTS ON WOMEN IN THE LABOUR FORCE

One of the major issues connected with women's equality in society is what "sphere" (domestic, workplace, both, neither) she fits into. In North America, a stereotypical view of the "traditional family" used to involve a husband who worked outside of the home to put food on the table and clothes on everyone's back, with a wife by his side to cook the meals, to keep the house in order, and to care for the children. According to Andrew and Moore-Milroy (1991, p. 7), this stereotype had been developing for a long time:

> the beginning of the twentieth century saw the transition to industrial capitalism in Canada, accompanied by an urban pattern of reproduction isolated in private homes away from spheres of production. This had obvious repercussions for urban structure - with the creation of residential suburban neighbourhoods - and for gender roles - with the full-time housewife in a nuclear family supported in the suburban home by the income of her husband.

Since the 1970s, however, a transition has been underway. Increasingly, women have become active participants in the paid workforce (see also chapter 2 in this book by Rennie).

While participation in the paid workforce has seen some blurring of older notions of a separation of home and work, it has been argued that it has not corresponded with a liberation of women from the domestic sphere. In fact, it has been suggested that despite their increased participation in the workforce, women continue to shoulder most of the household's domestic responsibilities as well. Cater and Jones (1989, 127) suggest that "it goes almost without saying that neither commodification nor socialization has completely eliminated the purpose of the women-centred family". Even though the 'modern woman' may be seen as being career-oriented and independent, she still has in many cases the primary responsibility for the domestic sphere. Cater and Jones go on to argue that it is still a widespread expectation that domestic labour is a woman's duty and that her primary obligation is to the home. The struggle to balance domestic and employment responsibilities is seen as an up-hill battle:

> ... the trend towards female economic independence is clearly one of slow, uneven and personally costly progress and does not represent a genuine reshaping of the male-female relationship. To quite a startling

> degree women in contemporary society are still locked within ... the domestic world of the family ... . To emerge from this, as growing numbers are now doing, and to enter the 'mainstream world' of paid work, they must overcome numerous obstacles including a continuing responsibility for domestic matters (Cater and Jones, 1989, 123).

It had been so long accepted that women should remain at home and have babies that it is hard to break away from that image and challenge this long-standing societal norm. When women do make the leap from the domestic sphere into the work sphere, there are many decisions to make and many obstacles to overcome. Issues range from affordable daycare for children to equality of pay and employment opportunities in the workplace.

Marx and Engels were among the first theorists to perceive the relationship between the state, the economy, the family, and relative gender status (Cater and Jones, 1989). From their perspective, women had to stay in a marriage to inherit money because they could not work outside the domestic sphere due to the fact that men controlled production outside the home. Marx and Engels theorized that women could end domestic exploitation by:

> joining men in productive labour outside of the home. Instead of an exploitive relationship between an economically dependent person (wife) and an economically independent person (husband), men and women would exist freely as equals. In addition, marriage as we know it would cease to be. Monogamy would no longer have an economic value attached to it once inheritance and ownership of private property was abolished (Elliot and Fleras, 1992, 105).

Today, while women do work alongside men outside of the home, there is still an economic value attached to marriage and the assets accumulated before or during marriage. Some people sign pre-nuptial agreements before they marry but, in a lot of cases, when two individuals separate it is not an equal economic split.

For those women who do decide to enter the workforce, jobs in the "caring" professions are among those most commonly entered into. These jobs include such general areas as education, welfare, and health. Women essentially end up engaging in the same activities in the workplace as they would if they were in the home (Cater and Jones, 1989). As well, women may often try to select jobs that will allow them to still maintain control over their family life, for example, by choosing to work only part-time. The amount of hours worked is a main concern for women with families. The type of job sought, and whether or not it is full-time or part-time, often depends on the children - how many there are and how old they are. It is also dependent on the amount of education and training the applicant has acquired.

Women with families who are engaged in paid employment must create a balance between their work and domestic lives. In making the transition from the domestic sphere to the work sphere, women must readjust their use of both time and space. Andrew and Moore-Milroy (1991, p. 23) suggest that:

> because women work both at home and in the wage sector, they are organizing services at the interface. Community day care centres, health advice centres, and alternative consumer services structure women's domestic working conditions, providing time for wage work, and creating employment. Women are creating their own jobs - looking after each other's children, sewing each other's drapes - jobs which are socially necessary to reproduce a family but are also remunerative and located at the intersection of the private home and the public wage economy.

With an increasing number of women entering the workforce, a growing concern is with the placement of children while their mothers are at work. This has, in part, led to an increasing demand for child care outside the home. In response to the dual tensions of the need for employment income and the need for suitable child care arrangements, one trend among women has been to create daycare facilities in their own home. These daycare operators fill the child care needs of working parents, they allow mothers to enter the work force, and at the same time they generate income for themselves while being allowed to remain at home with their own children.

Having women enter into the paid labour force has altered fundamentally the social and spatial organization of contemporary cities (Preston and McLafferty, 1993). An important consideration for the "working woman" is accessibility to her place of employment. It is not always possible for a family to have more than one vehicle so there could be difficulties in getting one member of the family to work. If the husband and wife do not work in the same area of the city, then either walking or public transit becomes a necessity. Women often try to find jobs that are closer to home and will lessen the time they spend in commuting. If this is not possible, then public transit is a next logical step. Preston and McLafferty suggest that "for women who often rely on public transit, failure to integrate routes and schedules may preclude commuting long distances and restrict access to jobs" (1993, p. 125). Add to this the need to connect with child care sites and it is clear that the location of employment in relation to the home is a very important consideration for working mothers and may seriously affect the way a family is able to function. Not only this, but such logistical constraints may actually restrict the type of job a woman is able to take.

Women in resource towns are placed in a similarly vulnerable position. Gender trends in existing resource base towns were examined in a study by Gill. Focusing on the mining community of Tumbler Ridge, Gill describes "a distinctive setting which has traditionally been viewed as male-dominated, with women functioning predominantly in a subordinate role to the main mode of production" (Gill, 1990, p. 347). In such cases, women are often very dependent on their husbands. Because it is usually the husband's work that brought them to the town, women's lives are seen as "being structured around their husband's jobs: thus, they are dependent on their husbands to an unusual degree for economic and psychological support" (Gill, 1990, p. 348). Nevertheless, in today's society there is the necessity for both husbands and wives to be wage earners. The employment trend for women in resource-based communities, however, is that:

> [m]ost women employed outside the home in mining communities are still working in traditional service and clerical occupations. Although a small proportion are employed in non-traditional jobs, there are still constraints on their entry into such positions. The main barriers include shift work schedules which often necessitate flexible child care arrangements, lack of training opportunities, and attitudes of managers (Peacock, 1985, p. 8).

Dependency on a husband for financial support can result in considerable financial hardship for women in the case of family breakup, when they suddenly find themselves as head of single-parent families and lack the skills and knowledge to get well-paying jobs to economically support their families. The growing trend of single-parent families has been a reality of the last few decades. Klodawsky and Spector suggest that:

> women lose experience and job opportunities when raising young children. When they do enter the labour market, they are often limited in the jobs that they are able to take and the hours that they are able to work. Given their initial low income levels, they are often unable to afford cars which help them seek and choose jobs, housing, child care, shopping, and other opportunities. Single parents are thus often caught in a web of poverty aggravated by a general loss of experience and social and physical mobility (1988, p. 153).

Some women can find the support they need within the community in which they live. They may be able to turn to extended families, neighbours, and services within the community to help them with child care, transportation, and household duties. The characteristics of single-parent families vary greatly and, therefore, different coping measures and mechanisms may be undertaken depending upon each circumstance. The group requiring the most comprehensive support are the never-married single parents (often under age

25, with infant children, and little job experience). Most social support services are constructed to target this specific group (Klodawsky and Spector, 1988).

As with employment and child care, finding affordable housing can be a very difficult task for a single-parent family. Roughly eighty-five percent of single parents in Canada are women, and most of their economic problems relate to the differentiated labour market in which women's employment income has traditionally been much less than for men (Klodawsky and Spector, 1988). This lack of financial resources often means single parent families end up taking less than desirable housing. People who find themselves in this circumstance generally end up living in multiple-unit apartment complexes in cities. Unfortunately, these buildings are not able to effectively accommodate young children and they do not usually offer the facilities that are appropriate and required for single-parent child rearing (Klodawsky and Spector, 1988). Shared housing is an option for the single-parent which can "help reduce housing costs, distribute various household responsibilities such as maintenance and child rearing, and, in some cases, encourage emotional support from empathetic peers" (Klodawsky and Spector, 1988, p. 152). Further, single-parents often find themselves short of time and money and have to turn to whatever resources that can be found in order to help keep the family going.

PRINCE GEORGE

The rest of this chapter will seek to relate the issues introduced above to the City of Prince George. We will begin by examining the stereotype of women being confined to the domestic sphere by addressing the questions: how are women participating in the paid labour force?, and what are the occupation and income consequences of this participation? This is followed by a discussion of the changing family, specifically the numbers of female-led lone-parent households in Prince George. Next, the issue of daycare facilities within the City will be examined. The way in which our society functions today has determined the need for multiple incomes and parents need a safe place in which to leave their children while they are working. Accessibility to the parent's work, to school, and to the home are very important variables when weighing the child care costs of time and monetary expense. Finally, available social support services for women will be considered, including the issue of housing - especially housing for low income single mothers.

Women and Work

Between 1981 and 1991 female presence in the Prince George workforce has dramatically increased (Table 5.1). In 1981 there were 14,085 women aged 15 and over who were actively participating in the paid labour force. By 1991, this had increased by just over 18 percent to 16,700. More important than the numbers is the changing participation rate - that is, the percentage of women who are in the City's labour force relative to the total number of women in the City. Between 1981 and 1991 the participation rate for females in Prince George increased approximately 5 percent. This is consistent with longer term Canadian trends that have seen a steady increase in female participation rates since 1960.

TABLE 5.1
Prince George Workforce

	1981	1986	1991
Males*			
number	21,510	20,540	21,545
participation rate	87.2	84.9	82.1
Females*			
number	14,085	14,140	16,700
participation rate	59.3	61.1	64.8

*persons 15 years of age and over
Source: Statistics Canada.

Interestingly, male participation rates fell about 5 percent over the same period - again consistent with other Canadian trends (this time due more to population aging and increased retirement levels). Reasons underlying this change for women include the number of single-parent households and, in two-adult households, the need for more than one income to meet rising household costs of living.

For those women who choose to stay at home, the federal government has taken a relatively small step towards recognizing the importance of unpaid housework to the Canadian economy. Caring for the family is important for the stability of our society and its value will be reflected in a new question found on the 1996 Census. For the first time since national census-taking began in Canada, unpaid housework is to be formally measured. The new household activity category asks Canadians to "calculate how much time was spent, during a specific week, on unpaid house and yard work and care for children and seniors. This includes time spent bathing or playing with children, helping them with their homework and talking to teens about their problems" (Southam Newspapers, 1996, p. A2).

Focusing only upon employment in the paid workforce, it is clear that there are significant differences between men and women. Table 5.2 summarizes some of these differences by beginning first with the issue of occupation. Even a cursory glance at the table indicates that male (m) and female (f) occupational employment opportunities are almost mirror opposites. Compare, for example, clerical to construction, or teaching to processing industry, occupations. Male employment from 1981 to 1991 clearly illustrates patterns common for resource-based industrial communities while female employment is in the service, support, or care giving occupations.

TABLE 5.2
Occupational Group Comparison for Prince George

	1981		1986		1991	
	m	f	m	f	m	f
Number in Labour force	21,510	14,085	20,540	14,140	21,545	16,700
Percent in each Occupational Group:						
Manager/Admin.	9.7	3.9	9.9	6.5	9.1	6.7
Teaching	2.6	6.8	2.4	6.7	2.6	7.3
Medical/Health	1.2	7.7	1.3	7.5	1.6	7.9
Tech./Art.	6.4	3.1	6.3	4.9	7.4	4.8
Clerical	4.8	40.5	4.6	35.9	4.5	33.8
Sales	8.9	10.9	8.8	9.9	8.6	10.7
Service	7.6	18.8	9.9	21.1	8.0	21.5
Primary	4.8	1.3	8.7	1.9	8.0	1.9
Processing	8.4	0.9	8.2	1.3	8.9	1.1
Machining	13.8	0.9	13.6	1.2	13.1	0.9
Construction	15.5	--	11.6	0.4	12.2	0.3
Transportation	8.3	--	7.5	1.1	9.1	1.3
Other	7.4	2.9	7.2	1.5	6.8	1.7

Source: Statistics Canada.

The structure of employment opportunities has a very important impact on levels of earned income. Table 5.3 includes information on average employment income for men and women in Prince George. While incomes have been rising over the 1981-1991 period, women continue to earn much less than do men. This applies to those employed full-time and those employed part-time. As suggested, part of the explanation lies in the structure of local occupational opportunities while another part lies in an historic undervaluing of work areas typically dominated by females.

TABLE 5.3
Employment Income Comparisons
Average Employment Income[1] in Prince George

	1981	1986	1991
Male *	no data		
full-time		$34,421	$42,161
part-time		$17,801	$21,904
Female *	$9,217		
full-time		$21,121	$25,142
part-time		$7,959	$11,205

[1]current year dollars
*persons 15 years of age and over
Source: Statistics Canada.

The Family

Over the years, the definition of the family has changed dramatically. Families need no longer consist simply of a mother, a father, and 2.2 kids. It is an ever-changing entity that has very permeable boundaries. Statistics Canada defines the Census family as involving "a now-married couple (with or without never-married sons and/or daughters of either or both spouses), a couple living common-law (again with or without never-married sons and/or daughters of either or both partners), or a lone parent of any marital status, with at least one never-married son or daughter living in the same dwelling" (Statistics Canada, 1991).

The profile of Census families in Prince George has changed subtly between 1976 and 1991 but still retains some central features (Table 5.4). The "husband-wife" family unit remains the norm for the vast majority of Census Families. The structure of "husband-wife" families remains one where more

TABLE 5.4
Census Families in Prince George, by Family Structure

TYPE	1976		1981		1986		1991	
	#	%	#	%	#	%	#	%
Total	14,645	--	17,420	--	17,780	--	18,735	--
Husband-wife								
total	13,205	90.2	15,290	87.8	15,145	85.2	15,980	85.3
with children*	(n/a)	(n/a)	10,705	70.0	10.550	69.7	10.250	64.1
no children*	(n/a)	(n/a)	4,585	30.0	4,595	30.3	5,730	35.9
Lone Parent								
total	1,440	9.8	2,135	12.3	2,635	14.8	2,750	14.7

figures may not add due to Census rounding
* means children living in the home
Source: Statistics Canada.

TABLE 5.5
Lone Parenthood In Prince George

LONE PARENT FAMILIES	1976 #	1976 %	1981 #	1981 %	1986 #	1986 %	1991 #	1991 %
TOTAL	1440	--	2135	--	2635	--	2750	--
Male Parent	n/a	n/a	375	17.6	470	17.8	460	16.7
Female Parent	n/a	n/a	1755	82.2	2160	82.0	2290	83.3

figures may not add due to Census rounding procedures
Source: Statistics Canada.

than two-thirds have children living with them at home. As seen in Table 5.4, the number of lone parent families is on the rise in Prince George. Over the 15 year period covered in the table, the proportion of lone-parent families has increased from approximately 10 percent to approximately 15 percent (or just above the Canadian average of approximately 13 percent).

Table 5.5 compares the distribution of male versus female lone-parents. While the number of male lone-parents has slightly decreased since 1986 and the number of female lone-parents has slightly increased since 1986, the far majority of lone-parent families in Prince George are headed by women. Among the reasons for the general increase in the numbers of lone-parent families include the growing numbers of total households in the City and the changing social norms with respect to single parent families. Reasons for the upward trend of female lone-parent households may not simply be the outcome of changing social trends but may also be the result of an increase in the number and types of services that have been constructed for women in the last few years. Women are no longer forced to stay with abusive or incompatible partners for financial support. There are now places for them to turn to obtain the emotional and financial support they need.

Mapping

Map 5.1 shows the distribution of lone-parent households across the City. As seen on the map, Census Tracts 5, 8, and 17 in the bowl area of the City have the highest shares, with over 10 percent of all lone-parents in the City living within each of these Census Tracts. In contrast, Census Tracts 1, 4, 9, and 12 have almost no lone-parent households - although (with the exception of Census Tract 4 which is the agricultural area of Cranbrook Hill) there are relatively few families living in these largely industrial and business oriented Census Tracts.

Map 5.1
Distribution of Lone-Parent Families across Prince George, 1991

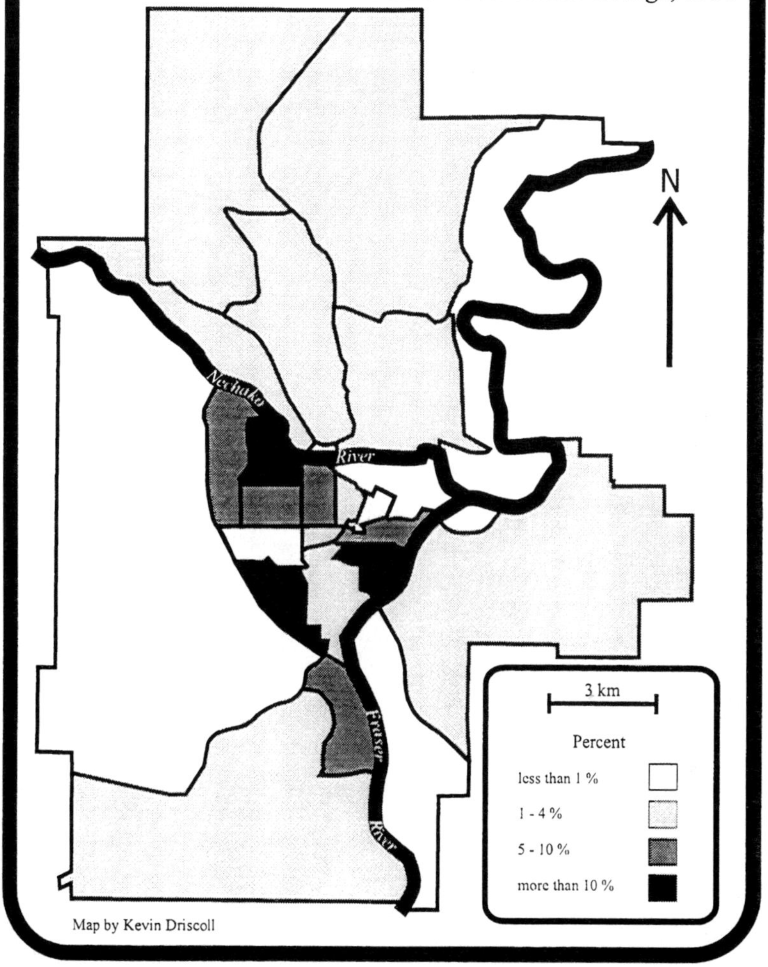

While Map 5.1 shows the distribution of lone-parent families across the City, Map 5.2 shows the relative concentration of lone-parent households within each of the City's Census Tracts. As such, Map 5.2 presents a comparison of the number of lone-parent family households to the total number of family households in each Census Tract. In other words, the map shows whether lone-parent households are a relatively common

Map 5.2
Lone-Parent Families as a % of All Census Families, 1991

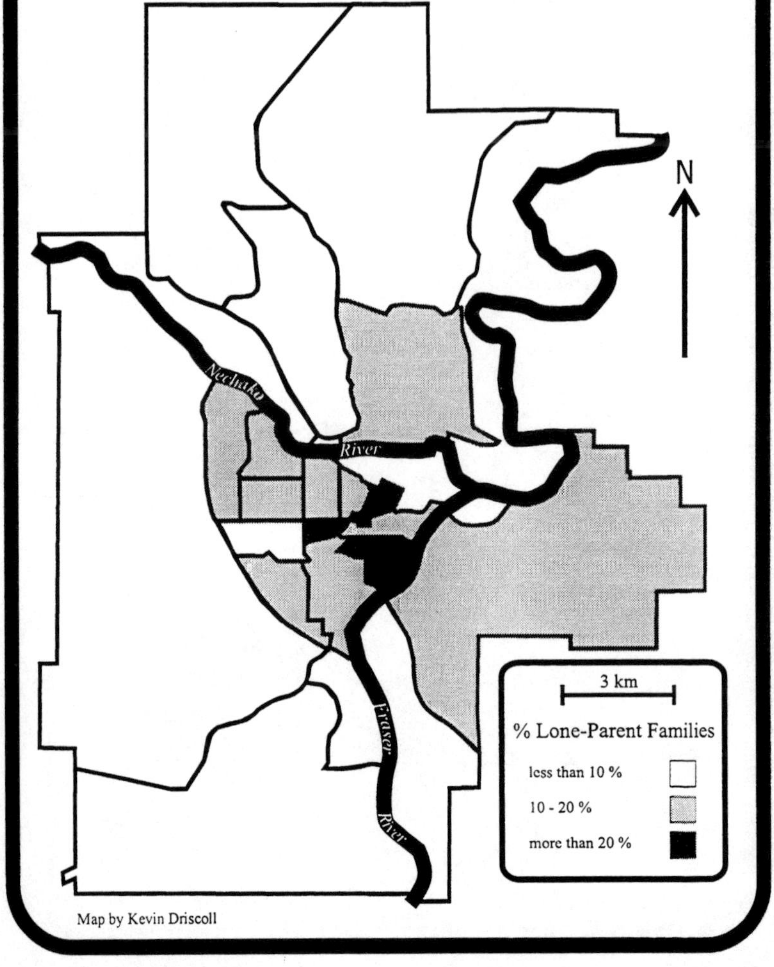

household type within each area. In Census Tracts 8, 10, and 12, more than 20 percent of Census families are lone-parents. In fact, in Census Tract 8, over 26 percent of families are headed by lone-parents (it should also be kept in mind that Census Tract 12 has relatively few households living within it relative to other Census Tracts in the City). Keeping in mind that the average share of lone-parent families for the City is approximately 14 percent, these Census Tracts can be said to be "over-represented" in terms of lone-parent households. Possible reasons for this pattern of concentration are likely connected with housing options and housing affordability, as well as proximity to schools, services, and public transportation.

Daycare

Daycare has become an important issue in the lives of today's working parents. Cost is a very important variable in selecting a daycare facility. The pressures and constraints of double incomes or single-parenthood often mean that more and more households make the decision to have their children taken care of outside the home for at least parts of the day. Garbarino (1982, p. 140) suggests that "supplemental child care can also be an instrument used to help a society meet its goals. Day care centres are viewed as a key to providing for full participation of adults in the political and economic life of the society, as well as for the socialization of children in a manner appropriate to societal goals".

However, those with a limited budget are also restricted to choosing only what they can afford. Child care can be expensive, and depending upon the complexity and length of the work day may involve two or more different caregivers. In this sense, the role of the school system in "caring" for children for a large part of the Monday-to-Friday workday is important. Individuals able to find part-time work opportunities where the hours fall between the 8:30 am to 2:30 pm (approximately) school day can make use of this "child care" facility with no additional loss in employment income for child care expenses.

Location also plays an important role in the selection process. Daycare centres must be close to home, work, and schools in order to serve the needs and limited time schedules available to working parents. Lone-parent households, or those who must rely upon the public transit system, face additional constraints on choosing daycare locations relative to the locations of the home and the workplace.

Daycare Licensing

Child care can be provided by formal or informal means. Individuals providing care to three or more children unrelated to the caregiver are required under the Community Care Facility Act and Child Care Regulation to be licensed (Northern Interior Health Unit, 1997a). While an Early Childhood Training certificate is not required to operate a licensed daycare, there are a number of requirements for both the caregiver and the facility. With respect to the caregiver, daycare course training and a valid first aid certificate are standard requirements, while for the facility a number of health and safety features must be met along with other requirements such as for indoor and outdoor play areas (Northern Interior Health Unit, 1997b).

There are various licensed services offered to meet the daycare needs of today's families. They include the following:

1) Group Day Care Centres - serve children from 30 months to Grade 1, or children from birth to 36 months. Full-day care is offered year-round.

2) Preschools (Nursery Schools/Playschools) - serve children from 30 months to Grade 1. Preschools are part-day programs.

3) Family Day Care - Family day care is offered in the caregiver's own home. They may provide care for children from birth to 12 years. Caregivers set their own hours.

4) Out of School Care - serve school age children who require care outside normal school hours. Some provide care both before and after school; others provide care only after school.

5) Special Needs Day Care - designed to serve children with a variety of special needs. Care may be offered on a full-time or part-time basis.

6) Child Minding - may provide care for children from 18 months to Grade 1. Children may attend no more

than three hours a day and no more than two days a week. Many programs are on a drop-in basis.
(Northern Interior Health Unit, 1997a)

However, formal care is often up to ten dollars a day more than informal care, and is harder to find (Bell, 1996). For low income households, where employment income is limited such as for many lone-parent female-headed households, costs are critical. A 1988 Statistics Canada study found that "the most common arrangement for children under six was with an individual, working independently or in a network supervised by a licensed agency" (Bell, 1996, 25). Other common alternatives for child care are: spouses arranging work schedules to accommodate children or having a relative, nanny, or part-time babysitter come into the home.

There are over two hundred formally organized daycare facilities in the Prince George region (and there are likely many more informal caregiving services). With the increase in the number of women participating in the workforce, there has been a steady increase in the number of child care facilities that have been established. In the City, the Prince George Child Care Resource and Referral service is available to help with finding and selecting childcare arrangements (Northern Interior Health Unit, 1997a).

TABLE 5.6
"Daycare" Services in Prince George

Year	Number of Daycares	Number of Pre-schools
1981 +	5	1
1986 +	5	5
1991 +	8	15
1997 +	16	13
1997 *	155	17

Sources: + Prince George Telephone Book, 1981, 1986, 1991, 1997.
* Northern Interior Health Unit, 1997a.

There is a perception that childcare services in the City are increasing as more and more women enter the paid workforce. While the information in Table 5.6 seems to confirm this, it is important to note that the sources of this information vary and that increasing awareness of both licensing requirements and the need to advertise can affect the trends as much as any change in the availability of daycare facilities.

Using the listing of Licensed Child Care Facilities for Prince George and area produced by the Northern Interior Health Unit (1997a), it is possible to map the distribution of such facilities. As illustrated in Map 5.3, the trend for daycare location in Prince George is that the concentration of the facilities are in the vicinity of either the workplace or the home. The bulk of the facilities are located in the Hart Highlands area. The second largest concentration is found in the College Heights and Southridge areas, and in the area between Foothills Boulevard and Tabor Boulevard. These areas are densely developed residential areas where households are likely to require daycare facilities. The people who live outside of town would often be required to bring their children with them on their way into work.

Day care facilities are also located at recreational facilities throughout the city. Fitness centres such as "Ladies Only Fitness" have child minding facilities on location to enable women to get out of the house and have their children near them at the same time (Plett, 1996). The "Family Y" has established many child care facilities across the City (Prince George Family Y, 1996). The "Tiny Y Nursery School" is for 3-5 year olds and operates either mornings/afternoons 2 or 3 days per week. This program has dedicated space at King George V School. The "Y Out of School Care Program" consists of 3 programs; after Kinder Care for Kindergarten aged children, after School Care for 6-9 years olds, and the Y Kids Club for 9-12 year olds. These programs are operated in several neighbourhood elementary schools (King George V, Spruceland, and Harwin).

Map 5.3
Number of Daycare Facilities by Census Tract, 1997

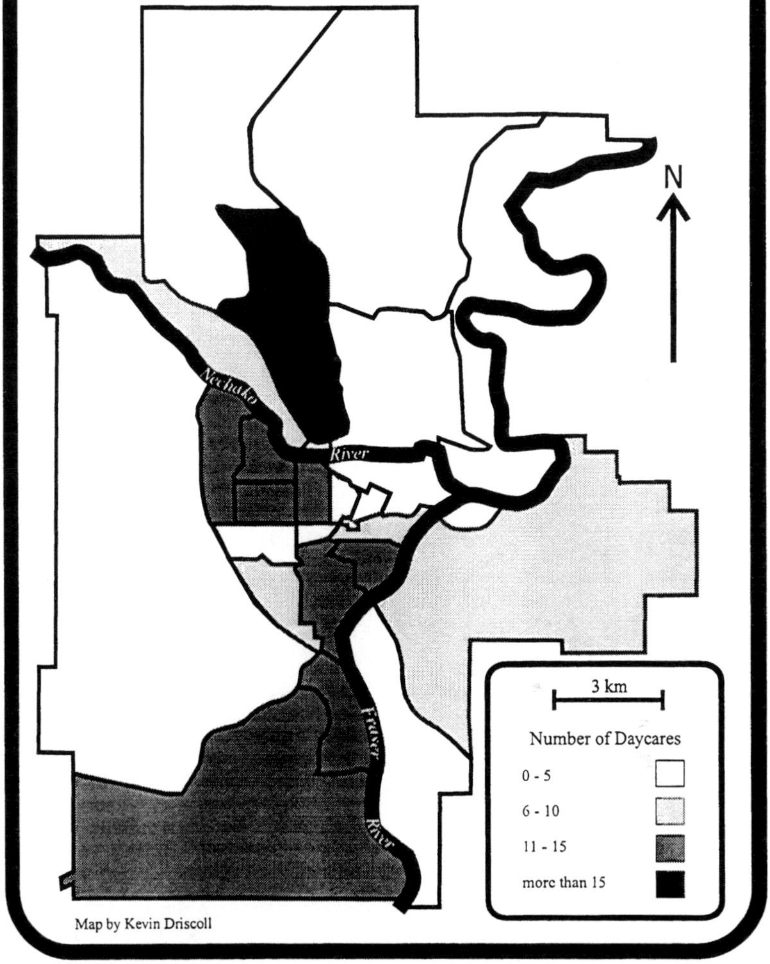

Access to education is one way for women to break the cycle of limited job opportunities and low wages. Along with an increase in the number of women entering post-secondary institutions goes the need for daycare facilities. Both the College of New Caledonia and the University of Northern British Columbia have made substantial commitments to provide on-site daycare services. The University of Northern

British Columbia took a step forward in making post-secondary education more appealing and more accessible to women with its January 2, 1996 opening of a $1 million day care centre to provide care for toddlers and preschoolers. About a dozen children were registered in the first month of operation, but the complex will eventually be able to accommodate about sixty children (Prince George, 1996b). The College of New Caledonia is also upgrading its child care services by including a more elaborate daycare facility within its $12 million remodelling project for the Prince George campus. As part of this remodelling, a daycare has opened with spaces for sixty-one children (Prince George, 1996a). The daycare facility was previously located in a portable on the College grounds but it is now located near the northwest corner of the College.

Support Services for Women

Beyond some of the potentially restrictive limitations already identified above, there are many reasons why a woman may need the help of a private or government agency in order to cope with everyday life. She may have had a male partner as her main source of income, and death, divorce, or abuse may have forced her into being on her own with much more limited resources. Whatever the case may be, there are many agencies in Prince George established for those in need of financial, physical, and/or emotional aid. A selection of these agencies and services are shown on Map 5.4 and corresponding Table 5.7. It should be noted that further discussion of the social services landscape of Prince George can be found in Chapter 7.

One such service in the Prince George area is the Elizabeth Fry Society (located at point #13 on Map 5.4). The Elizabeth Fry Society is one of the most publicized women's support services in the Prince George region. The front cover of its advertising pamphlet reads, "Elizabeth Fry Society: shelter for abused women and their children that emphasizes self-worth, self-help, and self-determination" (Elizabeth Fry Society brochure, nd.). They offer a safe place for women who are unable to continue living in their homes, and are equipped with programs and counseling for women and their children by on-site counselors. The provision of support to women in need is an essential aspect of the Society, as it offers support groups for abused women as well as providing court orientation, accompaniment, and transportation to court if required. If visits to the hospital or lawyers are needed, then the Society will help with referrals or arrangements for the women to obtain these services.

TABLE 5.7
WOMEN'S AND CHILDREN'S
SERVICES IN PRINCE GEORGE

1) Ministry of Social Services
2) Ministry of Women's Equality
Quebec St. Emergency Shelter For Women
& Advocacy for Women and Children
4) Wimmin's Connection
5) Healthiest Babies Possible
6) P.G. Crisis and Information Centre
7) Childcare Support Program
- Phoenix Transition Society
9) Prince George Regional Hospital
10) Northern Interior Health Unit
11) Project Parent North
12) Mom's and Kids' Drop In Centre
13) Elizabeth Fry Society

(numbers correspond with Map 5.4)

Further, the Society has connections to the crisis line, emergency social services, legal services, resources for children, and community agencies. In addition to counselling and support for victims of physical, sexual, or emotional abuse, the Society also offers education, life skills, computer training, and career preparation and work experience for single-parents. The Society provides a strong foundation and re-building tool for traumatized women. Whether the trauma stems from physical or emotional abuse, or financial hardship, the Society is a stepping stone that women can use to get back on their feet again.

Map 5.4
Women's and Children's Services

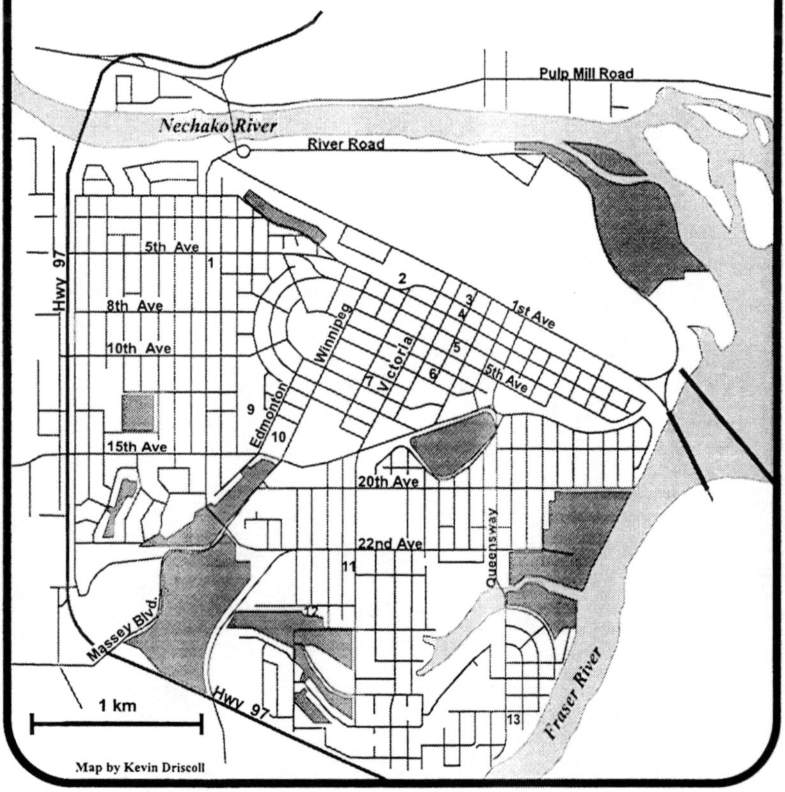

The Elizabeth Fry Society also offers a program for teen parents known as "Pathways" (Elizabeth Fry Society, Pathways brochure, nd.). The emphasis of this program is to provide aid for young parents while they are continuing their education. Located in a classroom at Duchess Park Secondary School, "Pathways" allows students to complete regular Grade 10, regular Grade 12, or Grade 12 equivalency programs. A daycare service is provided across the street from the school. Counselling is also available for these young mothers as well as peer support groups, workshops, and recreational activities.

Another support service for women in Prince George is the Wimmin's Connection[1]. The Wimmin's Connection has developed and opened a Women's Centre, (point #4 on Map 5.4). It was constructed in 1991 after the results of a survey conducted by the Elizabeth Fry Society indicated that there was a need for a central resource and referral centre for women in Prince George. The Wimmin's Connection is a "group of women who have worked to establish and operate a women's space and to be a liaison and central resource group for women of the Prince George area" (Wimmin's Connection, 1995). The Wimmin's Connection holds potlucks, film nights, women's dances, and a women's fair. They organize Prince George's annual "Take Back the Night March" (a public opposition to violence against women) and participate in other various public events regarding women and women's issues. It is an organization which provides women with a place to connect with one another and to familiarize themselves with the resources and services available in the Prince George area (Wimmin's Connection, 1995). It is not only a place for disadvantaged women to become connected or reconnected with the community, but also a place for women to connect with other women and themselves.

Healthiest Babies Possible is a Pregnancy Outreach Program of the Northern Family Health Society (Northern Family Health Society pamphlet, nd). Started in Prince George as a pilot project in 1988, Healthiest Babies Possible seeks to provide education and support to high risk pregnant women who would not normally access traditional pre-natal health services. Most clients come as "self-referrals", becoming aware of the program from family, friends, past clients, community organizations, or

---

[1] Editor's Note: as one reflection of the rapid state of change within the social services landscape of cities such as Prince George, it should be noted that since writing, the Wimmin's Connection has closed its offices.

health care professionals. About half of the women who make use of the program are single-parents. The program provides support, counseling, and education on nutrition, health, child birth and care. Base funding comes primarily from the Ministry for Children and Families. Staff includes 2 Registered Nurses (1 of whom is a Fetal Alcohol Prevention Worker), a nutritionist, and 2 outreach counsellors. In addition, Health Canada recently sponsored a "Fetal Alcohol Syndrome (FAS) Collaborative Community Network" project which seeks grassroots community solutions to FAS issues. The agency's central role remains advocacy, education, support, and referral work on behalf of mothers. Referrals may be made, for example, to services such as post-natal health and child care. In 1997, 170 babies were delivered to women participating in the program. Child minding and transportation is available to promote participation in programs which include a Cooking Club and a support group for pregnant and parenting women with substance misuse issues. The program serves up to 350 women each year.

Another set of services available to women in Prince George are those delivered through the Phoenix Transition Home (not identified on map). Operated by the Phoenix Transition Society, the Home has been an emergency shelter for women and their children since 1974 (Phoenix Transition Society, nd.). Services to women, beyond the safety of the emergency shelter itself, include group facilitation and individual counseling, as well as assistance through an outreach worker. The Society also works closely with other community agencies in developing plans to assist women. Recently, the Society has developed a "Children Who Witness Abuse" program which includes both group and individual counseling services. Though centred on children from pre-school age through to adolescence, these new programs incorporate parent education and support as well.

Family Services

Beyond the specific groups mentioned above, there are also many other services and agencies which can assist women and female-led lone-parent families. Parent Mutual Aid Support

Organizations (PMAO) are community support groups for families. Their motto is "Strengthening Families by Empowering Parents" (British Columbia, 1995). Services are provided by the Ministry of Social Services in collaboration with Carney Hill Neighbourhood Centre, Project Parent North (#11 on Map 5.4), Carney Hill Elementary School, Seymour Elementary School, Highglen Elementary School, and Highland School (British Columbia, 1995).

PMAOs are parent support groups that meet twice or more weekly. PMAOs provide an opportunity for parents within a community to interact with one another and to help conquer feelings of loneliness and social isolation (British Columbia, 1995). PMAOs can offer emotional support, educational support, community contacts/information, activities for children, and other projects. For example, the Family Maintenance Program helps provide support for single-parents and their children. Eligibility for the Family Maintenance Program is determined by whether an individual receives Income Assistance from the provincial government and at least one of the following situations applies to that individual:

> - You are separated from a legal spouse or common-law spouse;
> - You are divorced;
> - You are remarried or living in a common-law marriage with a child or children from a previous marriage; or
> - You are an unmarried parent. (Family Maintenance Program, 1993)

Once these prerequisites are met there are many services which can be utilized through this program. Those running the program try and reach consensus between a mother and the person responsible for maintenance, apply to Court for a Maintenance on the woman's behalf, assist if the person responsible for child or spousal support applies to Court to decrease payments, interpret and explain the language, procedures, and expectations of the Court system, and file orders with the Family Maintenance Enforcement Program (Family Maintenance Program, 1993).

Housing Projects

Affordable housing is in great demand in the City of Prince George. There are relatively few places available and many people who are in need. "Social housing" complexes are often the subject of many misconceptions. Community members too often associate the people who live in them with social problems, such as drugs, alcohol, and violence. While it may seem "politically correct" to encourage the development of these complexes to bring relief to the poor, it is often the case that nobody wants them in their own neighbourhoods. In Prince George, there are some presently some social housing complexes that face these same prejudices and there are also some new ones that are being considered for construction.

"We're no different", screams the headline of a Prince George This Week newspaper article from June 18, 1995. The article describes the 12-unit social-housing complex in the 4300 block of First Avenue. A group of mothers who live in this complex came out to oppose the negative connotations that are directed at the single-mothers who live in subsidized housing. They complained that they were wrongly being stereotyped as drug users and alcohol abusers and were "picked on and called partiers who don't take care of their kids" (Horth, 1995, p. 3). One woman and her children had to "leave a violent situation and would have had to live with relatives because she couldn't find a landlord who would rent to a single mother with children. Despite checking every classified ad, [she] says almost nobody was willing to give her a chance - only two landlords would even consider her as a tenant" (Horth, 1995, p. 3).

As the newspaper reporter covering this story wrote, it is difficult to distinguish this social housing project from any other multi-tenant dwelling complex (Horth, 1995). The "lawns are neatly trimmed, gardens are filled with colourful flowers, there's no broken windows or peeling paint" (Horth, 1995, p. 3). A commonly expressed fear of neighbours that the complex might attract violent boyfriends or ex-husbands is not seen as a problem for the tenants or landlord. It is the experience of all involved that "the tenants form fairly tight communities and support one another" (Horth, 1995, p. 3).

Rent in subsidized housing complexes is designed for families who have difficulty making ends meet and are based on the household's ability to pay. The tenants in this situation pay what they can afford for their housing arrangement and their rent increases as they move up to higher income employment. Rent in this type of complex may typically be set at thirty percent of the tenant's income. Subsidized housing units not only offer a sense of community but a flexible rent level which is especially important for single-parent women.

There is considerable pressure on available public housing in Prince George. The British Columbia Housing Corporation directly manages 126 units of public housing in Prince George - all but six are for low-income families. In 1995, there was a waiting list of approximately 155 applicants looking to get into this housing (Horth, 1995, p. 3). Examples of recent alternative low-cost housing projects are described in the 'Poverty and Homelessness' chapter by Kilden and Geisler (Chapter 4).

Conclusion

In our society today, the definition of the family is ever-changing. The family does not always consist of a mother, a father, and children who all live together in the same dwelling. The 1990s have shown us that there is an increasing trend in single-parent families, the majority of whom across Canada and within Prince George are headed by women. Along with this increase comes the need for support centres for women. Whether the woman requires physical, emotional, or financial assistance, she is more likely to be able to find it in today's society. We have seen the emergence in Prince George of such centres as the Elizabeth Fry Society and the Phoenix Transition Society. These types of organizations focus on supporting women and their children in times of crisis.

As a result of more and more women entering the workforce, there has been a greater demand for daycare facilities over the last decade. There are now over two hundred daycare facilities in the Prince George region and they are all in demand. Danielle Perry recently wrote in the Prince George

This Week newspaper that there are many improvements that could be made when it comes to child care but that it will require a change in attitude among the voters (Perry, 1996). Perry was referring to the huge cost of daycare for parents. She goes on to say that:

> if society valued the work of a stay-at-home parent, the government could provide tax breaks for those who care for their children at home. If society valued the service day care centres provided, the centre would be receiving donations for needed supplies and wages. More employers would provide on- or near-site child care centres for their workers. At the very least, they would provide a day care subsidy as an option on a benefits package just like dental or RRSPs (Perry, 1996, p. 13).

Affordable and quality daycare is difficult to find. Fortunately, government agencies such as the Ministry of Health and the Ministry of Social Services, and community groups are available to help in the decision-making process. As gender roles and norms shift over time, communities such as Prince George will struggle to deal with the different pressures and issues that may arise from time to time for both men and women. The social geography of a community is very much affected by this struggle over gender.

REFERENCES

Andrew, C. and Moore-Milroy, B. eds. (1991). *Life Spaces: Gender, Household, Employment.* Vancouver: University of British Columbia Press.

Bell, P. (1996). "Who's Looking After the Children?". *The Prince George Citizen.* January 19, p. 25.

British Columbia. (1995). *Parent Mutual Aid Organization.* Victoria: Ministry of Social Services pamphlet.

British Columbia Telephone Company. (1981). *Prince George.* Vancouver: British Columbia Telephone Company.

_______. (1986). *Prince George.* Vancouver: British Columbia Telephone Company.

_______. (1991). *Prince George.* Vancouver: British Columbia Telephone Company.

Cater, J. and Jones, T. (1989). *Social Geography: An Introduction to Contemporary Issues.* London: Edward Arnold.

Elizabeth Fry Society. (nd.). *Elizabeth Fry Society - Shelter for Abused Women and Their Children.* Prince George: Elizabeth Fry Society pamphlet.

_______. (nd.). *Pathways - A Program for Teen Parents.* Prince George: Elizabeth Fry Society pamphlet.

Elliott, J. and Fleras, A. (1992). *Unequal Relations.* Scarborough: Prentice-Hall.

Garbarino, J. (1982). *Children and Families in the Social Environment.* New York: Aldine de Gruyter.

Gill, A. (1990). "Women in Isolated Resource Towns: An Examination of Gender Differences in Cognitive Structures", *Geoforum*, 21 (3), 347-358.

Horth, D. (1995). "We're No Different". *Prince George This Week.* June 18, p. 3.

Klodawsky, F. and Spector, A. (1988). "New Families, New Housing Needs, New Urban Environments: The Case of Single-Parent Families". In *Life Spaces: Gender, Household, Employment*, C. Andrew and B. Moore-Milroy, eds. Vancouver: University of British Columbia Press. pp. 141-158.

Northern Family Health Society. (nd.). *Healthiest Babies Possible, "Pregnancy Outreach Program", Program Profile*. Prince George: Northern Family Health Society, pamphlet.

Northern Interior Health Unit. (1997a). *Licensed Child Care Facilities - Prince George and Surrounding Areas*. Prince George: Northern Interior Health Unit, pamphlet.

________. (1997b). *Child Care Licensed Child Care Facilities - Prince George and Surrounding Areas*. Prince George: Northern Interior Health Unit, pamphlet.

Peacock, A. (1985). "Tumbler Ridge: A New Style Resource Town", *Priorities*, 13, 6-11.

Perry, D. (1996). "Quality Caregivers Deserve Wage Equity". *Prince George This Week*, February 4. p. 13.

Phoenix Transition Society. (nd.) *Phoenix Transition Home*. Prince George: Phoenix Transition Society, pamphlet.

Plett, I. (1996). "Babies Welcome At This Workout". *Prince George This Week*, February 4, p. 8.

Preston, V. and McLafferty, S. (1994). "Gender and Employment in ServiceIndustries: A Comparison of Two Cities". In *The Changing Canadian Metropolis*, F. Frisken ed. Toronto: Canadian Urban Institute. pp. 123-150.

Prince George. (1996a). "City of Opportunity - College Undergoing Huge Changes". Prince George: The Prince George Citizen, March 21, p. 7.

________. (1996b). "City of Opportunity - University Expansion Comes Fast, Furious". March 21, p. 9.

Prince George Family Y. (1995). *Family 'Y' Licensed Childcare*. Prince George: Prince George Family Y pamphlet, January 4, p. 2.

Prince George This Week. (1996). "School Closures Won't Change Housing Plans", February 11, p. 8.

Southam Newspapers. (1996). "New Questions On Census". *The Prince George Citizen*, February 6, p. A2.

Wimmin's Connection. (1994). "The Wimmin's Connection". Prince George: Wimmin's Connection pamphlet.

Chapter 6

ETHNICITY IN PRINCE GEORGE

John Sardinha

INTRODUCTION

Various definitions can be applied to the term ethnicity. For example, ethnicity can be based on a consciously shared system of beliefs, values, loyalties, and practices that pertain to members of a group who regard themselves as different and apart (Elliott and Fleras, 1992). It can also refer to ways in which people define, differentiate, and organize themselves and others on the basis of certain characteristics such as birthplace, language, historical experiences, and religion (Elliott and Fleras, 1992). It is often these types of characteristics that allow a group of individuals to call themselves Croatians or French-Canadians, just to name a few. The goal of this chapter is to take the broad topic of ethnicity and apply it to the City of Prince George. This will be done by examining the history of ethnicity in Prince George, and the formation of ethnic groups and local ethnic facilities.

CONCEPTS AND THEORIES

In an increasingly diverse population, people must learn how to face the problems of living together. This is why an understanding of the issues connected with ethnicity is important. To begin, the concept of ethnicity is very complex and it is important to first touch upon some of the associated theoretical terms and definitions. These terms and definitions can assist in the clarification of some of the issues in contemporary ethnic relations.

Social Class

Like ethnicity, the concept of social class is often employed in attempts to classify individuals into categories (Cater and Jones, 1989). In the case of social class, affiliation is primarily based on the criteria of wealth and associated power status (Elliott and Fleras, 1992). It is important to consider the idea of social class when it comes to the study of ethnicity because income levels and educational attainment often appear to be affected by ethnic origins. As stated by Elliott and Fleras (1992, p. 89), social class is one basis "upon which inequality is constructed, organized and perpetuated". Under certain circumstances, class may overlap with concepts such as ethnicity to generate a segregated society. For example, throughout the history of Canada, various ethnic or racial groups have been used as labourers to fill menial jobs at different junctures of its development (Li, 1988). This process of control and segregation is often organized by the dominant group - those who hold the power. The consequence is the creation of different social classes, job segregation, wage discrimination, and unequal social treatment (Devore and Schlesinger, 1991, p. 51).

Ethnic Stratification

It has been argued that ethnic minority groups are often exploited for reasons that involve cultural and structural factors. One result is that class inequalities can develop. This is what is implied by the term "ethnic stratification". Ethnic stratification can be described in two ways. First, it refers to a hierarchial system in which scarce resources are unequally distributed among ethnically defined groups. Second, it consists of highly segmented systems in which different cultural groups occupy specialized occupational positions (Elliott and Fleras, 1992, p. 91-2). John Porter (1965), one observer of ethnic stratification in Canada, regarded policies of multiculturalism and language retention as impeding the achievement of equality of opportunity for individuals, irrespective of ethnic origin. In Canada, policies on multiculturalism have sought to reduce pressures of assimilation through encouraging the protection and celebration of ethnic identity and the participation of ethnic groups in the Canadian economy (Canadian Human Rights Foundation, 1987; Elliott and Fleras, 1992). Ethnic affiliation and concentration of ethnic minorities often leads to labour market clustering. While many reasons for this may affect individual cases, such labelling can restrict opportunities for upward mobility and at the same time reinforce existing inequalities.

Ethnic Communities

Due in part to the pressures mentioned above, some ethnic groups come together in the urban landscape to form ethnic communities. This may especially be the case when discrimination or other inequalities persist. In these types of situations people may come together to form a support network (Anderson, 1991). The term "ethnic group" can be defined as a collectivity of individuals who "possess a common ancestry, awareness of historical past, identification with select cultural elements as symbolic of their peoplehood, a set of related experiences, interests, history, origins, and descent, potential to interact with others up to and including the point of community, and a self-awareness of themselves as a people" (Elliott and Fleras, 1992, p. 331). Although the preservation of cultural traditions and/or language are important reasons for forming ethnic groups, it is also common for ethnic identities to be formed as a reaction to challenges associated with work, residence, lifestyle and pattern of sociability (Herberg, 1989; Fandetti and Gelfand, 1983). This often leads to the creation of segregated neighbourhoods, reliance on common institutions and services, and occupational concentration (Elliott and Fleras, 1992, p. 141). The larger the ethnic group, the greater are the opportunities to establish such services, and institutions.

The creation of ethnic communities within the urban landscape can support needed services and also set a foundation for cultural celebration and preservation. Language preservation is especially important. As described by

Devore and Schlesinger (1991, p. 31), "a common language provides a psychic bond, a uniqueness that signifies membership in a particular ethnic group, as well as a base for the coordination of activities both social and political". It is especially important that children are taught the language in order to enable communication with their parents. Rituals and celebrations are another important part of the ethnic community. Devore and Schlesinger (1991, p. 32) explain that "the excitement of celebrations might include folk music or dancing, or a sport. Religious practices are especially of great significance as members of ethnic groups might often centre their lives around churches, temples, mosques, or synagogues". These religious centres are usually places to affirm ethnic identity and beliefs (Devore and Schlesinger, 1991; Harney, 1985).

Often, one of the spatial outcomes for ethnic communities in urban places is the formation of ethnic enclaves, areas within which members of a particular ethnic group are concentrated. Ethnic concentration can be defined as the degree to which members of an ethnic group reside in proximity to one another (Herberg, 1989). It is often the people's common culture and language that brings them together to form such neighbourhoods. For members of the ethnic group, an enclave allows for the creation of social and support networks and often creates the critical mass to support ethnic shops and services. While these are all very positive benefits, isolation in ethnic neighbourhoods can also perpetuate such pejorative connotations of superiority-inferiority, majority-minority, and superordinancy-subordinancy which may create or contribute to existing inequalities (Anderson, 1991; Herberg, 1989). Being segregated usually implies being an outsider. Due to the lack of affiliation with mainstream society, socio-economic problems occasionally arise among ethnic groups. In large cities some ethnic neighbourhoods might end up being viewed or labelled as an ethnic ghetto or slum.

ETHNICITY IN PRINCE GEORGE

History

In the City of Prince George, various ethnic groups have made their own mark within the community. Historically, different immigration waves have created different ethnic landscapes. But before any recent immigration to the Prince George area can be discussed, it is first important to emphasize that the First Nations people were the first inhabitants of the region. When the first Europeans arrived at the junction of the Fraser and Nechako Rivers, the Carrier nation already had a long local history. Other surrounding aboriginal nations included the Denes, the Sekanis, the Babines and the Chilcotins (Runnals, 1946).

Statistics Canada did not start to collect census information on ethnic breakdowns until 1961. Prior to that date, very little was known about the ethnic make-up of Prince George. As Europeans settled the area in the late 1800s, a colonial concept of assimilation into western culture was pushed upon the aboriginal population. The Roman Catholic missionaries, for example, built churches in the area as they attempted to convert the native people (Runnals, 1946).

Out of all the European groups that settled in the Prince George area, British immigrants were the majority and held the top positions in local government and business. The few historical accounts written about British Columbia's Central Interior list only the contribution of the Anglo-Saxon dominant group (Hansen, 1981). However, other ethnic groups were present in the area and have played a part in the growth and development of Prince George. An influx of Scandinavian immigrants, for example, occurred in Prince George around 1915 after the completion of the railway. In fact, by 1917, 20 percent of the area's landowners were of Scandinavian origin compared to seven percent two years earlier (Hansen, 1981). Many settled on their own farms and homesteads working hard to eke out a living in this northern climate with its short growing season.

As the Danes, Norwegians and Swedes settled in the Central Interior, many quickly integrated into society. As noted by Ruth Hansen (1981, p. 10), "during the twenties; multiculturalism was not an accepted concept in Canada, and the Scandinavians sought to assimilate as quickly as possible". But even with integration taking place, old country traditions and culture still remained. The Lutheran Church, for example, became an important focal point as Scandinavians would gather for services at the Connaught Hill Lutheran Church, an institution also frequented by the local German population. During this early period, the midsummer dance, an old solstice ritual which was also an important cultural event, was celebrated annually. Hansen (1981, p. 14) describes the ritual in this manner: "hundreds of people showed up that night to dance to the music of violins and accordions. Everyone liked to come to the dances. There was good music, good food, and lively people. The midsummer dance lasted all night".

As early as the 1800s, a legacy of non-European and non-aboriginal visible minority groups is identified as having an influence on the area. Chinese immigration to the Central Interior was important during the Cariboo gold rushes (Chow, 1996). In Prince George, one particular individual played an important role in the City's early development. The February 11, 1996 edition of the Prince George Free Press newspaper contained the following:

> The Prince George area is the legacy of captain Owen Forrester Browne who stood at the helm of several local stern wheelers for 40 years. His most famous command was of the BX riverboat, the first to shoot Fort George Canyon without using lining to the shore. Captain Browne was part black and rumoured to be part Hawaiian. (p. A13)

Although there is evidence of visible minorities making an impact on the area, such as the case of Owen Forrester Browne, little has been written or publicized.

Many reasons can be given to explain why so many European immigrants made the trip across the Atlantic. Many came in search of economic prosperity and a better future for their families. The message across Europe was that there was great wealth in Canada. To the Portuguese immigrant, for example, "Canada was the land of a thousand opportunities; a country as big as Europe with a population as small as Portugal. And to the poor people, those uneducated in this type of activity, came the prospect of saving and struggling to attain the golden goal" (Tavares, 1975, p. 110).

For those who settled in the city, Prince George was often not their original destination. Many first arrived in larger metropolitan centres where they heard about the work opportunities available in northern resource towns such as Prince George. The lumber industry was a major employer in the area and many would take up jobs in sawmills and lumber camps. Once immigrants were settled in Prince George, others followed to be closer to family members. Immigrants who were already established often sponsored family members to come to Canada.

Since the 1970s, immigration to Canada has changed from that of mostly European origin in-migrants to more Asian origin in-migrants. While the search for better economic and employment opportunities is still a priority, many are now also escaping violent civil wars or other political conflicts in their homeland (Richmond, 1988). Table 6.1 shows the arrival of the immigrant population in ten year periods.

Table 6.1
Arrival of Immigrant Population to Prince George in Ten Year Periods, 1991

Period of Immigration	Number	Percent
Before 1961	2,520	31%
1961-1970	2,100	26%
1971-1980	2,260	28%
1981-1991	1,050	13%

Source: Statistics Canada 1991 Census

As of 1991, 31 percent of the immigrant population of Prince George had arrived prior to 1961. From 1961 to 1970, 26 percent arrived, while from 1971 to 1980, a further 28 percent arrived in Prince George. The period between 1981 to 1991 saw a decrease of immigrant arrivals compared to the previous decades. Of the 1,050 immigrants who did come between 1981 and 1991, it should be noted that 80 percent came from Asia.

Measuring Ethnicity

Attempts at measuring concepts such as ethnicity are confronted with many difficulties. Problems of how to define ethnicity in the Census, and how those completing the census forms will interpret the ethnicity categories, mean that the use of Statistics Canada Census data must be done with caution. As will be noted below, available categories for ethnic affiliation also change between censuses.

Figure 6.1 shows the population by ethnic group for the City of Prince George in 1961. That year, the census listed 21 ethnic sub-categories. Out of a total population of 13,877, the largest ethnic group involved 7,196 British people who made up 52 percent of the City's population. The second and third largest groups were Germans (1,668) at 12 percent of the population, and the Scandinavians (1,393) at 10 percent of the population.

Ten years later, the 1971 census shows that Prince George had a population of 33,020. Those from the British Isles still dominated, with a total of 17,470 people making up 53 percent of the population (Figure 6.2). The German ethnic category also continued to have a large share (11.5 percent) of the total population. There were very few differences in the way the 1961 and 1971 censuses studied ethnicity. In terms of ethnic categories, the 1961 census combined the Czechs and Slovaks into the same category while in 1971, each was separate. In 1961, the census listed general groups such as "other Europeans" and "other Asiatic", while in the 1971 census categories such as "West Indian" were added. In both 1961 and 1971, if an individual did not fit into the 21 listed ethnic categories, the remaining choice was "other".

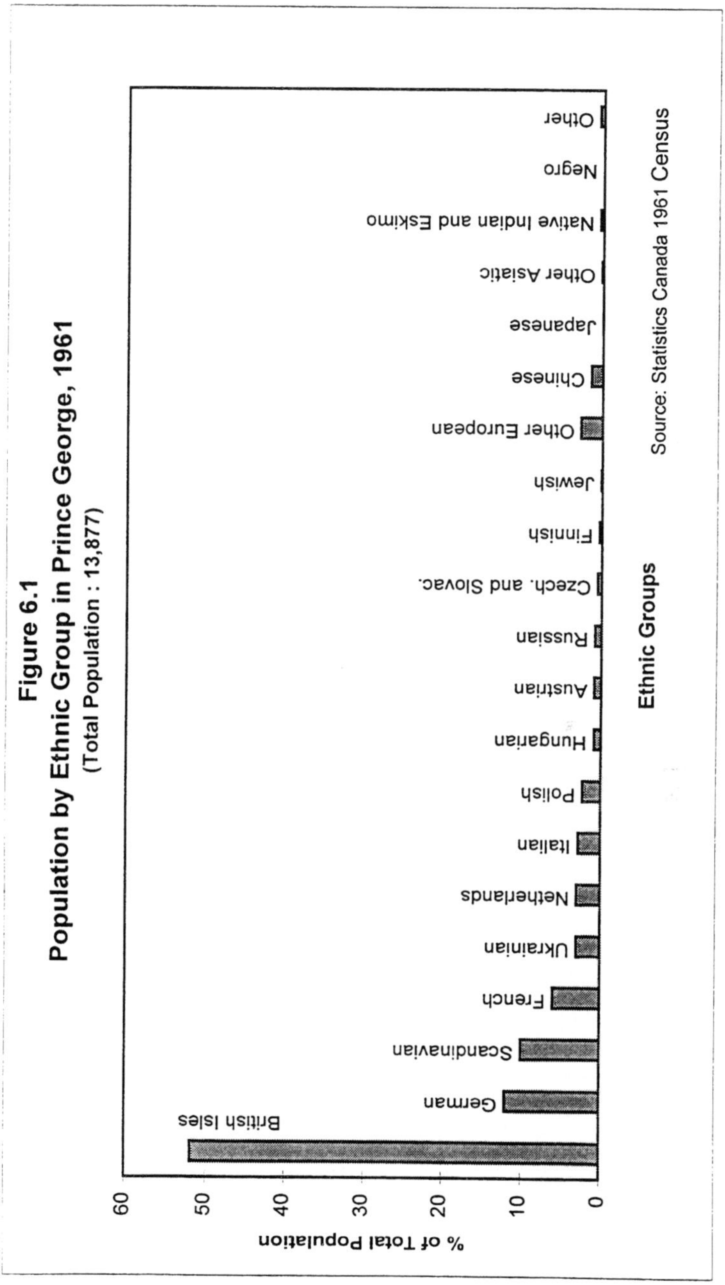

Figure 6.1
Population by Ethnic Group in Prince George, 1961
(Total Population : 13,877)

Figure 6.2
Population by Ethnic Group in Prince George, 1971
(Total Population : 33,020)

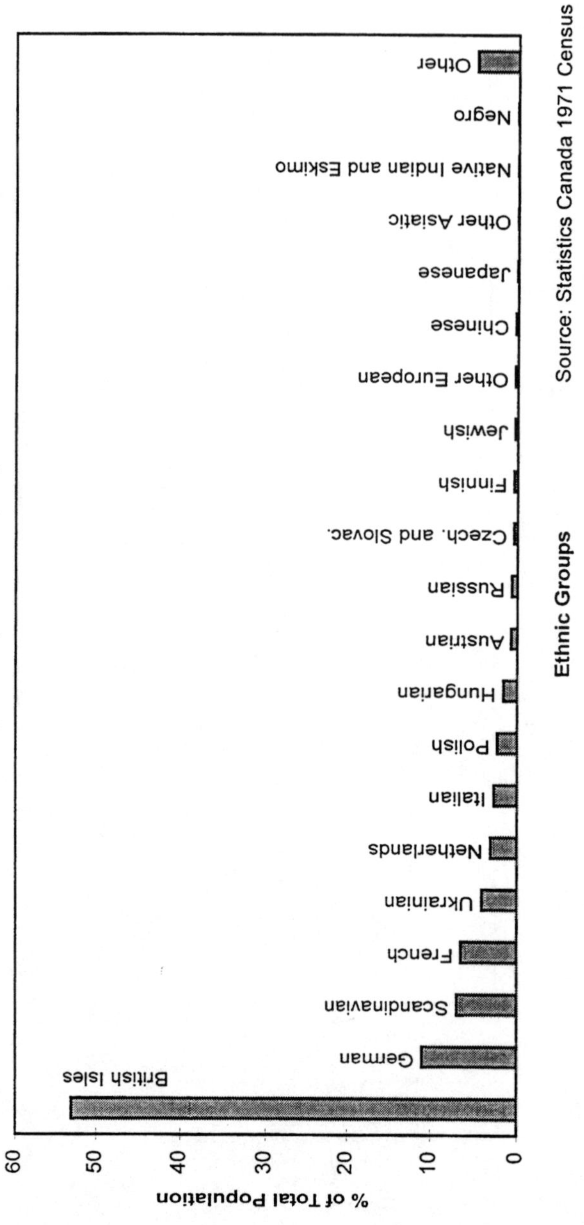

In Figure 6.3, the census breakdown of Prince George's population by ethnic origin for 1981 is shown. In terms of the way the census recorded ethnic categories there is little significant change from 1971. The one notable change, however, is that the census variable is no longer defined as "ethnic group", rather it is now labelled "ethnic origin". Such definitional changes on the part of Statistics Canada reinforce earlier comments about the need to interpret ethnicity data over time very carefully. Several of the general categories such as "Scandinavians" are still lumped together. In terms of the Prince George population, those reporting British ethnic origin still constitute the largest single group (48 percent). When those who reported multiple ethnic origins are added, those reporting British ethnic origin account for 58 percent of the local population. In terms of those who reported only a single ethnic origin, the next largest groups are German (8.4 percent), French (5.6 percent), and Scandinavian (4.1 percent).

Figure 6.4 shows the population by ethnic origin for the City of Prince George in 1991. There are now a large number of new and revised ethnic categories. The 21 categories from 1971 have become 30. The British Isles ethnic category had been divided into English, Scottish, Irish and other British. The same thing occurred with the Scandinavian groups as they were now divided into Norwegian, Swedish and Danish. One of the problems that comes with compiling ethnic information is the confusion that often arises from changing definitions. For example, the ethnic category of "Yugoslavian" might encompass all ethnicities within the Balkan region, such as Bosnian, Slovenian, and Macedonian, for example. A person who is of Bosnian descent may chose not to register him or herself as a Yugoslavian. As well, a number of specific Asian categories such as Vietnamese, Korean and Philippine have also been added. In recognition of the complexity of Canadian society, the "multiple origins" category is now the choice of the largest number of Prince George respondents.

The total population of Prince George in 1991 was 69,565. Figure 6.4 shows that 32,835 people (47 percent of the population) responded that they were of multiple origins. Of the 36,345 (52 percent) of Prince George respondents who

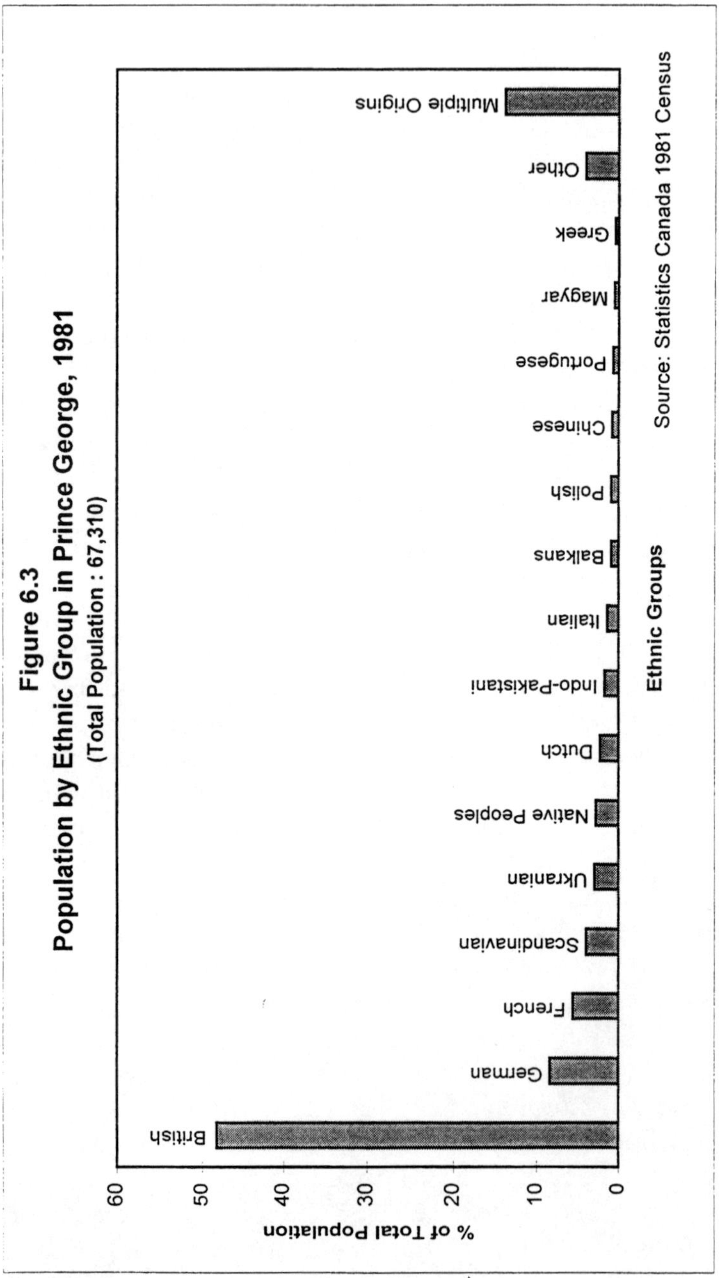

Figure 6.3
Population by Ethnic Group in Prince George, 1981
(Total Population : 67,310)

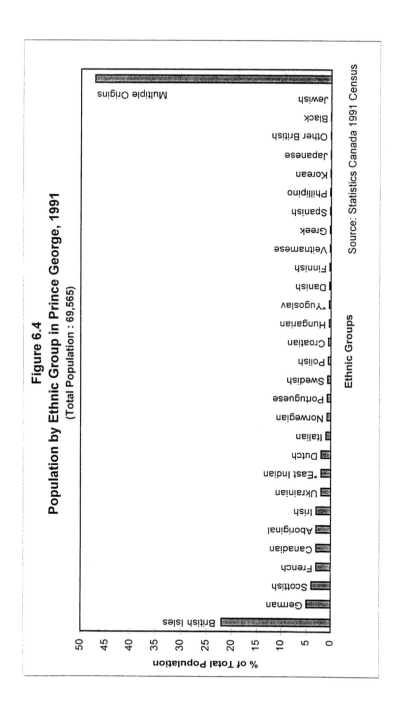

Figure 6.4
Population by Ethnic Group in Prince George, 1991
(Total Population : 69,565)

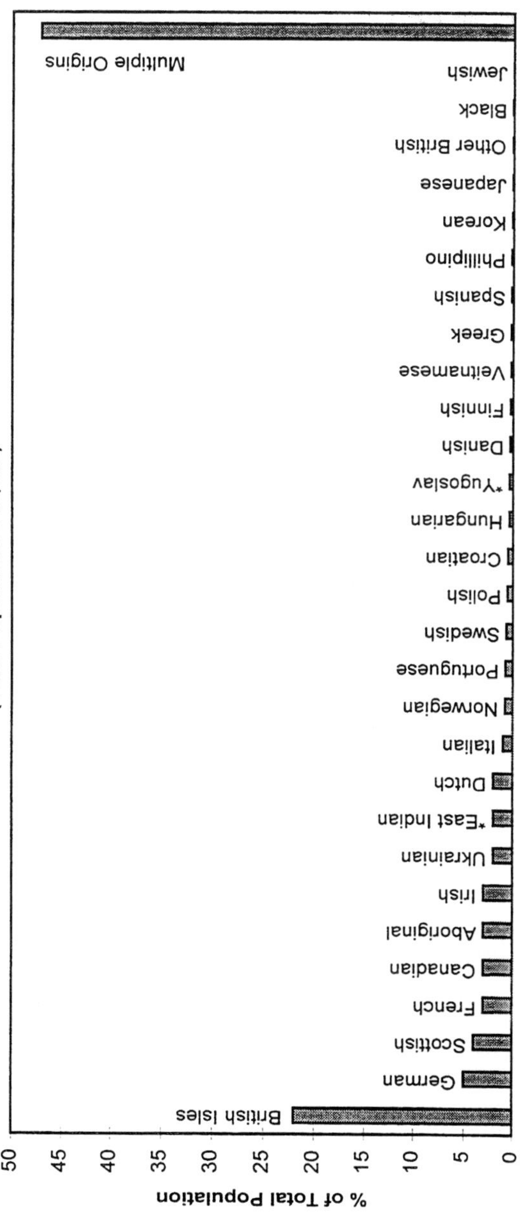

Source: Statistics Canada 1991 Census

reported single ethnic origin, the largest group was that of the English (15 percent), with the total "British Isles" categories accounting for approximately 42 percent. Other large ethnic origin categories include German, French, a category called "Canadian", and Aboriginal.

It is very difficult to directly compare Figures 6.1 and 6.2 with Figures 6.3 and 6.4. The categories have changed, the Ethnic Group definition has changed to Ethnic Origin, and there is a much more sophisticated understanding among members of the public regarding pride in ethnic heritage. In summary, while the ethnic makeup of Prince George appears to remain largely European, there is now a more significant representation of people with Asian and South Asian ethnic origins. As a final note, it should be mentioned that the recording of census information for First Nations / Aboriginal groups has been very difficult for Statistics Canada. Definitions and data collection procedures have been ineffective and it is quite common to have addenda to census publications caution readers about using First Nations /Aboriginal data due to inaccuracies.

PRINCE GEORGE'S ETHNIC LANDSCAPE

Ethnic Facilities

Ethnic facilities play an important part in the transmission of traditional culture, religion, and language. Facilities, such as social clubs, churches, and schools, often grow out of a need to organize and to keep old country ways alive. In Prince George, various ethnic facilities have been established. Map 6.1, entitled "Prince George Ethnic Facilities", shows the location of several different ethnic and cultural facilities in Prince George. Different ethnic groups have established these facilities with different purposes in mind. The French Canadian Club, for example, not only provides a location where cultural traditions can be carried out, but at the same time, a school has also been provided.

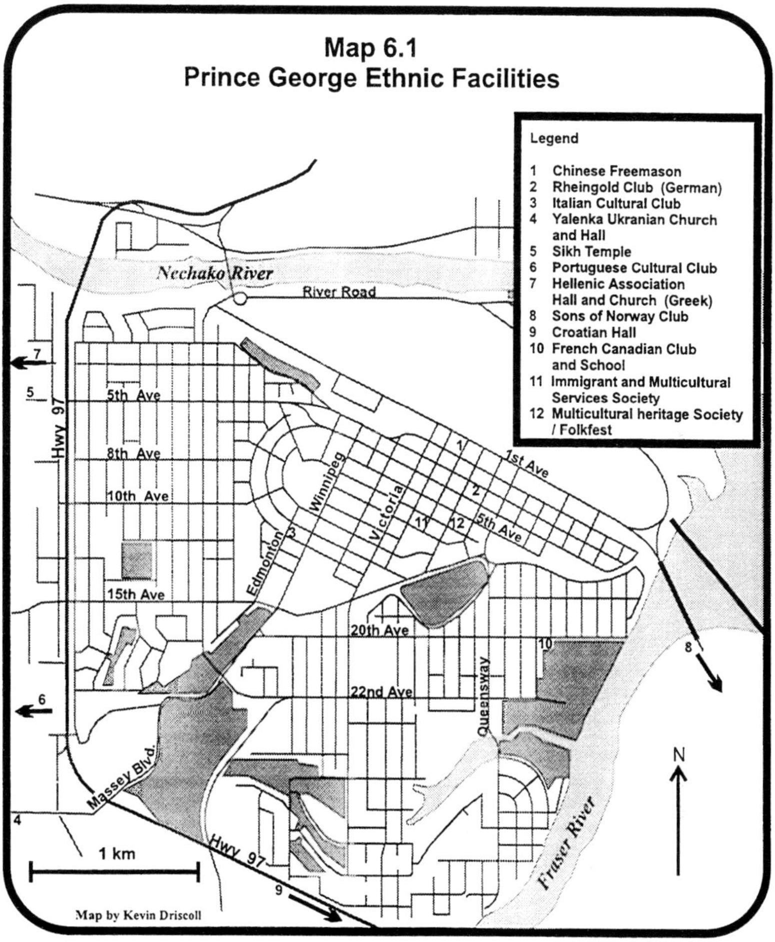

Map 6.1
Prince George Ethnic Facilities

Other ethnic groups, such as the Greeks, the Ukrainians, and the Sikh community, have established places of worship in the community. A church is often an important institution for ethnic groups; in some cases it is the basis for ethnic group identity (Herberg, 1989). In all cases, churches make an important visual statement on the city's landscape. The Ukrainian Catholic Church of Prince George is one such example. The idea of building the church was first conceived of by John Bihun in 1954 (Prince George Immigrant and Multicultural Services Society, 1994). Hampered by a lack of funds, the Ukrainian Catholic community first purchased a building from the Sacred Heart Catholic Church. Then in 1974, John Bihun's dream of constructing a Ukrainian Catholic Church was realized when the building, which now stands on Massey Drive, was completed.

In Prince George, various ethnic clubs and facilities have been established to keep old traditions and culture alive by carrying out ethnic activities such as dances and games, and to also celebrate ethnic holidays. Some local facilities include the Rheingold Club, the Italian Cultural Club, the Portuguese Cultural Club, and the Sons of Norway Club.

The Portuguese Cultural Club, located on Gillette Street, provides a social place where people of Portuguese origin and descent can come together to watch televised soccer from Portugal. People might also come to socialize or to partake in other activities such as card games, but one of the main activities remains watching soccer games from Portugal. A satellite dish was acquired in April of 1994. Since then, people have been gathering every week between two and sometimes five times a week. On weekends, people gather every Saturday and Sunday morning to watch league games. Since there is an eight hour difference between Portugal and Prince George, games usually take place at 8:00 a.m. or at 11:00 a.m. in Prince George. Usually, during these early weekend games someone will make breakfast for everyone either before or after the game. A breakfast fee of $5.00 might be charged. People sometimes also gather on Tuesdays, Wednesdays, and Thursdays to watch European championship games, or occasionally to watch the Portuguese national team play international games.

Just like the Portuguese Cultural Club, the Rheingold Club is an important institution to the German community. Besides providing a place where people of German descent can come together, the club also has a library for the German community which includes a collection of German books and videos. Like the Portuguese Cultural Club, the Rheingold Club also serves as a link to the homeland via the different forms of communication available to the people. German films are shown on weekends and cultural events take place at the club during different times of the year.

Other ethnic facilities that assist in cultural preservation can include those enterprises or services that supply specialty goods. Ethnic food stores, for example, have been established in Prince George to cater to specific needs. Some of these stores include Il Mercado - specializing in Italian and Mediterranean foods, Jet Lin Noodle - catering to the Chinese community, and also Bobby's Discount Centre which sells East Indian foods. Along with food stores, restaurants may also assist in preserving and transmitting ethnic cultures in the form of food and/or decor. Map 6.2 shows the location of ethnic restaurants within the central business district of Prince George. Perhaps the best represented of ethnic restaurants are those featuring Chinese cuisine. Other ethnic groups represented with a multiple number of restaurants include five Greek restaurants and four Italian restaurants. Other ethnicities represented in Prince George's culinary landscape include Hungarian, German, Japanese, Spanish, Mexican, East Indian, and Caribbean.

Ethnic Activities

Now that we have discussed ethnic facilities within our landscape, it is also important to discuss the communities that built them, and to also observe some of the kinds of activities associated with them. Perhaps we can once again observe the Portuguese Cultural Club. Soccer is one of the elements that defines this community. Besides soccer, however, individuals are also bounded by the love they feel towards the country they came from. For many, it is a way to keep up with the culture they once knew before immigrating to Canada. Once the community members step into the Portuguese Cultural Club, it is like making a return to Portugal. Everything from the posters on the walls, to the language that is spoken, to the commentating on the television is in Portuguese. Once an individual leaves the clubhouse and the company of the

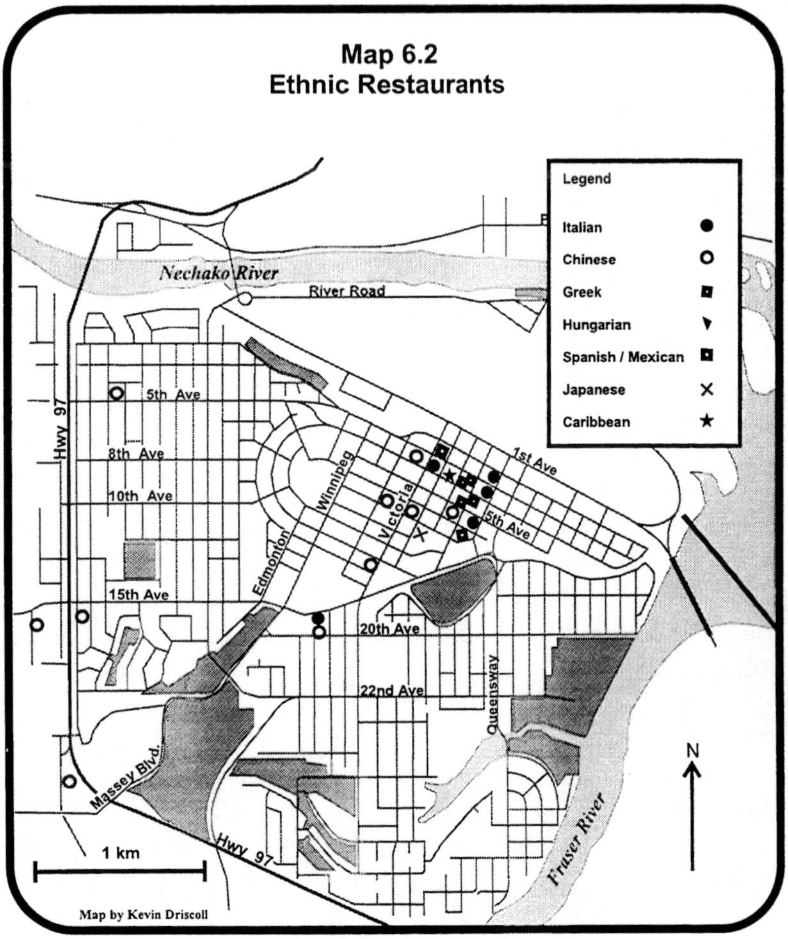

community, it is like once again leaving Portugal and returning to Canada.

When discussing ethnic groups, it is important to consider the many different aspects of the community. Within the broader ethnic community there is often an internal diversity. As explained by Elliott and Fleras (1992, p. 142-143):

although sharing a common land and cultural

> background each community may consist of members with an almost unmanageable range of interests and histories ... Ethnic community members converse not only to promote corporate interests but also to jockey for leadership and status. An image of corporate unity is maintained, but primarily for the benefit of the outside world. Beneath the constructed facade may lurk internal tensions that threaten to undermine community solidarity.

In discussing the group that gathers at the Portuguese Cultural Club, one is observing a sub-group within the broader Portuguese community. It is one of two associations organized by the Portuguese people of Prince George. The Portuguese Cultural Society celebrates Portuguese culture. This organization holds different celebrations during different parts of the year. For example, Portuguese Carnival is celebrated in February, Portugal Day is celebrated on June 10th, and in September grape harvesting and wine making festivities are held. The Portuguese Cultural Society also used to have their own television program on Shaw Cable 10 along with Portuguese classes at D.P. Todd Secondary School. Both of these operations no longer exist "because of differences and disagreements that have taken place" (Personal communication, 1996).

The other local Portuguese group is the Portuguese Catholic Association. Organized around the Catholic Church, its role is to celebrate the Catholic religion and to organize Catholic celebrations relevant to the Portuguese Catholic community. Two specific celebrations are especially of great importance during the calendar year. The first takes place on the 13th of May and the second on the 13th of October. On these two days the Feast of Our Lady of Fatima takes place.

As observed, ethnic groups organize to maintain culture, language, ritual and custom. To the elders it is especially important to pass these ideas and traditions down to the next generation. As a way of carrying out some rituals and customs, social activities are often created by ethnic groups. Dance groups, for example, are often created as a way to celebrate one's culture. Various ethnic groups in Prince George have created their own dance groups. The Philippine Cultural and Dance Group, the Yalenka Ukrainian dancers, and the Scottish Highland Dancers, are just a few examples. These dance groups play an important role in maintaining culture. A specific dance garb represents the group's ethnic origin while the music also serves as a way of communicating culture. Sports organizations are also created by ethnic communities. For example, there are two ethnic soccer clubs in Prince George, the P.G. Croatia Soccer Club which is made up of members of the Croatian community, and the GGST Soccer Club, composed of individuals with an East Indian background. Another example is the Prince George Cricket Club which was founded by residents of Prince George from the West Indies.

Language

Another important part of maintaining one's culture is language preservation. In order for many ethnic groups to preserve their culture, it is important to communicate in their own language. One way of measuring language retention among ethnic groups is to look at which language is used in the home. But before such discussion is to take place, it is first important to define the difference between home language and mother tongue. "Home language" is the language used to communicate at home and with family on a daily basis. "Mother tongue", on the other hand, is the first language one inherits in life. So even though a person's mother tongue might be Punjabi, for example, their home language might be English, if that is the language presently being spoken at home.

In examining language retention, 15 ethnic groups in Prince George are listed in Table 6.2. Of note is that aboriginal languages scored the lowest. Of the 2,070 aboriginal people in Prince George, only 10 individuals, or one-half of one percent of the native population reported that they actually use an aboriginal language at home. The second lowest scores were registered by the Germans and the Hungarians with four percent. Perhaps an explanation for the lower scores among these two ethnic groups is because many of the individuals have been settled in Canada for a long period of time and may consist of second or third generation residents.

Table 6.2
Ethnic Language Retention, 1991

Ethnic Groups	Ethnic Group Population	Ethnic Language as Home Language	Percentage (%) retaining Ethnic language at home
Aboriginal	2,070	10	0.5
Chinese	420	250	60
Croatian	360	155	43
German	3,565	140	4
Greek	145	40	28
Hungarian	255	10	4
Italian	945	255	24
Japanese	65	10	15
Korean	90	45	50
Portuguese	525	230	44
Polish	385	25	6
Punjabi	1,205	945	78
Spanish	130	30	23
Filipino	115	10	9
Vietnamese	155	95	61

Source: Statistics Canada 1991 Census

The highest percentages in Table 6.2 were registered by the Punjabi speaking population with 78 percent, followed by the Vietnamese with 61 percent, the Chinese with 60 percent, and the Koreans with 50 percent. As discussed earlier, Asian immigration to Canada increased dramatically during the 1980s. In comparison to the German and Hungarian populations, the Punjabi, Vietnamese, Chinese and Korean populations are more likely to be new or first generation arrivals into Canada. Language retention, therefore, is more likely to be higher.

As it has been discussed, community is of great importance to an ethnic group. But within the community an even stronger element often exists. That element is the family. Let us examine, for example, a family from South Asia. It is common to often more than one generation of a South Asian family living in the same house. As expressed by one community spokesperson, "it is important to keep up with the language and the values for it is beneficial in communicating with family" (Personal communication, 1996). If the only language spoken by the grandparents is that of Punjabi, then it is important that the children also speak Punjabi in order to communicate with their elders.

Immigration and Multicultural Services Society and the Multicultural Heritage Folkfest Society

The Immigration and Multicultural Services Society (IMSS) and the Multicultural Heritage Folkfest Society are two community service groups that work with immigrants and ethnic organizations in Prince George. The Immigration and Multicultural Services Society is often associated with assisting immigrants and minorities. One of their roles is to help orient the lives of newly arrived immigrants and to assist them with getting through the hardships and frustrations often brought by the encounter with a new country and culture. This is done through various services, such as English as a Second Language (ESL) classes. Offered to landed immigrants and refugees, ESL programs are run in conjunction with Prince George School District #57 and are held at the College of New Caledonia. According to one spokesperson, "all immigrants and refugees are encouraged to take ESL because equality is not likely to occur if English is not known" (Personal communication, 1996). In order to participate in ESL and other programs offered by IMSS, an individual must be 19 years of age or older.

Another service offered by IMSS is the Multicultural Employment Service (MES). MES is sponsored by the Canada Employment and Immigration Centre in order to help people fulfil their short and long term employment goals while they are unemployed, under-employed, volunteering, holding part-time jobs or pursuing further education (Multicultural Heritage Society, *New Service Announcement* pamphlet). Along with the MES program, group and individual career counseling is also offered. Finally, IMSS helps families find daycare services and assists in integrating children into the school system.

Translators are often available if needed.

The Multicultural Heritage Folkfest Society was formed in 1974 as an umbrella organization for ethnic groups in Prince George. Originally intended as a platform for staging multicultural events on July 1st, it has evolved to meet the needs and aspirations of the multicultural communities it serves. Now, in addition to organizing cultural and heritage celebrations, the Society provides a wide range of services aimed at the development of cross-cultural awareness and sensitivity, harmonious inter-group relations, and racial acceptance (Multicultural Heritage Society of Prince George, pamphlet). Currently, the Society has 12 member groups (Table 6.3). The Society's role is to organize and coordinate these members when celebrating annual events. These events may include Canada Day celebrations, International Food Festival, International Human Rights Week, Multiculturalism Week and Anti-Racism Day. The Society is also responsible for various multicultural programs such as organizing conferences, workshops, seminars, public forums, and lectures on multiculturalism and race relations, and the provision of cross-cultural educational services to schools, government agencies, businesses, voluntary groups, and the public. Both the IMSS and the Multicultural Heritage Folkfest Society play an important role in defining the ethnic landscape of Prince George.

Table 6.3
Multicultural Heritage Society of Prince George
1996 Membership

Atlantic Provinces Association of Northern BC	Nechako Fraser Junction Metis
Chinese Benevolent Association	Philippine Cultural and Dance Group
German/Canadian Rheingold Club	Prince George Celtic Group
Hellenic Community (Greek) of Prince George	Prince George Italian Club
Jamaican-Integrated Benevolent Society	Sons of Norway Rondane Lodge 71
Native Friendship Centre	Yalenka Ukrainian Cultural Society

adapted from Multicultural Heritage Society of Prince George pamphlet.

CONCLUSION

All Canadian cities are composed of a mix of ethnic groups. In this respect, the ethnic landscape of Prince George is really no different from other urban places. Historically, Prince George has encountered its share of discrimination and both individuals and groups have experienced processes of assimilation into “mainstream” culture. Recent shifts in Canadian immigration patterns from traditional to new source countries is being experienced within Prince George. Ethnic communities form for many reasons; to preserve culture, to retain the language, to create a source of identity, and for defence purposes in the case of outside hostility. In looking at the social geography of ethnic groups in Prince George, some remnants of ethnic enclaves do exist. Even as such enclaves fade into the general residential landscape, there are visible reminders of the City's varied ethnic heritage through buildings and facilities. The creation and perpetuation of ethnic social activities and celebrations also have a lasting impact on our social geography. In Prince George, one can see this on the landscape and in our daily social lives.

REFERENCES

Anderson, K.J. (1991). *Vancouver's Chinatown - Racial Discourse in Canada 1875-1980*. Montreal: McGill-Queen's University Press.

Canadian Human Rights Foundation. (1987). *Multiculturalism and the Charter -A Legal Perspective*. Vancouver: Carswell.

Cater, J. and Jones, T. (1989). *Social Geography - An Introduction to Contemporary Issues*. New York: Edward Arnold.

Chow, L. (1996). *Sojourners in the North*. Prince George: Caitlin Press.

Devore, W. and Schlesinger, E.G. (1991). *Ethnic-Sensitive Social Work Practise* (3rd edition). Toronto: Collier MacMillan.

Elliott, J.L. and Fleras, A. (1992). *Unequal Relations - An Introduction to Race and Ethnic Dynamics in Canada*. Scarborough: Prentice-Hall Canada.

Fandetti, D.V. and Gelfand, D.E. (1983). *'Middle-Class White Ethnics in Suburbia: A Study of Italian-Americans' Culture Ethnicity, and Identity*. W.C. McCready ed. Toronto: Academic. pp.138-161.

Hansen, R. (1981). *The Scandinavians in Prince George 1910-1935*. Prince George: College of New Caledonia Local History Seminar essay.

Herberg, E.N. (1989). *Ethnic Groups in Canada - Adaptations and Transitions*. Toronto: Nelson Canada.

Li, P.S. (1988). *Ethnic Inequality a Class Society*. Toronto: Thompson Educational.

Multicultural Heritage Society of Prince George. (nd.). *New Service Announcement*. Prince George: Multicultural Heritage Society of Prince George, pamphlet.

_______. (n.d.). *Multicultural Heritage Society*. Prince George: Multicultural Heritage Society of Prince George, pamphlet.

Porter, J. (1965). *The Vertical Mosaic*. Toronto: University of Toronto Press.

Prince George Free Press. (1996). "Black Legacy in Prince George". February 11, p. A13.

Prince George Immigrant and Multicultural Services Society. (1994). *We Canadians - Unity and Diversity*. Prince George: Prince George Immigrant and Multicultural Services Society.

Richmond, A.H. (1988). *Immigration - an Ethnic Conflict*. New York: St. Martin's.

Runnals, F.E. (1946). *A History of Prince George*. Prince George: City of Prince George.

Tavares, C.M. (1975). Canada: Land of Opportunity. In *Immigration and the Rise of Multiculturalism*, H. Palmer, ed. Vancouver: Copp Clark. pp. 110-111.

Chapter 7

SOCIAL SERVICES

Cherie Allen

INTRODUCTION

The social service sector of North American cities plays an important role in the growth and prosperity of our society. In Canada, the social service sector has been developing since the 1920s to assist people and provide the necessary means to maintain social well-being. A wide variety of services are now available, ranging from health and welfare to housing and shelters. The social services sector is very prominent in Prince George, where new types of social services continue to establish in this once small, resource-based, community. The coming of the pulp and paper mills to Prince George in the 1960s, together with more recent population growth, has led to the need for more social services for a more diverse local community.

This chapter will examine the social services sector of Prince George. This will be accomplished by reviewing the historical importance of social service distribution in urban areas, followed by an illustration of the availability and distribution of such services in Prince George. These service location maps reinforce the reciprocal relationship between the location of services and the location of dependent populations. In order for a service provider to assist the greatest number of people, a central and accessible location is usually critical. The final section of the chapter will present a case study of street youth residing in the city, and of the organizations attempting to address and aid this group. Even though many residents of Prince George may be unaware of the extent of this problem, the fact remains that efforts need to be taken in order to help these street kids.

SOCIAL SERVICES IN URBAN AREAS

A social geography of social services provision must include an understanding of the geographic location of services and the connection to the people they are serving. This relationship, between the dependent population and the social services, is a reciprocal one and must be considered when discussing the geographic location of services within an urban area. Hodge and Qadeer (1983, p. 169) suggest that:

> poverty is not the result of bad luck or laziness. The system that produces affluence also creates poverty. These are the material and ideological realities of modern life, and they have become a part of the national ethos ... community needs are goods, services, organizations, and regulations deemed necessary for the effective and equitable functioning of a group. There is a common stake in the availability of such a good or service, although some individuals may be the direct beneficiaries. Community needs are anchored in the institutional, economic, and technological framework of a locality.

Historically, social services have been located in urban areas in order to meet the needs of the greatest number of people requiring assistance. The need for services in rural areas is evident, yet "marketplace measurement of programs is particularly unfavorable to rural community services simply because it costs more to serve a dispersed population than a concentrated one" (Fitchen, 1991, p. 155). Such "cost-effective" and "efficiency" based models quite often have "a negative impact on [the] distribution of services for low-income residents in rural areas" (Fitchen, 1991, p. 157). The existence of poverty and, in many cases, a continuing lack of services in rural areas forces many people to move to adjacent towns or cities. For many, this forced move may also create a dependency on social services in order to survive in the city.

As cities can act as magnets for people requiring help, the need to have services situated in certain areas of the city to serve local dependent populations is logical. Dear and Wolch point out the result is often a 'service hub', which is a "diverse collection [of] small-scale, community-based facilities so close to each other that interaction between them is facilitated...Hence, [the service hub] can address the needs of a wide variety of client groups" (Dear and Wolch, 1993, p. 306).

Services which are designed to cater to specific clients, such as the handicapped, poor, homeless and unemployed, are generally situated in the inner city (Rubenstein, 1996). Many social service providers prefer this inner city location to be "close to the deprived populations they serve" (Pinch, 1985, p. 113), and to give their clients opportunity to preserve anonymity and not devalue them as people. The best location is accessible and minimizes the costs and distances clients must travel, therefore, social services concentrated in the downtown core provide better access to more people.

Social Service Location in the Urban Landscape

Despite obvious logical reasons to situate social services in the city centre, other locational factors affect the final destination. Many suburban neighbourhoods do not want specific types of services located near their homes. Conflict is common, especially when service providers "attempt to open residential facilities [such as abuse shelters or rehabilitation centres], they typically face organized and angry neighbours... . A common result is exclusion of services from the rejecting community" (Dear and Wolch, 1993, p. 307). In most cases, neighbourhood opposition is based on fear, ignorance, concern over increased disturbances and rowdiness, a possible decline in property value, and a "not-in-my-neighbourhood" reaction (Personal communication, 1996). It is this opposition that tends to direct the social service sector to areas of least resistance - normally the city centre (Knox, 1995). The geographer Steven Pinch strongly argues that "middle- and upper- income groups are better organized both to resist the location of facilities which are likely to lower house prices in their neighbourhoods, and to attract and retain those facilities which will lead to an increase in local amenities" while those in the lower-income brackets, because of a lack of wealth, power and knowledge, are less successful in voicing their opinions (Pinch, 1985, p. 113).

Efficiency and *equity* are other factors which need to be taken into consideration when interpreting social service location. An efficient location pattern is generally considered to be "one in which some societally predetermined level or volume of service is met at minimum total system costs" (Morrill and Symons, 1977, p. 216), while an equitable or 'just' location involves the notion that location "may be considered equitable if no more than some acceptably small proportion of people are more than some critical distance from a good or service provided by a facility..." (Morrill and Symons, 1977, p. 217). In theory, there should be no conflict between efficiency and equity, yet "ideas of efficiency and equity frequently conflict with the optimal degree of centralization or concentration of activities" (Morrill and Symons, 1977, p. 220). Locational patterns of efficiency and equity vary due to income, scale and population density. Either one area or group will have close access to a specific service, therefore, depriving other distanced areas or groups, and vice versa. The centralization of facilities is undertaken in an attempt to accommodate as many of those involved as possible; for social services, this often equals the inner-city.

History and Role of Social Services

Canada's social service sector began to develop in the early 1900s in response to a growing public demand. Since the early twentieth century, the range and scope of the available services has continually widened. The British North America Act (BNA Act) of 1867 stated that "social welfare was regarded as a matter that could be best handled by charitable individuals, religious institutions, or local government" (Weeks, 1991, p. 471). Yet gradual changes in the economy resulted in new roles being assumed by the state concerning social reform. In 1919, the federal government's Department of Health was established "to draw together the isolated federal government health responsibilities that had grown up over the years and to respond to new needs deemed to require federal assistance" (Meilicke and Storch, 1980, p. 4). A number of programs were established in the 1920s, and these programs "appear to have paved the way for the 1927 Old Age Pension Act which was Canada's first nationwide income support plan and the first major, continuing, federal-provincial cost-shared social security program..." (Meilicke and Storch, 1980, p. 5).

The economic depression of the 1930s was a significant factor in the development of social security programmes in Canada. The depression was:

> so devastating in its effects that it brought home to the average Canadian the interdependence of citizens in an industrial society...[and] the concept of local responsibility for the relief of the unemployed was replaced first by the assumption of provincial and then of federal responsibility. From this point on, unemployment was seen as a national problem rather than a purely local or regional one. (Wharf, 1990, p. 175)

Although initial social service policies were reactive and 'ad-hoc' problem solving, changes have led to the establishment of a wide variety of programs to serve Canadian citizens. Social service programs have been developed to provide a measure of security, as well as address the serious social problems in our society. Frank McGilly (1990, p. 12) states: "whether the social services are designed to forestall damage institutionally or to repair it residually, their development is likely to parallel those changes in social life that have been recognized as posing difficult challenges". These changes often arise from the uncertainty generated from economic or employment disruption, or from the consequences of rapid population growth. Brian Wharf argues that social services, although difficult to define, include three main elements: income security, personal social services, and social planning Table 7.1 provides a set of definitions and descriptions of these elements.

TABLE 7.1

Income Security Programs:

"any federal, provincial or municipal program having as its main objective the provision of direct financial benefits to individuals and families" (Wharf, 1990, 170). Types of programs:

A.) Demogrant programs - "pay benefits to or on behalf of citizens in a defined range regardless of their financial situation," such as family allowances and old age pensions (Wharf, 1990, 170).

B.) Social insurance programs - the responsibility of the federal government, and include the Canada Pension Plan and Unemployment Insurance programs.

C.) Income-tested programs - commonly federal programs, yet a number of "provincially administered income supplement programs for families and the elderly have been developed," such as the Child Tax Credit and Guaranteed Income Supplement (GIS) for the elderly (Wharf, 1990, 171).

D.) Needs-tested programs - designed to provide an income to the indigent who are not covered by any of the above (Wharf, 1990).

Personal Social Services:

"programs designed to support individuals and families and to protect vulnerable individuals such as children" (p. 173).

Typical types of services include counseling, homemaker, home care, daycare, as well as "substitute care facilities for those individuals who can no longer remain at home or live on an independent basis" (Wharf, 1990, 173). Personal social services include both:

A.) statutory facilities - required by legislation, like those dealing with child abuse and neglect, and

B.) non-statutory facilities - not required by law, but have been developed in response to the needs of the citizens, such as family counseling, homemaker and daycare programs (Wharf, 1990).

Social Planning

"systematic and research-based efforts to identify causes of social problems, to develop programs to remedy these problems, and to identify the social consequences of other kinds of planning activities" (Wharf, 1990, 173).

This type of planning includes the involvement of citizens in the social planning process, and is usually referred to as "locality development" or "community organization."

SOCIAL SERVICES IN PRINCE GEORGE

The social service sector in Prince George is a thriving part of this community. Due to the City's growth, size, and central location within the province, it is the logical site for a variety of social services for northern British Columbia. Exactly the same characteristics have provided the impetus for Prince George's growth as a retail centre for much of northern and central British Columbia. Prince George's downtown core houses a large percentage of the community's social services. Through the use of maps, the following section highlights the concentration of services in the downtown area and illustrates the notion that the geographic location of social services is essential in attempts to serve dependent populations.

There are a variety of services in the city, and a majority of these social services are located in the downtown area in order to serve a local dependent population. Many of Prince George's social services are also found in close proximity to one another so as to cut down travel time and increase overall accessibility for those utilizing the services. Government assistance, counseling, health and welfare, and financial assistance services are all located close to one another in downtown Prince George - a locational outcome which very nearly approximates "one-stop-shopping". Despite the wide range of social services available, this chapter concentrates on five specific types which address specific social groups and areas of importance in the community. The maps in this section illustrate the distribution of "counseling", "health", "government", "Aboriginal", and "women's and children's" services. This selection of services demonstrates clearly the geographic patterns of concentration and clustering.

Counseling Services

Map 7.1 illustrates the availability of family, personal and crisis counseling services in Prince George. Despite a few exceptions, such as the Prince George Regional Hospital, Northern Interior Health Unit, Elizabeth Fry Society, and St. Patrick's Transition House for Alcoholics, one can see that there is a definite

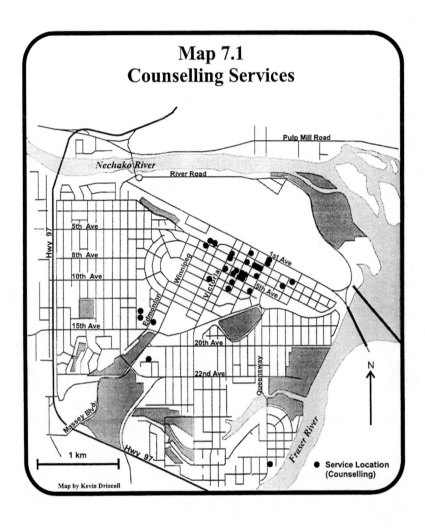

Map 7.1
Counselling Services

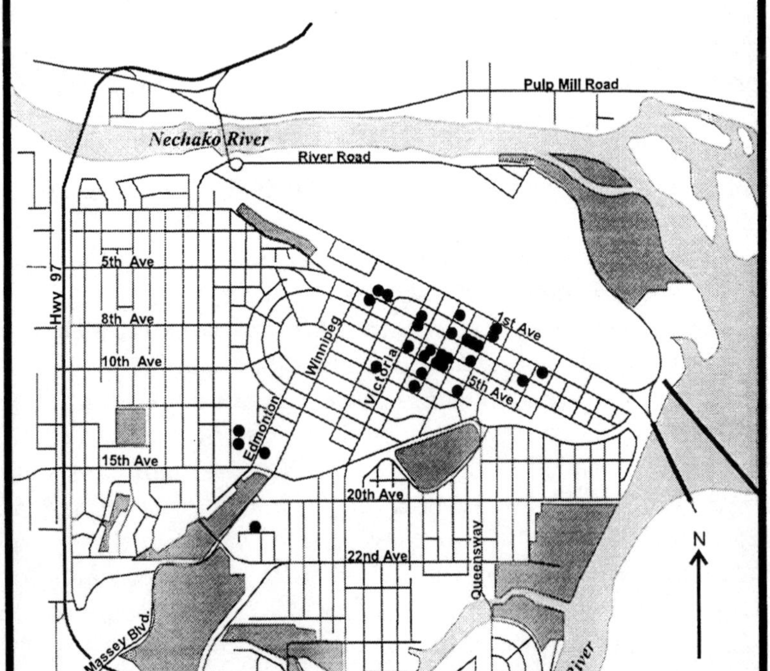

concentration of counseling services in the downtown core. Although in close proximity to the downtown core, services such as those like the Elizabeth Fry Society, are located in more suburban areas. Due to the type of services offered by the Society, such as shelters for abused women and children, victim services and youth programs, a more residential setting with a non-threatening atmosphere was sought.

There are a variety of counseling services in Prince George which serve a specific purpose, such as alcohol and drug treatment centres. Some of these programs include the Salvation Army Addictions Treatment Centre, Detox Assessment Clinic, Prince George Native Friendship Centre's Alcohol and Drug Program, Nechako Centre, Prince George Alcohol and Drug Services Society, and St. Patrick's Transition House for Alcoholics. These services are available for those dealing with alcohol and drug related problems and are mainly located in the City's downtown area.

Another set of available services involves those for marriage, family, child and individual counseling. Some of these services include the Prince George AIDS Society, Prince George Family Services, Intersect Youth and Family Services, Native Courtworkers and Counseling Association, and Healthiest Babies Possible. Due to the many other social services available in Prince George, counseling services are logically situated in the downtown area in order to provide a type of one-stop-shopping accessibility.

Finally, a range of general counseling services are also found in the City. Some of these include the Prince George Crisis and Information Centre, Central Interior Native Health Society, Canadian Mental Health Society, and Northern Interior Health Unit. Although there are a large number and variety of counseling services available in Prince George, Map 7.1 illustrates their concentration in the downtown core.

Health Services

Map 7.2 illustrates the distribution of most available health services in Prince George. Again, as suggested above, most of these services are located in the City's downtown core. The health services mapped include those funded by both the federal and provincial governments. Some fundamental services such as the Prince George Regional Hospital, the Northern Interior Health Unit, and the Spruceland Medical Centre, are situated adjacent to or just outside of the downtown core. Map 7.2 is also somewhat misleading, since numerous services are often located within one building. One example is the Oxford

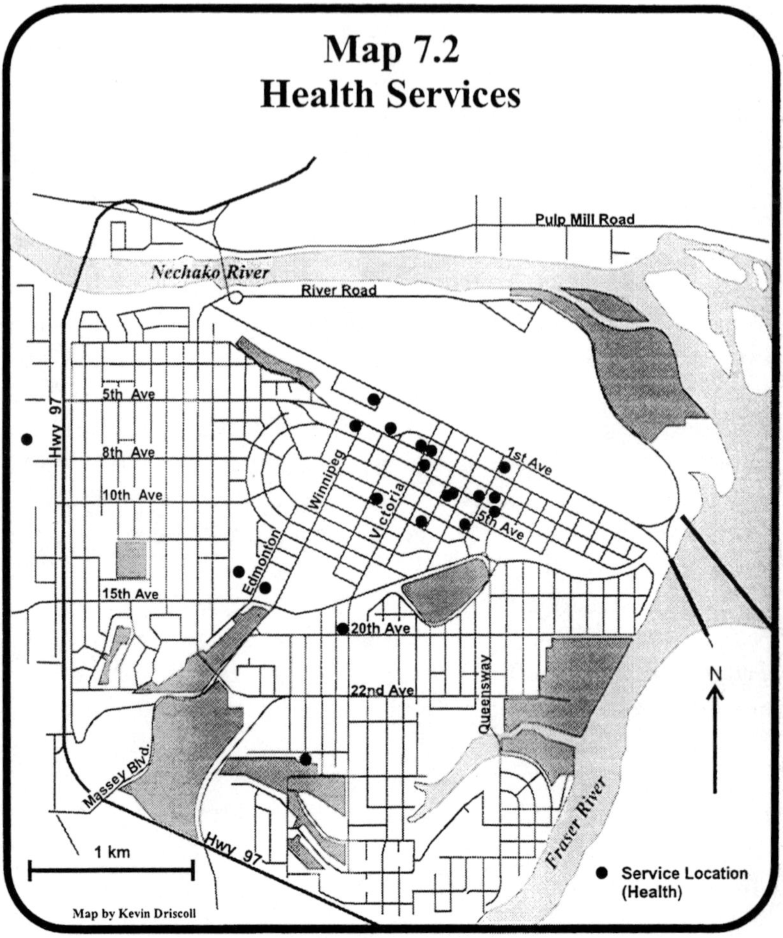

Building on Victoria Street, where numerous government health services are situated, including Inuit and Health Services, Environmental Health Services, and Health and Welfare Canada. Another example where a number of services are situated within one building, and represented by only one symbol on the map, is the Kiwanis Building on Quebec Street. The services located here include the Canadian Diabetes

Association, Healthiest Babies Possible, Heart and Stroke Foundation, Canadian National Institute for the Blind (CNIB), Dyslexia Resource Centre, and Multiple Sclerosis Society. Finally, a number of personal medical and dental offices are also distributed around the city, especially at shopping centres where the principle of client accessibility continues to play a role in location choice.

Government Social Services

Map 7.3 illustrates the distribution of government social services available in Prince George. Federal and provincial government services are an integral part of the social service sector of any city, and this applies to Prince George as well. As indicated in earlier sections, the role of the government in the implementation and maintenance of social services is essential to a community's social well-being. A wide variety of services are directly delivered by a government agency or depend upon government funding to function. The challenge for government to provide necessary social services is a continually changing process.

Government social services address many areas of need, such as health, counseling, un/employment assistance, and financial assistance for those who require help. The provincial government's Ministry of Social Services is responsible for the direct delivery of many social services in our community. In Prince George, the Ministry has a number of offices in the City's downtown core. These various offices deliver job services, income support programs, family and children's services, district offices and child welfare resources.

As was seen with the other maps, it is often the case that several social services are housed within one location. The government building on Second Avenue and Dominion Street, for example, is the site of the Unemployment Office, Aboriginal Training Centre, Canada Pension Plan, and Old Age Security offices. Another central location of government services is at the provincial court building on Third Avenue. Youth Probation and Family Court Services, Family Court, Counseling Services, Hospital Programs, and Human Resources Office - Northern

Map 7.3
Government Social Services

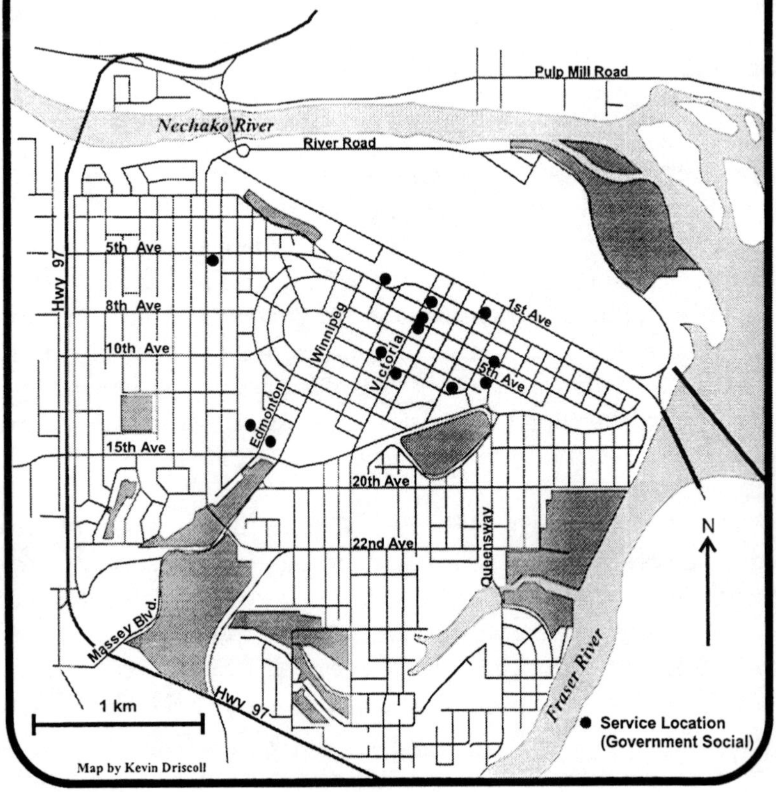

Region are located at this site.

Other government services, such as the Northern Interior Health Unit, Citizenship and Immigration, Forensic Psychiatric Services, Services for Community Living, and Health and Welfare Canada, are located in Prince George's downtown. While there has been some dispersal of a couple of offices outside the downtown core, Map 7.3 reinforces the trend of a concentration of social services in the city's core. Access to clients, accessibility by transit, and proximity to other social service providers assist in making the City's downtown area attractive as a social service hub.

Aboriginal Services

The location of various Aboriginal organizations available in Prince George are shown on Map 7.4. The Prince George Native Friendship Centre (PGNFC) is one such establishment that offers a wide variety of services. Established as a "non-profit, non-sectarian organization dedicated to servicing the needs of Native people residing in the urban area and improving the quality of life in the community as a whole" (PGNFC *Organizational overview pamphlet*, p. 2), the PGNFC offers a variety of public services. These include the AIDS Prevention Program, Alcohol and Drug program, Native Healing Centre, Sexual Abuse Treatment Services (SATS), career training opportunities, single men's hostel, Native halfway house (Ketso Yoh), and a variety of other educational and social services. This organization is continually growing and adapting to serve the Aboriginal and non-Aboriginal population in Prince George. In 1997, the PGNFC moved some of its operations into larger premises in the former Provincial Court Building.

Other Aboriginal organizations in the city include those serving the Métis population. Organizations such as the Apehtaw Kosisan Métis Child and Family Support Society, Prince George Métis Housing Society, Central Interior Métis Women's Society, Nechako Fraser Junction Métis Association, and Prince George Métis Elders Society are important organizations for this particular community within the City. Other various Aboriginal services include the British Columbia Native Housing Corporation, Aboriginal Training Centre, United Native Nations, Carrier Sekani Tribal Council, Native Courtworkers and Counseling Association, and the Central Interior Native Health Centre. Although there is a broad range of services for the Aboriginal population in Prince George, Map 7.4 illustrates that the majority of these organizations are located in the downtown area. Again, as seen on the other

Map 7.4
First Nations Services

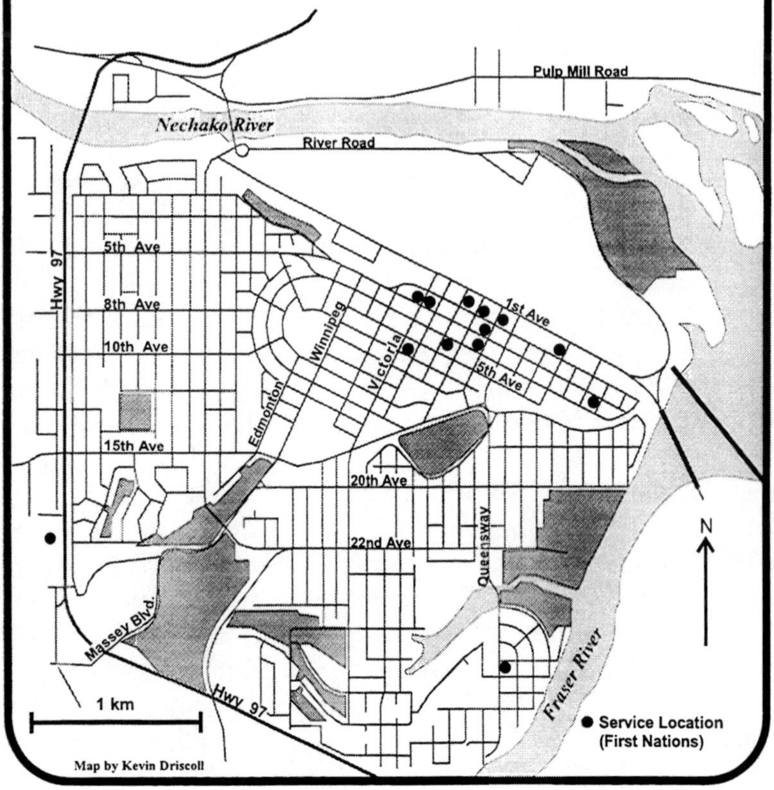

maps, some service locations in fact house many services.

Women's and Children's Services

The need for services to address women's and children's social service needs has been growing over the past two decades. Certain circumstances such as abusive situations, financial assistance, and counseling are all factors involved in the organization of services aimed at aiding women and children. In Prince George, a large number and wide range of such services is now available (Map 7.5). Examples include the Elizabeth Fry Society, AWAC (Advocacy for Women and Children), the Quebec Street Emergency Shelter for Women, and the Phoenix Transition Society to name but a few.

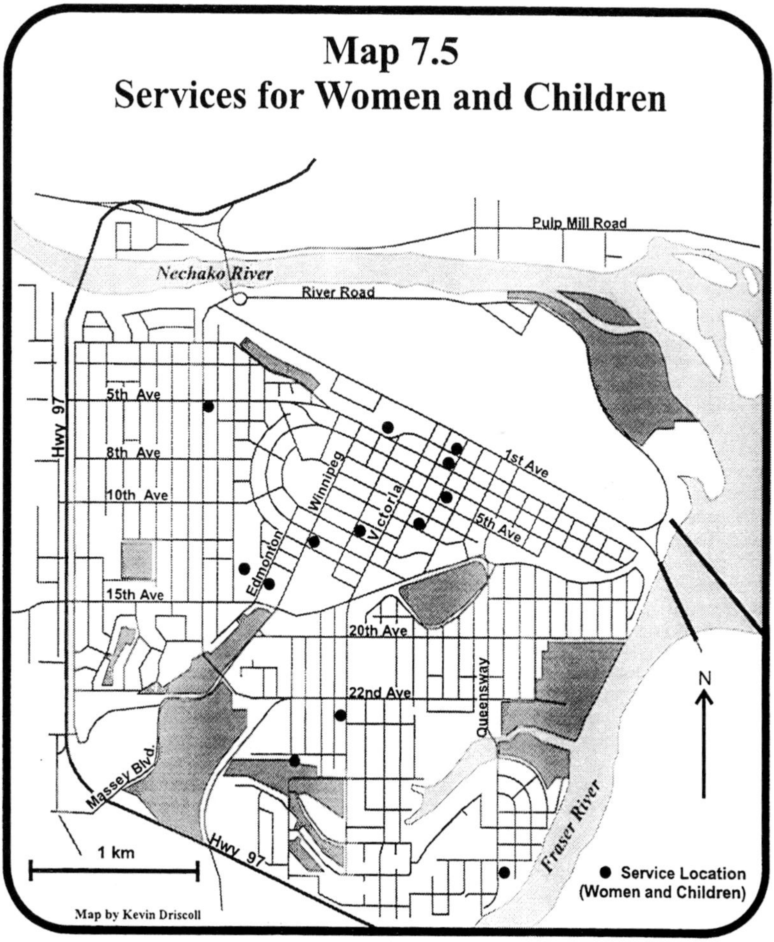

The list of services designed to address the needs of women and children is continually growing, and the map illustrates that a majority of these services are once again located in Prince George's downtown area. One difference between this map and the others is something of a decentralization of particular services into more suburban neighbourhood areas. Organizations such as the Child Development Centre, Elizabeth Fry Society, Project Parent North, and Moms' and Kids' Drop In Centre are located outside the immediate downtown core. Possible reasons for this move can be attributed to lower land prices, increased accessibility for families, as well as the service provider's desire to establish itself in a less threatening atmosphere than in the inner city.

The other services utilized by this group include the Ministry of Social Services, Northern Interior Health Unit, Women's Centre -Wimmin's Connection, Healthiest Babies Possible, Prince George Crisis and Information Centre, and Ministry of Women's Equality. The above mentioned services are merely a sampling of the list of services designed to address the needs of the women and children in the City. Although there are many other social services utilized by this group, these services have specific programs aimed at aiding the women and children of Prince George and surrounding rural areas.

Social Services Summary

In summary, this review of social services in Prince George highlights a very centralized distribution pattern (Map 7.6). With only a few exceptions, such as the Prince George Regional Hospital, the Northern Interior Health Unit, the Spruceland Medical Clinic, and the Elizabeth Fry Society, most social services available to the community are located in close proximity to one another in the downtown core. The need to establish services designed to cater to specific clients, and to situate these services in close connection to the dependent population is a key element in this location pattern. The literature on social services location suggests that the concentration of social services in a city's downtown core is

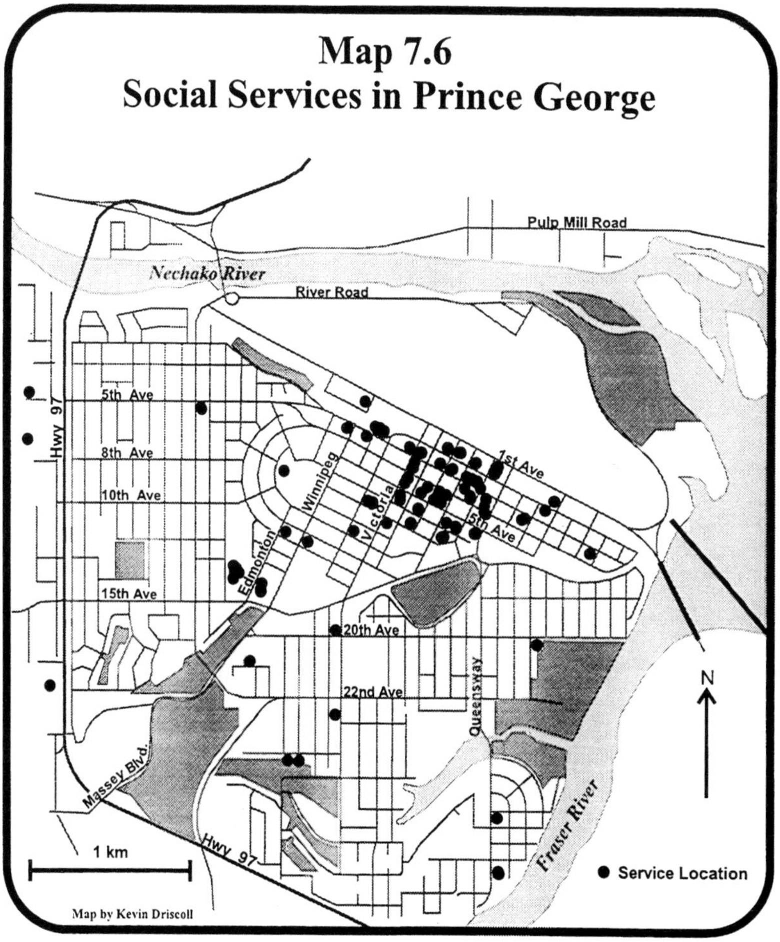

essential in order to serve a dependent population and Prince George is a prime example of this reciprocal relationship. At present, there are a variety of social services available in Prince George, and this service sector is continually growing and adapting to meet the needs of the City's diverse population.

STREET YOUTH IN PRINCE GEORGE

The number of youth living on Canada's streets is growing. The term 'street youth' is an ambiguous one for which there is as yet no single definition. Current definitions vary from person to person, but often call forth images of "young vagrants and street urchins who sleep in alley ways and eat from garbage cans" (King *et al.*, 1988, p. 110). This is definitely not an accurate portrayal of all street youth. A more useful working definition of street youth is: "young people who hang out on the city streets and have little or no connection with their families or community services" (PGNFC, *Streetworker Program* pamphlet). The degree to which such youth spend all of their time actually "living" on the streets does vary. A study done by Queen's University in 1988 indicates three general patterns of youth living on the street: some youth literally live on the streets, some youth periodically run from the supervision of social services, and others live at home yet spend a great deal of time on the street (King *et al.*, 1988).

Although there are a variety of reasons why youth turn to the streets, many young people do not run to the streets but rather, run away from situations within their homes. This is contrary to a commonly held belief that these youth have refused the responsibility of employment and education (King *et. al.*, 1988). In reality, many youths are from dysfunctional families and may have been abused or abandoned. Others live at home where physical, verbal, and sexual abuse are common, yet they remain to protect other siblings and turn to the streets as a temporary escape or as a place to earn some money. Still others are 'thrill seekers', attracted to the excitement of the city's downtown (Clarke, 1994b). Whatever the case may be, many of Canada's youth who turn to the streets as a survival option often fall into the trap of drug or alcohol abuse, prostitution, or petty crime. In her book *Street Kids: The Tragedy of Canada's Runaways*, Marlene Webber describes a vivid image of life on the streets: "life on the streets is a scavenger's existence, a restless hunt for cash or for anything that can be converted into cash or a bed or a meal or drugs to sustain the hunter for one more day" (Webber, 1991, p. 14). Figure 7.1, adapted from the 1988 Queen's University study, illustrates the diverse elements of street life existing in Canadian cities. Often it is through drugs, alcohol, prostitution, and theft that street youth are able to endure the dangers and pressures of living on the streets (Kostash, 1994).

Figure 7.1
Types of Street Youth

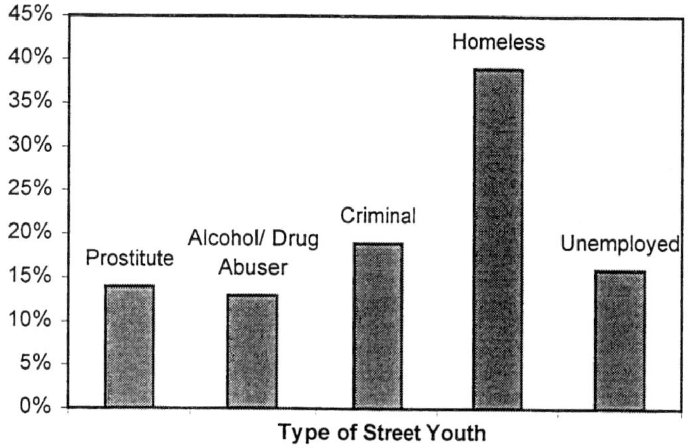

Source: King et al. 1988, 109.

Prince George, like many other urban centres, has a large number of street youth attempting to survive on its city streets. Despite the challenge, Prince George is trying to tackle this problem. The Prince George Native Friendship Centre's Streetworker Program (or Reconnect) is part of a provincial program for street kids. This program operates in 34 communities throughout British Columbia, and is designed "to help those who are on the street to leave it for a healthier and safer lifestyle and to prevent other young people from becoming street youth" (PGNFC, *Street Kids* pamphlet). According to Reconnect, "most kids need help and support to reconnect with family and community .... The constant struggle for survival puts them at risk of being victimized. More time on the street increases the risk, alienation and the difficulty youths have in using community resources" (Ministry of Social Services, 1993). Streetworkers provide services such as: connecting with children who are on the street, identifying young people who are new to the street scene, referring youth to appropriate agencies, and providing outreach counseling on lifestyle alternatives for young people. Although the program has been in Prince George for many years, the number of youth on the City's street, and the attempts to aid and address their problems, continues to be a challenge.

The Prince George Reconnect program works with an average of 200 clients at any one time. With the coming of summer, the number of youth frequenting the streets increases (Reconnect, 1995). Despite the number of street youth in the City, one of the main challenges to the streetworkers is the time needed to build a relationship with new clients. Since they often live dangerous lives (for some this may involve crime), street youth are transient and it is hard to keep track of them (Clarke, 1994b).

The typical experience of street youth in Prince George involves some connection to drugs, alcohol, prostitution, theft, and sometimes even death. The death of two teens, Leah Germaine, and Roxanne Thiara, both aged 15, in Prince George in 1995 has been a tragic eye-opener for all those living on the city's streets. The deaths of these two young women occurred within four months of one another. Even though there is no reported evidence of a direct link between the two murders, Leah and Roxanne seemed to have had something in common. Both had vowed to abandon the seedy world of prostitution and drugs in Prince George and turn their lives around. Unfortunately, their lives were cut short before this was accomplished (Mallam, 1995). Although these murders generated fear among the street youth population at the time, any apprehension would not likely have a lasting effect on Prince George street life. Street people fear for their lives since they live in a dangerous atmosphere, but the fear is short-lived when it comes to obtaining the things they need for survival.

A story by Sayers (1991) in the *Prince George This Week* newspaper provides an in-depth look into the life on one person living on the City's streets. "Anne's" story is said to be typical of other street youth in Prince George. She grew up in an atmosphere where physical and sexual abuse were a daily occurrence. Anne found relief in the arcades and on the downtown streets. It is here where she met other kids in the same situation as her. As time went on, Anne was introduced to drugs and alcohol. Even though she returned home occasionally, she decided the people who cared about her were those on the streets and not her parents. In an interview, Anne stated: "it didn't matter to my parents whether I came home at night. The only thing that mattered to them was the welfare cheque and getting drunk. The street became my family" (Sayers, 1991, p. 5). Unfortunately, drugs and alcohol became a big part of Anne's life. If Anne could not find any food she went without eating. If she could not find a house to pass out in, depending on the weather, she would spend the night on a park bench, in a doorway, or even in a car. Although she was living on the streets, Anne tried to look as if she came from a good home. She went to great measures to keep herself well-dressed and clean, often getting clothes from wherever she could. Anne saw 12 and 13 year old girls dressing themselves up as 18 and 20 year olds, and for many, prostitution was a popular way to make ends meet (Sayers, 1991). Anne realized that standing on the street corners was not for her, yet she slept with guys who could help her. Anne fell into the same trap as others on the streets: resorting to any measure to survive.

In the summer of 1991, Anne made a decision to change her lifestyle and turned to the Streetworker Program for help. At the time the newspaper article was written Anne was making plans to finish high school and eventually go on to college (Sayers, 1991). Social services enabled her to work towards this goal by helping her get a place to live and by providing money to pay for living expenses. Anne is an example of the situation of Prince George's street youth, and service providers such as Reconnect's Streetworkers are continually striving to help the City's youth get off the street.

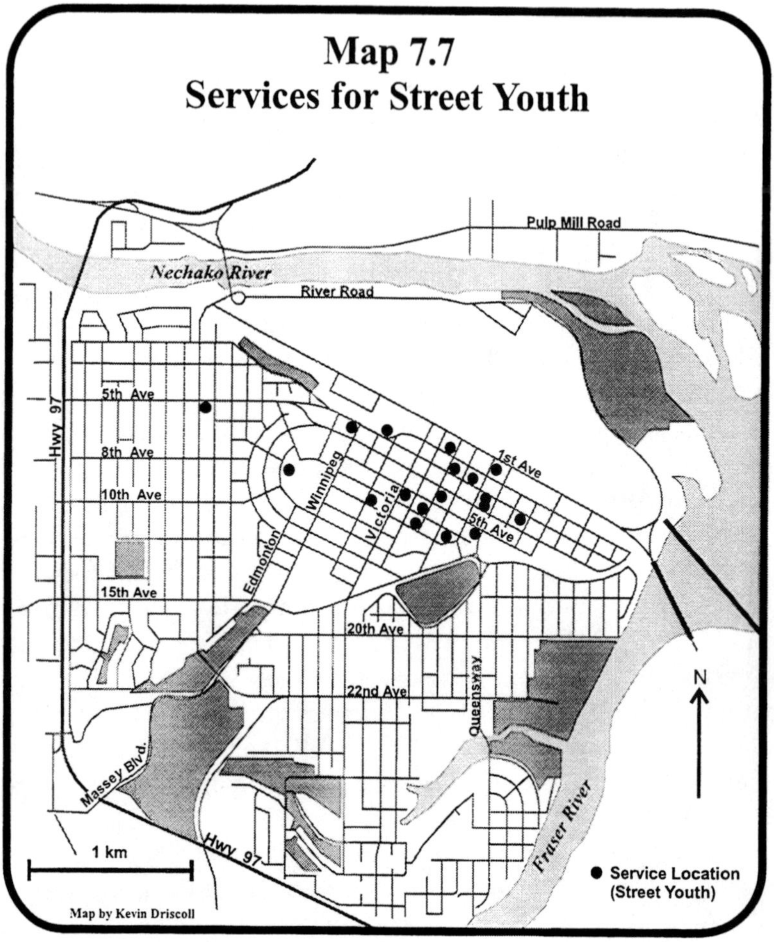

Map 7.7
Services for Street Youth

Street Youth Services

As understanding of street youth in Prince George has grown, so too have the number of social services available to assist this group. Since these youths are residing in the downtown area, it is logical to locate the services here as well. Map 7.7 illustrates the distribution of services available to street youth.

One of the main organizations serving this group is the Prince George Native Friendship Centre. Established twenty-five years ago as a grassroots organization, the PGNFC offers many services to assist those living on the streets. The Reconnect program, Youth Drug and Alcohol program and educational programs are all integral services provided by the centre. The latest addition is the Friendship House, a new safe house for youth-at-risk aged 12 to 18. Although its location is not visible on the map (due to discretion) the safe house was opened in January 1996. This six-bedroom facility provides 24-hour supervision to its residents. According to the director, "the home provides youth with a safe place and gives them opportunity to make long term decisions" (Prince George This Week, 1996, p. 3).

The Friendship House is based on the successful Los Angeles-based 'Children of the Night' program. Clients are able to stay a maximum of six weeks, and they are expected to help with chores, stay clean and sober, and participate in school, recreation and leisure activities. The Friendship House also employs a teacher who assesses each resident's skill in various subjects and refers them to an education program, such as the Storefront School or alternative education. Although the clients are considered youth-at-risk, "the children at Friendship House are just like many others their age. All they need is a chance to succeed" (Prince George This Week, 1996, p. 3).

Another important service provided by the PGNFC is the AIDS Prevention Program. Its objective is to provide medical services such as medical examinations, AIDS and Sexually Transmitted Disease testing and counseling, pregnancy testing, condom distribution, community education, as well as an intravenous needle exchange program (Clarke, 1994a). This organization is used by street youth but is also open to the public. Its location in the downtown core makes it accessible to those requiring some type of aid.

The Youth Housing Registry is another service aimed at street youth. A project of the Prince George Crisis Intervention Society, funded by the Ministry of Skills, Training and Labour, the Youth Housing Registry's main objective is to assist youth in finding affordable housing, a key obstacle commonly facing many street youth. (Prince George Crisis Intervention Society, *Youth Housing Registry* pamphlet, p. 1). Many landlords are apprehensive about renting to youths, but the aim of the Youth Housing Registry is to find landlords who are willing to rent to youths, and to provide information regarding the legal rights of youths as tenants. Other services which address the needs of street youth include the Ministry of Social Services, Intersect Youth and Family Services, Advocacy for Women and Children (AWAC), Healthiest Babies Possible, Youth Probation and Family Court Services, the Salvation Army and St. Vincent de Paul's. Growing recognition of youth on the street has prompted many organizations to set up programs to aid these teens. Despite this, continued involvement and interest is required to help these youths.

CONCLUSION

The social service sector plays an integral role in the maintenance, growth, and prosperity of our communities. As Prince George has grown into an urban centre, so too has the need for social services and its capacity to provide a range of services and facilities. The purpose of this chapter has been to help interpret how social services fit into the complex social geography of the City. Historically, social services have been located in urban areas in order to meet the needs of the greatest number of people requiring assistance. A central location enables service providers to be in a close proximity to the population they are serving. It also coincides with locations of affordable housing and public transportation networks. In Prince George the majority of social services are indeed located in the downtown core. Such close proximity to one another cuts down travel time and provides increased accessibility for the dependent population. Some of these services, however, are moving out of the direct downtown and into residential areas. Such moves enable particular organizations to provide adequate access to their clients, while at the same time providing a somewhat calmer and safer environment.

The final section of the chapter explored the reality of youth living on our streets. There are many services now available within the City for this group, and these services are also located in the downtown core. Although the youth in northern BC and Prince George turn to the streets for various reasons, such as physical abuse, family problems, peer pressure, and drug and alcohol abuse, many inevitably fall into the trap of prostitution, theft, drugs, and alcohol. For a few, the ultimate consequence may be tragic. Prince George faces the same problems as many other urban centres in its challenge to address and help street youth. The continual growth of the City will require a further expansion of the social service sector in order to address the changing needs, demands, and realities of the population.

REFERENCES

Clarke, T. (1994a). Intravenous Drug Use A Community Problem, *Prince George This Week,* 26 January, p.14.

_______. (1994b). Reconnecting Street Kids, *Prince George This Week*, 16 October, p. 17 and 19.

Dear, M. J. and Wolch, J. (1993). Homelessness. In *The Changing Social Geography of Canadian Cities*, L.S. Bourne and D.F. Ley eds. Montreal and Kingston: McGill-Queen's University Press. pp. 298-308

Fitchen, J.M. (1991). *Endangered Spaces, Enduring Places: Change, Identity, and Survival in Rural America*. Boulder, Colorado: Westview Press.

Hodge, G.D. and Qadeer, M.A. (1983). *Towns and Villages in Canada - The Importance of Being Unimportant*. Toronto: The Butterworth Group of Companies.

King, A.J.C, Beazley, R.P., Warren, W.K., Hankins, C.A., Robertson, A.S., and Radford, J.L. (1988). *Canada Youth and AIDS Study*. Kingston: Queen's University.

Knox, P. (1995). *Urban Social Geography: An Introduction, 3rd ed.* Essex, England: Longman Scientific & Technical.

Kostash, M. (1994). Surviving the Streets: One Teen's Story. *Chatelaine* October, pp. 103-105.

Mallam, T. (1995). Fatal Attempts to Leave the Streets. *British Columbia Report*, p. 32.

McGilly, F. (1990). *An Introduction to Canada's Public Social Services: Understanding Income and Health Programs*. Toronto: McClelland and Stewart Inc.

Meilicke, C.A. and Storch J.L. (eds.) (1980). *Perspectives on Canadian Health and Social Services Policy: History and Emerging Trends*. Michigan: Health Administration Press.

Ministry of Social Services. (1993). *Reconnect: Services for Street Youth.* Victoria: Ministry of Social Services, pamphlet.

Morrill, R.L. and Symons, J. (1977). Efficiency and Equity Aspects of Optimum Location. *Geographical* Analysis, vol. 9, pp. 215-225.

Pinch, S. (1985). *Cities and Services: The Geography of Collective Consumption.* New York: HarperCollins Publishers.

Prince George Crisis Intervention Society. (nd.). *Youth Housing Registry*. Prince George: Prince George Crisis Intervention Society, pamphlet.

Prince George Native Friendship Centre. (nd.) *Prince George Native Friendship Centre: Organizational Overview.* Prince George: Prince George Native Friendship Centre, pamphlet.

________. (nd.) *Street Kids, The Forgotten People*. Prince George: Prince George Native Friendship Centre, pamphlet.

________.(nd.) *Streetworker Program*. Prince George: Prince George Native Friendship Centre, pamphlet.

Prince George This Week. (1996). "Youth Safe Haven". *Prince George This Week*, 18 February, p. 3.

Reconnect Program. (1995). *Current Statistics*. Prince George: Reconnect Program, pamphlet.

Rubenstein, J.M. (1996). *The Cultural Landscape: An Introduction to Human Geography, 5th ed.* New Jersey: Prentice-Hall, Inc.

Sayer, J. (1991). Life on the Streets. *Prince George This Week*, 2 October, p. 5.

Weeks, E.P. (1991). Some Geographical Aspects of Social Policy and Evaluation. In *A Social Geography of Canada*, G.M. Robinson ed.. Toronto: Dundurn Press. pp. 471-491.

Wharf, B. (1990). Social Services. In *Urban Policy Issues - Canadian Perspectives*, R.A. Loreto and T. Price eds.. Toronto: McClelland and Stewart. pp. 170-188.

Webber, M. (1991). *Street Kids: The Tragedy of Canada's Runaways*. Toronto: University of Toronto Press.

Chapter 8

A GEOGRAPHY OF CRIME IN PRINCE GEORGE

Laura Ryser

INTRODUCTION

Crime has increasingly become a focus for social geographers. Society is realizing that the distribution of many crimes are space specific. In some ways, crime - and perhaps more importantly our perceptions of crime - influences almost every aspect of our lives; from *where we go*, to *where we live*, to *when* we go to different places in our community. This chapter examines a social geography of crime within the context of the City of Prince George. To start, a number of possible explanations, or theories, that concern the geography of crime are described. Following this, the distribution of specific crimes, such as residential break and enters, across Prince George are mapped. Through mapping, we can see if crime concentrations correspond with our expectations from the various theories about criminal activity. The chapter will then look at how crime prevention through environmental design can reduce the risk of break-ins on residential property. This will include looking at design elements that will influence the natural surveillance of an area, as well as reducing the opportunities for crime to take place. To show how crime prevention through environmental design can work, a case study looking at the University of Northern British Columbia is provided.

Two points must be made at the outset. The first is that crime statistics are problematic. Too often such statistics represent more the geography of policing than they do the geography of crime, as many crimes in communities go unreported and unrecorded. A related issue is the question about whether such data refer to crime events, police arrests, criminal charges laid, or criminal convictions. Therefore, when talking about the incidence of crime we must remember that the collection of crime statistics is a complex issue. A second point is that a great many issues influence criminal behaviour and go well beyond the scope of a social geography investigation. As a partial consequence of these two points of caution, this chapter will focus only upon residential property crime.

THEORIES OF SPACE AND CRIME

This section will look at a number of theories which attempt to explain the geographic patterning of residential crime. The purpose in setting out these ideas about why certain crimes tend to occur in particular areas of a city is to suggest specific variables which may influence the geography of crime. Two key variables, distance and architectural form, appear to play a role in the geography of residential crime.

Social Disorganization

Most forms of law violation are also correlated with city size (Cater and Jones, 1989). Urban areas as a whole record higher crime rates than do rural areas. Even more so, the crime rates of particular neighbourhood areas within our communities will be influenced by changes in economic status, family status, and minority and youth composition of those neighbourhood areas (Covington and Taylor, 1993). Such changes can reflect shifts in a neighbourhood's role in the larger community. "Social Disorganization" is the label used to describe the consequences of large scale neighbourhood change. Thus, neighbourhoods experiencing transition through rapid population turnover are more likely to exhibit higher crime rates due largely to the fact that community institutions of social control are either absent or function imperfectly. As Cater and Jones (1989) describe this process, the inhabitants are not fully integrated into the dominant moral order of the city. While it is transitional neighbourhoods which are most at risk, such neighbourhoods are most typically found in the central city areas of urban places.

Neighbourhood communities provide a source of personal identity and mutual support for its members - they function as the territorial base for community life. Community organization can be a force for channelling energies into positive and constructive outlets such as voluntarism, entrepreneurship, property ownership, and self-advancement through education (Cater and Jones, 1989). In neighbourhoods undergoing continual change or transition, such positive outcomes are less likely.

Common Attributes of Known Offenders

Common attributes of known offenders, such as their demographic and socio-economic characteristics, can provide insight as to where crime in Prince George will most likely be concentrated. At a general level, Cater and Jones (1989) suggest that offenders are often associated with four sets of characteristics. First, offenders often tend to come from large families, broken homes, or minority groups. Second, they also often tend to be male, single, and young. Offenders also commonly have little income and little education, and may be unemployed and unskilled. Finally, offenders often tend to live in overcrowded areas of the community; areas marked by rental accommodations and a high population turnover.

Demographic Influences - Youth

One social disorganization element important in residential crime commonly involves unsupervised local teens or groups of teens. The lack of supervision usually results from breakdowns in both community and familial controls (Covington and Taylor, 1993). In communities with high residential turnover rates, adults are often reluctant to intervene with youths involved in minor delinquency because the youths' parents are strangers with unknown values. Adults may also refuse to become involved because they see offending youths as the responsibility of their own parents; they may also fear being seen as nosy or they may fear retaliation (Covington and Taylor, 1993).

Socio-Economic Influences - Poverty

Crime and civil disorder frequently result from class struggle over space. Studies have shown that law breaking, especially residential crime, in the most urbanized and industrialized areas tends to be concentrated in small pockets within poor and lower income neighbourhoods (Cater and Jones, 1989). For a few individuals a lack of income, a lack of education, a lack of parental supervision or other suitable role models, and despair over a perceived continuing lack of opportunity may push them towards criminal activities.

Neighbourhood Influences

Spatial variations in offender rates are associated with variations in household tenure. Herbert, Baldwin, and Bottoms found that neighbourhoods dominated by owner-occupied dwellings exhibit the lowest crime rates, likely because property ownership exerts a stabilizing influence and is usually connected with other positive factors such as employment, education, etc. (Cater and Jones, 1989). Crime concentrations, then, are often localized within neighbourhoods with large shares of rented housing, whose occupants are not only economically marginalized but also penalized by a form of housing which gives little material, financial, or psychological satisfaction (Cater and Jones, 1989). Such rental neighbourhoods also often have high turnover rates and this can then lead to processes of social disorganization. Anne Power (1989) suggests that this alienation can be reversed by encouraging and supporting community organization, which in turn helps the development of local social networks.

Fundamental elements include the need to feel secure, the need to feel a sense of control, and the need to feel "at home" within the neighbourhood (Power, 1989). In high turnover neighbourhoods, people may not even know who is legitimately going into their neighbour's house.

Influence of Distance on Crime Rates

Two aspects of space, distance and architectural form, very often determine whether a place is a potential target for crime. The bulk of crimes against property are perpetrated close to the offender's residence. This is due to the way familiarity and opportunity so often affect crime, and to the time and money involved in any journey to a scene of crime. The need for personal security tends to confine offending activity to familiar territory where the offender will feel comfortable and not draw attention to himself/herself. For example, if the criminal has an older vehicle, they are less likely to prowl a higher class neighbourhood where this vehicle will stand out (Personal interview, 1996). Offenders and their victims are often, though not always, highly localized in the same areas. There are, however, certain areas - most notably the central business district of urban communities - which will draw offenders from a wider radius (Cater and Jones, 1989).

Influence of Architecture and Design on Crime Rates

Architectural layout and design has been identified as an important factor in determining whether or not a potential target is readily accessible and at low risk to the criminal. Newman's theory of "defensible space" links crime directly to the form of the built environment (Cater and Jones, 1989). The concept of defensible space is, therefore, connected with a planning and design approach which seeks to create streetscapes, building entrances, and interior spaces which are more open and provide many opportunities for natural surveillance. As Leung (1989, p. 6) writes, "land use planning controls over the location, density, bulk, forms of construction, and occupancy are aimed at ensuring a healthy and safe environment for the user and the public ... [including] security against crimes". Gigantic, depersonalized, structures full of dark empty spaces which are often screened from the public and have no forms of natural surveillance are threatening areas. Newman identified large-scale high rise apartment projects as disproportionately prone to vandalism, assault and burglary because buildings of this type are the very negation of defensible space (Cater and Jones, 1989). Corridors, stairs, elevators, entrance halls and fire-escape exits are a kind of territorial limbo over which residents exercise little collective responsibility. These areas belong to all residents, but in practice they belong to no one.

Furthermore, modern house design which emphasizes a desire for privacy rather than for neighbourhood interaction reduces opportunities for the natural surveillance of activities on the streets. At one time, front porches took people out of their house and made them more visible (Jacobs, 1961). Criminals would be less reluctant to target these houses (Personal communication, 1996). Modern houses are recessed on the lot and have no functional front porches. Coming out of a desire for increased privacy, these homes create a setting which discourages interaction within the neighbourhood as people spend their time either inside the home or in the back yard surrounded by high fences. These solid fences are not the best way to discourage crime since they do not provide for natural surveillance. In fact, such fences may actually attract residential crime activity since once a criminal gets over the solid fence, they can do virtually anything undetected. Chain-link fences would be a better alternative since they allow for more natural surveillance (Personal communication, 1996).

A CRIME RATES COMPARISON

Before attempting to compare Prince George crime rates with those of other cities in British Columbia, we must discuss problems that arise when trying to compare crime rate data. Crime statistics let community residents know in broad terms what their risk is and how well their police department is doing (Friedman *et al.*, 1991). However, crime statistics do not in themselves lead to solutions in the fight against crime. The geographic and social contexts of the incidents, including what might have brought the victim and/or offender to that location, and other environmental factors such as the type of street lighting, amount of traffic, etc., are not usually captured by the incident reporting system because they will ordinarily not contribute to the arrest or trial of the offender (Friedman *et al.*, 1991, p. 21).

As suggested at the outset of the chapter, crime statistics are problematic. For example, in the collection and recording of such statistics there are a number of stages at which decisions must be made. Decisions can include under which category to record an incident, or even whether to record an incident at all, with the result that statistics may be tainted or biased. As well, crime data does not reflect the many contributing factors which may lead to incidents and this makes it difficult for society to pinpoint the causes of specific incidents. Pitfalls with official crime records include the extensive under-reporting of crime by victims and witnesses, together with the extensive social biases which focus attention from time to time upon the reporting, recording and prosecuting of particular types of offenses or offenders (Cater and Jones, 1989). The police can also exercise a great deal of discretion as to whether a particular act should be defined and processed as a crime. Cater and Jones (1989) suggest that recorded crime patterns and statistics are not the true geography of crime, but instead are the geography of police patrolling. Statistics may be affected by aggressive and intrusive policing in particular areas of a community. Because of limited police manpower resources, differential policing which is concentrated in areas stigmatized as "trouble spots" produces particular patterns within the crime statistics.

An extension of the geography of policing issue is that police resources may be very different from one community to another. Table 8.1 shows a comparison of RCMP Detachments for four communities whose crime rates are often compared. The RCMP detachments in these four areas are generally similar in size, the populations served (with the exception of Kelowna) are generally similar, but the Prince George

Detachment must patrol an area at least 5 times the size of their southern British Columbia counterparts. As a result, we can expect that a much different geography of police patrols and work must occur around Prince George - at the very least, patrols in some areas will be much less frequent and response times to some locations will be longer. This in turn will affect both crime and crime statistics.

TABLE 8.1
RCMP Detachment Comparisons - 1995

City	RCMP Force Size	Population Served	Area Patrolled (sq.km.)
Prince George	117	76,550	24,161
Kamloops	99	77,421	4,810
Kelowna	106	92,032	4,528
Nanaimo	101	71,582	1,239

Source: Police Services Division (1996) Municipal Crime Rate Report. Prince George RCMP Detachment.

One consequence of the difficulties associated with crime statistics is the need to interpret carefully the patterns which they may suggest. For example, high crime rates are not uncommon in municipalities which serve as a “core” city for a larger area, or which serve as tourist destinations (Police Services Division, 1996). Core cities are usually surrounded by other small towns or unincorporated rural areas which have significant populations. These cities are the business and entertainment centres for a large number of people who reside outside of the municipality. The problem is that local crime rates are generally based on the population of the municipal jurisdictions within which the crime incidents occur and this population base excludes commuters, students, tourists and other part-time residents. If this larger population was included, local per capita crime rates would be smaller than presently calculated. The result that core cities and tourist destinations often record higher than average per capita crime rates is, therefore, something of an unfair characterization of those communities.

Every municipality has unique problems that will influence crime rates. As mentioned, high crime rates could indicate that a municipality is a "core" city. The question also needs to be asked if a municipality's crime rate is influenced more by the boom and bust cycles of the resource economy, by the transportation or tourism activity passing through the community, by its role as a core urban centre for a larger hinterland population, or some other locally specific factor. Some of these effects are suggested from the crime rate data in Table 8.2 as many places with high per capita crime rates are small towns. For example, communities such as Williams Lake, Quesnel, Parksville and Terrace function as core cities for much larger regional populations - and most of these communities also have significant tourism and transportation functions as well.

TABLE 8.2
Per Capita Crime Capitals of British Columbia - 1993
Rate: Offences Per 1000 People

1. Williams Lake: 285	6. Dawson Creek: 207
2. Quesnel: 254	7. Langley: 201
3. New Westminster: 222	8. Victoria: 200
4. Prince George: 210	9. Parksville: 200
5. Prince Rupert: 210	10. Terrace: 200
	[15. Vancouver: 190]

Source: "Cariboo has top crime rate." The Prince George Citizen. April 27, 1994. 1

Some writers have suggested that rapid population growth may also influence crime rates, directly or indirectly, depending on how services and programs handle the sharp increases and stresses from growth. For example, in cities like Prince George, Nanaimo, and Kelowna, increases in crime rates (Table 8.4) after 1990 somewhat correspond with increases in population growth (Table 8.3).

TABLE 8.3
Community Population Growth

Municipality	1986	1987	1988	1989	1990	1991	1992	1993	1994	1995	% Change 86-95
Prince George	70,361	70,169	69,901	70,446	70,964	71,678	72,327	74,161	76,079	76,550	8%
Coquitlam	72,643	74,643	78,306	81,463	84,377	86,473	90,062	93,822	97,383	100,956	28%
Kamloops	64,275	65,175	65,805	66,603	68,034	69,007	70,689	72,969	75,100	77,421	17%
Kelowna	63,779	65,468	67,277	70,137	74,333	78,158	83,307	87,795	90,219	92,032	31%
Nanaimo	51,249	51,694	53,239	55,728	58,665	62,183	64,630	67,377	69,810	71,582	28%
Victoria	69,212	70,126	70,472	71,257	72,023	73,299	73,624	74,361	75,540	76,635	10%

Source: Police Services Division (1996).

TABLE 8.4
Community Crime Rates

Municipality	1986	1987	1988	1989	1990	1991	1992	1993	1994	1995	% Change 86-95
Prince George	170	166	174	159	168	197	230	210	204	179	5%
Coquitlam	134	126	114	114	118	123	116	126	116	116	-15%
Kamloops	138	152	131	144	161	164	166	153	162	138	0%
Kelowna	137	153	124	116	130	130	155	183	172	176	22%
Nanaimo	184	192	192	166	190	229	221	226	216	201	8%
Victoria	209	196	184	198	207	237	234	236	234	216	3%

Note: The municipal crime rates are the number of Criminal Code Cases per 1,000 population.
Source: Police Services Division (1996).

However, while this relationship between population growth and crime rate change tends to exist quite frequently, we must be wary that this explanation does not work in all cases. Again for example, in Coquitlam a 28 percent increase in population over the 1986 to 1995 period corresponded with a 15 percent decline in the local crime rate. We also see exceptions within the City of Prince George, where a decline in population for 1988 did not correspond with a similar decline in the crime rate for that year, and likewise, an increase in population for 1995 did not result in an increase in crime rates for that year. Population change does not, therefore, correlate directly with changes in crime rates as quite clearly a range of other variables may also come into play as well in explaining local patterns.

Finally, another possible reason for an increase in crime rates and offences after 1990 could be the influence of the economic recession during the early 1990s. It is, however, difficult to assess the effects of a recession. Not all municipalities saw a significant increase in crime rates during the recession. This may or may not be correlated with the degree to which certain towns, and certain types of economies and industries, were hit especially hard by the recession. The linkage between crime and economic recession can only be made at a very general level. For example, one cannot estimate the exact impact which the 1989 recession in the forest industry had on Prince George crime rates. Without examining each individual criminal case, it is impossible to determine who committed the crime and what were their motivations.

PERCEPTIONS ABOUT CRIME IN PRINCE GEORGE

Perceptions about crime play an important role in the way local citizens view their community. A neighbourhood with low crime rates can boost morale and give its inhabitants pride. High crime rates can bring down this morale. One reason why crime is able to play this role is because signs of crime can be imprinted onto the landscape, shaping community perceptions (Trick, 1994). In Prince George, the downtown core has especially suffered negative perceptions because of crime.

Broken windows are signs of breaking and entering, broken liquor bottles along the street are signs of alcoholism, and graffiti or other physical damage are signs of vandalism. This type of landscape can induce both concern and fear amongst the local population and, therefore, influence what crimes and in which areas police concentrate their patrol efforts. When we fight crime, we are attempting to gain back pride in our community.

For some time, local government, merchants, and the public have been discussing the issue of downtown revitalization. In fact, the City hopes that the new courthouse complex will have a positive influence on downtown revitalization (Personal communication, 1996). However, some merchants realize that unless we improve the general perceptions of social problems such as crime in the downtown area there is little point trying to "beautify your place if someone comes along and tears it apart" (Personal communication, 1995). Loss of businesses and the presence of empty stores contributes to a loss of natural surveillance and, therefore, a loss of defensible space. This loss of safe space potentially increases the perceptions of danger and fears about crime, and may discourage the general public from shopping in the area. Anything which discourages the general public will have a reciprocal impact on the viability of businesses. If people do not feel safe in the downtown core, they may chose to shop at malls that have uniformed security guards.

BREAK AND ENTERS IN PRINCE GEORGE

The objective of this section is to illustrate a geography of crime in Prince George. Table 8.5 lists the most common crimes as reported and recorded for the City of Prince George. Again, the cautionary remarks made earlier about crime reporting and crime statistics are important here. Since it is beyond the scope of this chapter to break down the geography of all types of crimes, this section focuses specifically on "break and enter" crimes only. Break and enters are of particular interest to the geographer because the physical landscape provides opportunities for this crime to occur.

TABLE 8.5
Most Common Crimes in Prince George

1. Property damage (less than $5,000) - includes broken windows, broken car windshields, car radio antennas snapped off, broken fences, etc.
2. Motor vehicle theft.
3. Assaults.
4. Break-and-enters.
5. Traffic tickets.
6. People drunk in public.

* Note: These are in descending order of frequency.

Source: "Prince George not Canada's Crime Centre." The Prince George Citizen. August 30, 1995. p. 2.

The reason for studying break and enters in the city is because Prince George was reported to have the highest break-in per capita rate of any large municipality in British Columbia (Storie, 1994). In fact, Prince George has more than twice the number of break and enter offences than Kamloops, and a significant number of more break and enter offences than other cities of similar size in British Columbia (Table 8.6). This may be an indication that Prince George is not only a "core city", but it may be that there are more opportunities for an offender to commit a break and enter. What is worse, some homes are even broken into two or three times as those who commit break and enters may return in several weeks because they expect the appliances stolen the first time to have been replaced (Strickland, 1994b).

TABLE 8.6
Break and Enter Offences for 1993

Municipality	Number of Offences	Charged Adults	Charged Youth
Prince George	2,328	139	124
Nanaimo	1,732	83	68
Kelowna	1,686	99	51
Kamloops	911	60	53

Source: Bell, K., Davidson, B., and Slack, M. (1994).

TABLE 8.7
British Columbia Youth Offenders Charged with Break and Enter from 1984 to 1993

Type	1984	1985	1986	1987	1988	1989	1990	1991	1992	1993
Business	844	937	1,199	909	829	791	845	1,155	897	1,053
Residential	1,563	1,920	2,096	1,998	1,854	1,444	1,478	1,689	1,673	2,179
Other	635	739	629	617	498	345	545	434	409	332
Total	3,042	3,596	3,924	3,524	3,181	2,580	2,866	3,278	2,979	3,564

Source: Bell, K., Davidson, B., and Slack, M. (1994).

Nationwide, eighty-five percent of the people accused of break and enter crimes last year were males under the age of 35, while people 45 years of age and older made up only two percent of those accused (Bronskill, 1995). The provincial statistics (Table 8.7) for youth offenders charged with break and enters fluctuate to such a degree that it is difficult to pinpoint trends. Tables 8.6 and 8.7 highlight how important it is to recognize the critical data collection difficulties with crime statistics as 'incidents', 'arrests', and 'formal charges' are each very different parts of crime activity reporting. In Table 8.7, there did appear to be an increasing trend of residential break and enters (as measured by number of offenders charged) by youth between 1989 until 1994. However as stated earlier, without looking at individual cases it is difficult to determine underlying rationales for fluctuating youth crime rates.

Similar to trends at the national level, Table 8.8 shows that youth make up a significant share of those charged with break and enter crimes in Prince George. Kevin Ball, a College of New Caledonia student who took part in conducting a youth crime report, noted: "Youth feel alienated everywhere because of unemployment and the sense that the economy has no useful place for those not going on to colleges or university to pursue a middle-class career" (Strickland, 1994a). Beyond the general issue of youth alienation are the very noticeable differences between males and females with respect to this issue. In Table 8.8, not only are approximately one-quarter to one-third of break and enter charges in Prince George laid against youth (defined in this case as falling under the jurisdiction of the Young Offenders Act), but almost all of these are laid against young men. When reported in the newspapers, the level of young male involvement in break and enter charges often reinforces stereotypes and preconceptions about who is responsible for crime in our City.

Table 8.8
Youth Crime Comparison
Adult vs. Youth Total Charges for Break and Enters in Prince George

Year	Male Youth	Female Youth	Total Youth	Total Youth & Adult	Youth as % of Total
1990	71	6	77	311	24.8 %
1991	83	2	85	220	38.6 %
1992	105	7	112	315	35.6 %
1993	83	2	85	220	38.6 %
1994 *	13	1	14	54	25.9 %

* incomplete data for 1994
Source: Bell, K., Davidson, B., and Slack, M. (1994).

These break and enter statistics, together with the reports on youth alienation, underscore a current debate in Prince George about activities and services for "at-risk" youth. Most recently, a "Youth Violence Committee" comprised of local educators, police, and civic leaders has been holding public meetings to identify strategies for dealing with youth crime and violence issues (Strickland, 1998). Against this backdrop of recent action is a longer history of efforts to assist at-risk youth. For example, a number of organized services in the community already seek to deal with street youth and runaways. The Prince George Native Friendship Centre supports "Reconnect", a program which offers a range of counseling, skills and advice services (Clarke, 1994), while the local RCMP has been trying to expand on this by bringing "Operation Go Home", a liaison service between youth and their families, into Prince George (Prince George This Week, 1997).

Providing a safe and welcoming place for youth is also the goal of a number of more general efforts directed at addressing the "boredom" and restlessness of the City's young people. Safe hangouts or drop-in centres connected with the youth music scene or with skateboarding have been suggested (Keeling, 1995a). While a new civic Youth Centre has been discussed and abortively initiated a number of times (Keeling, 1995b; Prince George Citizen, 1996), a couple of informal drop-in centres opened late in 1997 (Schaffer, 1997). Housed in the Hart Pentecostal Church along the Hart Highway, and in a trailer behind the College Heights Baptist Church, these drop-in centres hope to provide a creative way for youth to spend idle time on weekend evenings. Clearly the community has identified services for youth as a serious issue.

Distribution of Break and Enters in Prince George

An examination of break and enter concentrations in the City of Prince George is hampered by difficulties with the data. First, there is a lack of data available prior to 1986. Further, the reporting boundaries have changed over time which makes it difficult to compare local crime rates over time. Maps 8.1 and 8.2 attempt to show the distribution of break and enter activity for 19 neighbourhood areas across the City for 1989 and 1990. These neighbourhood areas correspond to the Policing Data Areas maintained by the local RCMP detachment and do not coincide with the census tract maps used in many of the other chapters in this book. The data table for this map information is found in an Appendix to this chapter. Map 8.3 shows the distribution of Block Watch groups functioning in each of these Policing Data Areas in 1995.

The years 1989/1990 are used for this examination of break and enter statistics because the neighbourhood areas for which the data were collected are much smaller than the neighbourhood areas used for the 1995 data. This enables us to pinpoint activity more specifically. For example, while the downtown did not have the highest crime rate, the central part of the City (including areas I, M, H, and G) reported the greatest amount of break and enters.

In mapping break and enter statistics, a clear patterning is evident both in terms of break and enter activity as well as the response of local residents to those patterns. Map 8.1 shows the distribution of total break and enter activity across the City for 1990. The first item of note is the strong concentration of break and enters around the downtown core. The large number of commercial, industrial and residential properties in this downtown core area certainly provides many opportunities for

Map 8.1
Total Break and Enters - 1990

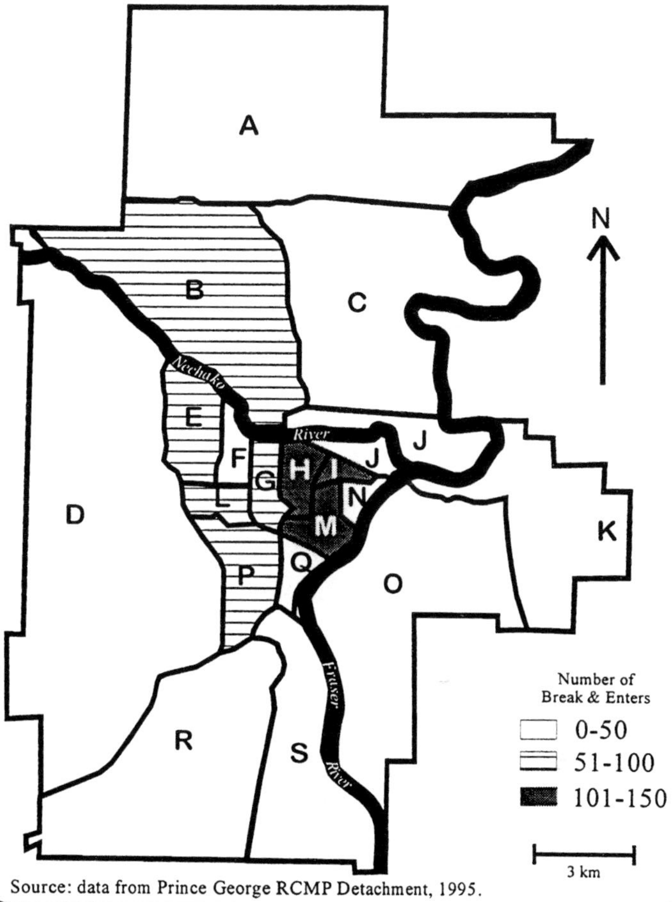

Source: data from Prince George RCMP Detachment, 1995.

such activity. The next item of note is that there is an intermediate band of break and enter activity in the residential districts of the 'bowl' and out towards North Nechako Road. This result supports the theory that the geography of delinquency tends to have a steady downward gradient from the central city to the outer perimeter (Cater and Jones, 1989).

Map 8.2
Residential Break and Enters - 1990

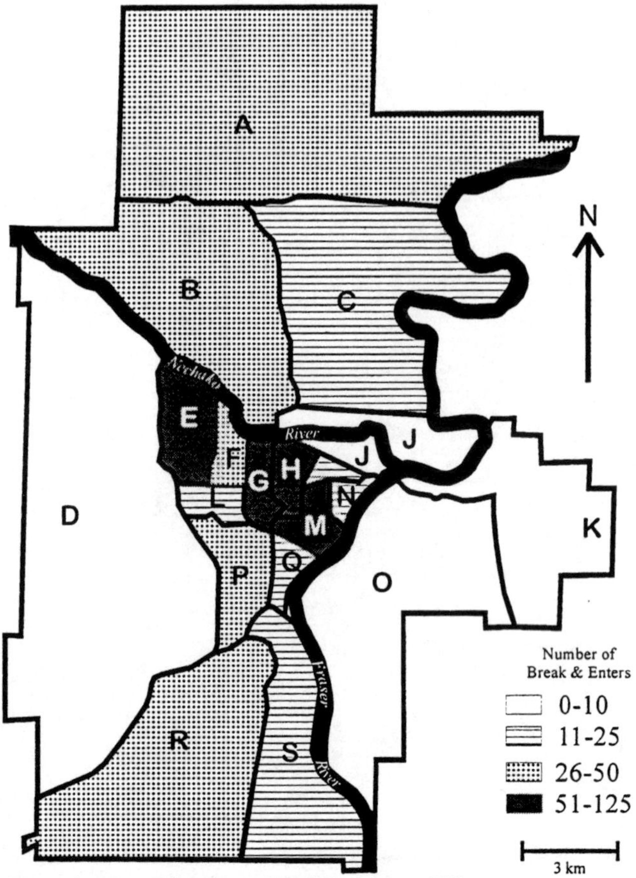

Source: data from Prince George RCMP Detachment, 1995.

Map 8.2 includes only residential break and enter information. While the legend on the map is different from Map 8.1 (because there are fewer incidents recorded) a similar pattern in the distribution of break and enter incidents is evident. The neighbourhoods immediately adjacent to the downtown core report the highest levels of break and enter activity. This is followed by other neighbourhoods in the "bowl", areas along the Hart Highway, and the rural areas along Highway 16 heading south to the City boundary. Since the maps show "number of break and enters" it is important to note that not all areas have the same number of residential properties and that some areas show up on Map 8.2 in the "high" break-in category yet this may simply reflect the higher density of homes in that area.

One of the explanations for residential crime suggested earlier in this chapter concerns property tenure and turnover. We recall that property ownership can have a stabilizing influence on social behaviour. In contrast, rental property is often characterized by a higher turnover in residents with a resulting lack of ties between neighbours. In addition, there are many unobserved spaces such as hallways, stairways, and parking garages and it is these "common property" areas which often provide potential entry points for criminals. The map of rental as compared to owner occupied housing from Chapter 3 of this book (Map 3.2 in Marchuk, 1998) identifies the inner city neighbourhoods of Prince George as having large shares of rental accommodation. But not all areas of the City with high frequencies of break and enters are dominated by rental housing. Clearly other explanations must also be important, including questions about the geography of opportunity for break and enter crimes; that is, the design of the neighbourhoods and housing may make some areas more accessible to criminals. Still, without having looked at each individual case, it is difficult to say that housing tenure types were a principal factor in break and enters in Prince George.

Block Watches

Police are not able to patrol all neighbourhoods at all times of day and night. A common neighbourhood response to residential break and enter crimes has been the creation of Block Watches or other similar preventative measures. Neighbourhood involvement projects such as Block Watch advocate a joint effort against crime and have been heralded as a means of reducing the risk of break and enters because there would be an increase in neighbourhood surveillance.

Unfortunately, Block Watches are seldom created in a vacuum and are most usually a direct response to perceptions of criminal activity in a neighbourhood (Strickland, 1994b). In 1995 there were approximately 110 Block Watch organizations in Prince George taking in about 1,462 homes, or about 6 percent of Prince George's approximately 25,000 households.

Map 8.3
Block Watches by Neighborhood Area - 1995

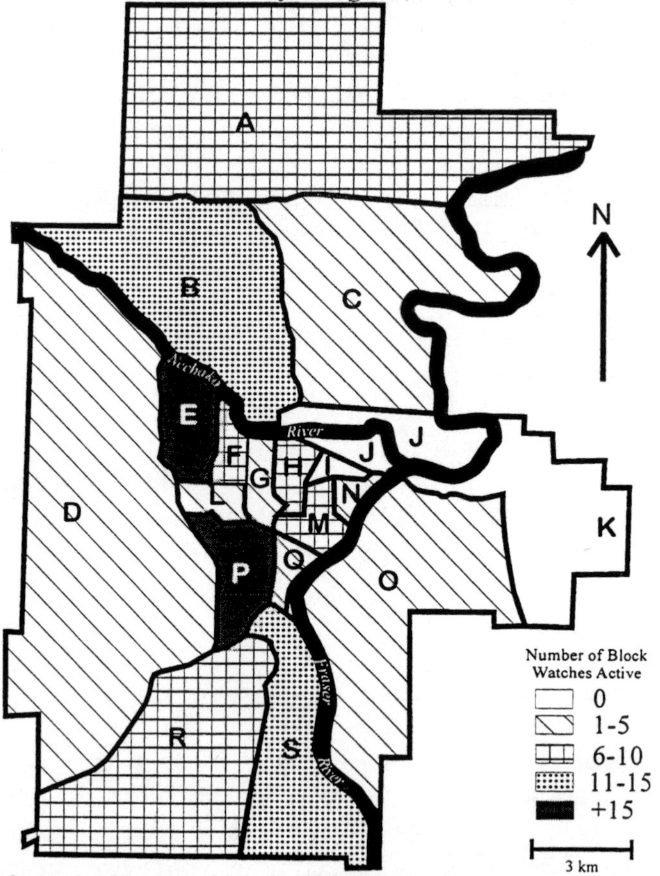

Source: data from Prince George RCMP Detachment, 1995.

Map 8.3 shows the distribution of Block Watches across Prince George in 1995. We can see that the distribution of Block Watches appears to be connected to levels of break and enter activity but that this is moderated by whether an area is dominated by rental or owner occupied housing. For example, some of the bowl area neighbourhoods located west of Central Avenue recorded a number of residential break and enters on Map 8.2 and a number of Block Watch organizations on Map 8.3. These neighbourhoods are largely comprised of owner occupied housing. In contrast, some inner city neighbourhoods near to the downtown core which recorded numbers of break and enters on Map 8.2 had few active Block Watch organizations in 1995. These neighbourhoods include large shares of rental housing.

Comparing Maps 8.2 and 8.3, the College Heights area stands out as an interesting neighbourhood. While the number of residential break and enters in 1990 was not very high relative to other parts of the City, a large number of Block Watch organizations were functioning in 1995. Here, residents appear to have taken a proactive stand through participation in preventative crime programs.

One final item of interest in this examination of break and enters in Prince George is that there appears to have been a significant drop in break and enter incidents since 1989. In 1989, there were 1,089 break and enters (Prince George This Week, 1990a). In 1990, the total incidents for break and enters dropped slightly to 1,021 (Prince George This Week, 1990b). By 1995, the total number of break and enters was almost cut in half, totalling just 546 incidents (RCMP, 1996). This could be an indication that Block Watch, defensible space, and other crime prevention programs are working.

CRIME PREVENTION THROUGH ENVIRONMENTAL DESIGN

One suggestion for decreasing the levels of crime is through the use of routine police patrolling. Police are now considering increased patrolling and the expanded use of community based officers (Poyner, 1983). In Prince George, there has been a development and expansion of the Community Policing Access

Centres. However, the geographical areas in which crime can occur are so great that the probability of a patrolling officer discovering a burglary or robbery in progress is small. Poyner suggests that many incidents occur in private places, beyond the reach of even the most efficient police patrol. The objective of Crime Prevention Through Environmental Design (CPTED) is to prevent crime by changing the situation in which crime occurs through changes in the design of products, buildings, and public places (Lemaitre, 1995b; Poyner, 1983).

The purpose of CPTED is to extend the sense of "turf" from private to semi-private and public space. This can be achieved by designing spaces, such as fountains, benches, and playgrounds, around buildings so residents can meet there. General clean-up of a neighbourhood will also show that residents have "taken ownership" of the public space in their community. Without this sense of territorial ownership or control, an area can be more susceptible to crime. For instance, if a broken window does not get fixed, an impression is left that people do not care, and vandalism increases (Personal communication, 1996).

Proper landscaping can help to reduce hiding spaces around points of entry. An example of poor landscaping would be bushes around windows which obscure natural surveillance. Low level shrubs and rose or raspberry bushes can provide aesthetic greenery that would also be uncomfortable for someone to try to climb through. Proper lighting can help to reduce crime and the fear of crime, and improve the ability of residents to identify suspicious activity. In order to accomplish these objectives, lighting must be positioned to illuminate points of entry. Light fixtures on corners can illuminate two walls, thus reducing shadows and hiding spots. Areas that will not provide an opportunity for crime to occur are generally those that are well lit, well travelled, and where one can see a good distance ahead and others can see you.

Natural surveillance occurs when the public can easily view what is happening around them during the course of everyday activities. In commercial areas it is better to include a variety of uses in the same building to help ensure that someone is around the building more frequently (Poyner, 1983). Avoid corners that people can hide behind and ensure gradual changes in grades and elevations. Neighbourhood design can create natural surveillance by clustering dwelling units, such as in cul-de-sacs, where many houses are visible from one another (Leung, 1989). Residents should design landscaping to allow clear, unobstructed views of surrounding areas. Replacing solid barriers such as walls, hedges, and fences with chain link fences will open up the view. Pruning of shrubs is also a good idea, especially where such vegetation would obscure the natural surveillance of a door or a window and thus provide a hiding spot for a criminal.

CPTED Case Study - UNBC

When the University of Northern British Columbia was being created, there was a conscious effort to build a safe environment. Parking lots were located on the same side as three and four story buildings with many windows overlooking the parking lots (Personal communication, 1996). People are less likely to commit crime if they feel they are being watched.

The university security office is located in the centre of the campus to give easy access to or from any location on campus within two minutes (Personal communication, 1996). This central location is accessible for students using the "Safe Walk" program. A Safe Walk program is designed to provide student escorts to other students who may have to walk alone into areas where they may feel or be unsafe (such as the far corners of a parking lot late at night). Campus Security is also located close to the Winter Garden pub - a central location. Student Services Street locates all student facilities in one central area to eliminate the need to travel all around the campus for services. The one main focal point of the campus is the courtyard, which draws the line of sight and activities to the centre of the campus rather than to obscure places all over campus.

Current design questions include the locker area. Tall lockers create hiding places and the lockers currently located in the middle of the locker area of the Laboratory Building should only be half the height to increase natural surveillance

(Personal communication, 1996). Seats in the locker area would make it more inviting and more social, which would increase traffic and natural surveillance that would further deter criminal activity. While some security measures are in place, increased natural surveillance in areas such as the computer labs would help prevent unauthorized use or theft. On some other university campuses, such computer labs have been located next to a cafeteria, with a glass wall separating the two, in order to provide greater natural surveillance.

As well, there are many bike riders and walkers who cut through the parking lots to go down the hill along University Way. At night, this connecting area is not well lit and does not have regular surveillance. As a result, people are in an unsafe situation with respect to animal encounters or assault from possible attackers (Personal communication, 1996). In fact, security staff recall an incident where a cyclist was cutting through the parking lots and was chased by a bear. A well lighted and cleared path would provide a safer route.

CONCLUSION

Crime Prevention Through Environmental Design is the one of the best passive methods through which to fight crime since it reduces the opportunity for crime to take place by increasing natural surveillance. It is well noted that police patrolling cannot be everywhere at once. It will remain concentrated in troubled areas, real or perceived. Still, the RCMP are trying their best to decentralize surveillance by using Community Policing Access Centres, by supporting programs such as Block Watch, and by educating the public in crime prevention.

Fighting crime will also be enhanced by compiling more crime maps, such as the publicly accessible break and enter map at the Community Policing Access Centre near Spruceland Mall. Clear connections need to be made between crime, neighbourhoods, housing tenure, or other factors, otherwise general statistics will not assist with educating the general public on the steps they can take to reduce their risk of crime. Until police reporting boundaries are smaller, stabilized, and co-ordinated with census areas over a period of time, it will be difficult to predict or clarify the causes of crime in certain areas. In the meantime, the best offense to fighting crime is defence through environmental design and numerous programs that co-ordinate efforts like Block Watch.

REFERENCES

Bell, K., Davidson, B., and Slack, M. (1994). *Youth Crime Trend Analysis: Prince George, B.C.* Prince George: College of New Caledonia manuscript.

Bronskill, J. (1995). "Lowest level since 1989: Break-in rate plummets". *The Prince George Citizen.* September 26, p. 6.

Cater, J. and Jones, T. (1989). *Social Geography: An Introduction into Contemporary Issues*. London: Edward Arnold.

Clarke, T. (1994). "Reconnecting street kids". *Prince George This Week*. October 16, p. 17.

Covington, J. and Taylor, R. (1993). "Community Structural Change and Fear of Crime". *Social Problems*, pp. 374-391.

Friedman, W. *et al.* (1991). *Mapping Crime in its Community Setting: Event Geography Analysis.* New York: Springer-Verlag.

Keeling, A. (1995a). "Yearning to express themselves". *The Prince George Citizen*, June 15, p. 3.

_______. (1995b). "If you build it, they will come - demand grows for 24 hour drop-in centre". *The Prince George Citizen*, June 14, p. 3.

Jacobs, J. (1961). *The Death and Life of Great American Cities.* New York: Random House.

Lemaitre, S. (1995a). "Block Watch Locations". Prince George: Prince George RCMP Detachment, handout.

_______. (1995b). "Crime Prevention Through Environmental Design (CPTED)" . Prince George: Prince George RCMP Detachment, pamphlet.

Leung, H-L. (1989). *Land Use Planning Made Plain.* Kingston, Ontario: Ronald P. Frye and Company.

Police Services Division. (1996). *Municipal Crime Rate Report.* Victoria: Public Safety and Regulatory Branch, Ministry of Attorney General.

Power, A. (1989). "Housing, Community and Crime". In *Crime and the City*, D. Downes ed. London: MacMillan Press Ltd. pp. 206-235.

Poyner, B. (1983). *Design Against Crime: Beyond Defensible Space.* London: Butterworths.

Prince George Citizen, The. (1994). "Cariboo has top crime rate". April 27, p. 1.

_______. (1995). "Prince George not Canada's Crime Centre". August 30, p. 2.

_______. (1996). "Youth centre fund drive launched". November 14, p. 13.

Prince George This Week (1990a). "Prince George Crime Statistics for November 1989". January 3, p. 7.

_______. (1990b). "Prince George Crime Statistics to Date". December 19, p. 6.

_______. (1997). "Operation Go Home helps youth return to families". June 8, p. A16.

R.C.M.P. (1996). *R.C.M. Police Operational Statistics Reporting System: Detailed Crime*. Prince George: Prince George RCMP Detachment, March 20.

Schaffer, D. (1997). "New youth centres open this weekend". *The Prince George Citizen*. November 28, p. 13.

Storie, M. (1994). "Break-in rate B.C.'s highest". *The Prince George Citizen*. November 14.

Strickland, P. (1994a). "Report: City youth crime rate high". *The Prince George Citizen*. September 21, p. 1.

_______. (1994b). "We are not helpless in our homes". *The Prince George Citizen*. January 29, p. 3.

_______. (1998). "Youth Violence: Educators, police want to know what you think". *The Prince George Citizen*. February 23, p. 1.

Trick, B. (1994). "New Downtown Plan Pushed". *The Prince George Citizen*. December 16, p. 3.

APPENDIX
Prince George Break and Enter Crime Statistics

Policing Data Area	Statistics Year to date for Oct. 10, 1989 Res.	Bus.	Total	Statistics Year to date for Oct. 10, 1990 Res.	Bus.	Total	Block Watches 1995
A	55	5	60	31	4	35	8
B	41	8	49	50	5	55	14
C	14	9	23	22	6	28	2
D	13	1	14	10	3	13	2
E	77	2	79	83	8	91	20
F	68	3	71	36	9	45	9
G	98	7	105	69	5	74	5
H	121	28	149	95	55	150	6
I	23	60	83	31	89	120	0
J	3	1	4	6	7	13	0
K	13	3	16	9	3	12	0
L	5	21	26	14	48	62	1
M	201	13	214	111	25	136	9
N	36	1	37	20	4	24	2
O	3	12	15	10	15	25	1
P	56	5	61	39	20	59	17
Q	18	2	20	19	2	21	4
R	36	1	37	30	7	37	8
S	22	4	26	17	3	21	12

Sources: Lemaitre. (1995a).
Prince George This Week. (1990a). "Prince George Crime Statistics for November 1989." January 3, p. 7.
Prince George This Week. (1990b). "Prince George Crime Statistics to Date." December 19, p. 6.